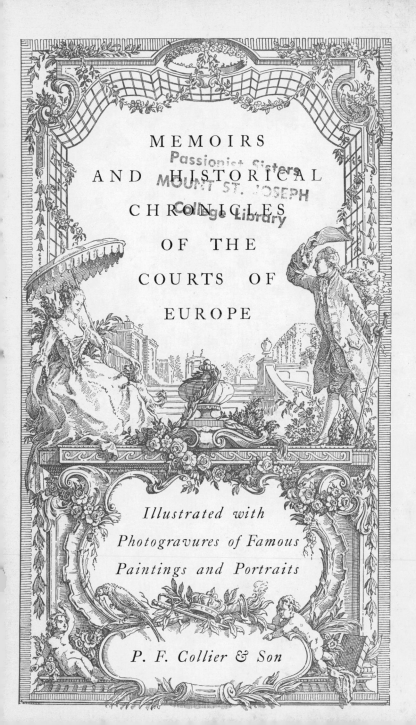

MEMOIRS
AND HISTORICAL
CHRONICLES
OF THE
COURTS OF
EUROPE

*Illustrated with
Photogravures of Famous
Paintings and Portraits*

P. F. Collier & Son

MEMOIRS OF
THE COURTS OF BERLIN
AND ST PETERSBURG

BY COUNT OF MIRABEAU
(Honore Gabriel Riqueti)

*With a Special Introduction
and Illustrations*

VIGILANS ET AUDAX

NEW YORK
P F COLLIER & SON
PUBLISHERS

CONTENTS

CONTENTS

CONTENTS

CONTENTS

INTRODUCTION

A TWOFOLD interest centres in this volume of secret history written by the Comte de Mirabeau,—the interest attaching to its remarkable author no less than to the work itself.

"Mirabeau!" exclaims Victor Hugo. "It is not a man, not a nation, but an event which speaks—an immense event—the fall of the Monarchy of France. His entry into public life was a veritable event. It was Revolution which accompanied him on the stage."

Widely famed as author, statesman, orator, letter-writer and roué; in turn the favourite and sport of fortune; buried by the French nation and mourned by all Paris as one of her illustrious dead, and two years later his body taken from its honoured place in the Pantheon and flung into a common grave, to make room for Marat,—this surely was no common man!

His life is a record more enthralling than fiction. He has inspired playwright and novelist. From birth to death all may read him as an open letter, in which we have preserved the turbulent gamut of passion and ambition through which he ran. He was the product of Revolution, that Revolution which saw Louis Capet and his queen bow their proud heads to the will of a frenzied people.

Honoré Gabriel Riqueti, Comte de Mirabeau, was born at Bignon, near Nemours, France, in 1749. His father was a well-known writer on political economy, and the son inherited a natural talent for politics, and a natural genius for oratory. He was, however, the ugly duckling of the family, being a wild dissipated youth of unpleasing exterior. His father endeavoured to correct the faults of character by severe discipline, and finally caused the young man to be imprisoned. But upon each release Honoré plunged into new excesses. He was especially noted for a succession of scandalous amours, despite his ugliness of feature. "Never was there child more ugly in face and feature," says one biographer; "nor more passionate and uncontrollable. Nature seemed to have played a prank on the world in producing him. He defied law, morals, authority; and because of defiance was sent by his father to the dungeons of Castles If, and Joux, and Vincennes, in hopes of his death by sickness, or starvation, or despair, or suicide. Yet from each he managed to get release, and ever through grosser immoralities as would now be said; through intrigue, and friendship, and the collusion of officials, as was said then." With escape came fresh problems—flight into Switzerland, or England, or Holland. And the worst of it was that he was not always alone. Perhaps it was the young wife of an old marquis whom he persuaded to accompany him—the "Sophie" to whom he dedicated a volume of passionate epistles; again it may have been the wife of an army officer, or only some poor misguided girl who followed him despite his ugliness and the poverty which dogged his footsteps.

To support himself in this precarious roving life he turned to writing. He issued pamphlets, on the "Order of Cincinnatus," the "Bank of Spain," the "Bank of Discount," the "Water Company of Paris," and many more. Those attacking the rotten system of French finance had the merit of being true and were instrumental in bringing about needed reform, but they also caused yet another flight on the part of the author to prevent arrest.

At the age of thirty-one he had sowed most of his wild oats and was done with prison life. He now set himself earnestly in the current of political life, and endeavoured to curry favor with the authorities, in hope of being given some prominent post. He found, however, that he had created a following for himself more powerful than officialdom. His pamphlets on finance had been widely read. During his imprisonment he had restlessly written an essay on "Despotism" and a daring booklet entitled "Lettres-de-Cachet." These attacks upon the monarchy were quickly suppressed. But the times were ripe for them and they passed from hand to hand and mouth to mouth. The spirit of Revolution was beginning to assert itself, and the new party was looking upon Mirabeau as one of its chosen leaders.

To escape a clash with the ruling powers he went to England in 1784, where his brilliance in writing and speaking won him friends, and also gave him entrance into literary and political clubs where he gained many ideas. Upon his return to France he made his peace with the Minister, M. de Vergennes, who evidently saw use for Mirabeau's peculiar talents abroad rather than at home, for he was sent in 1786 upon a secret mission to Prussia, with the aim of reporting to the Ministry the effect which would be produced in Prussia by the expected death of Frederick the Great; and also to sound the inclinations and temper of Frederick's successor.

With his usual "push," Mirabeau made his way into the good graces of the aged king, was present at his death, and at the inauguration of Frederick William II. With characteristic boldness he wrote a memorial to the new ruler giving him some advice upon conduct and reform—a pamphlet of some 84 closely written pages from a past master in the subject! Whether the recipient profited by all this gratuitous advice, history does not say. But Frederick William had no particular love for Mirabeau, who remained at the Court for only a few months (until January, 1787).

It was during this time that he wrote to M. de Calonne the remarkable series of letters now known to English readers as "Memoirs of the Courts of Berlin and St. Petersburg." They sum up with much accuracy the personal traits of the dying Frederick the Great, and the character of his successor, Frederick William II. Included in them also are many personal details of the inner life of Catherine II. of Russia, whose career, he intimates, is tarnished with the breath of scandal. The whole series of 66 letters, in fact, is written in a satirical vein and with the outspoken brusqueness and lack of sympathy for which the writer was always noted. Hence it created an uproar when, in 1789, it was published under the title of "Histoire sécrète de Cour de Berlin, ou correspondance d'un voyageur français depuis le mois Juillet, 1786, jusqu'a 19 Janvier, 1787" ("Secret History of the Court of Berlin, or letters of a French traveller, from July, 1786, to January 19, 1787").

The work, while giving an excellent insight into the methods of foreign courts, useful views, and highly interesting observations, created such a scandal at the time, that parliament was forced to order it burned by the hand of the public executioner. The king's advocate in a speech against the book, February 10, 1789 (still preserved in the Parliamentary Register), said: "Frederick II, whose name alone was sufficient to preserve that balance of power which assured to Europe general peace and happiness, still reigned.

But the prince was fast declining. It was at the moment that the self-styled 'Voyageur français' endeavoured to ingratiate himself with the greatest personages of the state, in order to gather any stray scraps of conversation, and to endeavour, in the midst of the trouble and commotion caused by the unforeseen changes of a new ruler, to surprise ministerial secrets, to detect the aims and ambitions of the nobles, to expose the intrigues of courtesans, and to fathom the plots of the Court.

"It is not enough to have showered invectives on the uncle of the new king, the king himself, his august family, the princesses of the blood and the ministry; in fact the whole court is treated with such a criminal indecency that we should blush to repeat the infamous expressions of which the author has made use."

This arraignment, as the reader may suspect, was dictated from motives of royal policy. Louis upon his tottering throne could not afford to pass by free-spoken criticism of a neighbouring court in silence. Such material was dangerous, and the book was accordingly destroyed. The original manuscript, however, was stolen from the royal archives, sold to Malassis, a printer of Alençon, and published by him as a work by "an unknown traveller who had died a year previous in Germany." Several editions, totalling 20,000 copies, were quickly issued to meet the wide-spread demand; and a few months later it was translated into English. It was not, however, until Mirabeau attained his larger fame as the head of the Revolution, and the offended authorities were no more, that his name was placed upon the work as author.

In respect to the charges of the king's advocate and others, that the work includes scandalous revelations and other confidential material, it must be remembered that the "Secret History" covers precisely the ground it was intended to cover. Mirabeau was sent upon a secret mission to report all he saw at Court. This he did, conscientiously, in letters addressed to a single individual, and not intended, at the time, for publication. Indeed, it has been asserted that their issue in book form was entirely contrary to the author's wishes. He had busied himself, also, while in Berlin upon a lengthy study of the "Prussian Monarchy," published in 1788, to which he proposed to give his name, and which gave proof of his far-reaching grasp of matters political, financial, and legislative.

It is in these letters, however, that he has preserved for us an interesting epoch in European life. The great Frederick was passing away. The Court of France was crumbling. All was unrest and upheaval, and Mirabeau by tongue and pen was a vital influence. In these historical memoirs he is consistently himself, revealing his own personality quite as much as the court life he describes. He has preserved the reputation of telling the truth, and it was this trait which made him the great popular leader of later years.

After reading the memoirs of his checkered life, written by his contemporaries, Goethe exclaimed: "At last the wonderful Mirabeau becomes natural to us, while at the same time the hero loses nothing of his greatness! . . . . The French look upon Mirabeau as their Hercules, and they are perfectly right. But they forget that even the Colossus consists of individual parts, and that the Hercules of antiquity is a collective being—a gigantic personification of deeds done by himself and by others."

MEMOIRS OF
THE COURTS OF BERLIN
AND ST. PETERSBURG

LETTER I

July 5th, 1786.

S IR,—I have the honor to write to you by the
first post, to inform you that the Berlin mail, for
which I waited before I would enter my carriage, has brought me no letter. It is possible, but not
probable, that the letter of my correspondent has been
sent too late for the post. It is also possible, and very
likely, nay, if the Comte de Vergennes has received no
intelligence it is almost certain, that the great event
either approaches or is past; for I hold it as infallible
that, when death becomes inevitable, the couriers will
be stopped. This, sir, deeply engages my attention,
and I shall hasten with all expedition to Brunswick,
where I shall gain certain information; there I shall
remain several days if the King is living.

I have at present only to add, I shall think no labor,
time, or trouble too great if I can but serve you, monsieur, and the cause of the public.

I shall not repeat any of our conversations, but shall
take the liberty to offer you my advice, solely founded
on my personal attachment; of which you cannot
doubt, since, independent of that amiable seduction
which you exercise with power so irresistible, our

interests are the same. The torrent of your affairs, the activity of cabals, the efforts of every kind which you so prodigally are obliged to make, render it impossible that you should yourself class and arrange the grand projects which your genius has brought to maturity, and which are ready to bud and bloom. You have testified some regret that I, for the present, declined performing this office for you. Permit me therefore, monsieur, to name a person who is, in every respect, worthy of this mark of your confidence.

The Abbé de Périgord, to consummate and practical abilities, joins profound circumspection and inviolable secrecy. You never can select a man more to be depended upon; or one who will with more fervent piety bow before the shrine of gratitude and friendship; who will be more anxiously active in good, less covetous of others' fame, or one with superior conviction that fame is justly due to him, only, who has the power to conceive and the fortitude to execute.

He possesses another advantage. His ascendency over Panchaud represses the defects of the latter, which have been so described to you as to inspire fears, and sets all his great qualities and uncommon talents, which daily become more necessary to you, in action. There is no man who can guide and rule M. Panchaud like the Abbé de Périgord, who will momentarily become more valuable to you the better to effect a grand money measure, without which no other measures can be effected. You may confide that delicate business to the Abbé de Périgord, which, especially in the present moment, ought not to be trusted to clerks. The noble, the enlightened, the civic project of drawing inferences from the numerous false statements that infest the accounts of Ministers (and which, being compared to the true statements, caused, or rather obliged, the King to determine that decisive measures should give France a national credit, and consequently a legal constitution) cannot be better realized than by the joint labors of these two persons. One of them has long been devoted to you; and the other will be, whenever any single act of benevolence shall excite his emulation. Condescend to believe, monsieur, that you cannot act more to your own interest.

I was desirous of writing thus to-night, because it would neither be delicate nor decent for the person interested to read what I have written; and this letter is the last you will receive that must not pass through the hands of a third person. My attachment, monsieur, to you, and your fame, induces me to hope you will place some confidence in this counsel, if I may so venture to call it; and that it will not be ranked among the least of the proofs of the most devoted respect with which I am, etc.

LETTER II

BRUNSWICK, *July 12th,* 1786.

THAT the King is very ill is very certain; but he is not at the point of death. Zimmermann, the famous Hanoverian physician, whom he sent for, has declared that, if he would be careful, he might still live; but he is incorrigible on the article of abstinence. He still mounts his horse, and he even trotted fifty paces some days since, with a man on each side of him; but it is nevertheless true that he has the dropsy; and in reality, he has not been any better since my departure.

I shall not see the reigning Duke of Brunswick before this evening; he is in the country. He has powerfully supported the election which the Chapters of Hildesheim and Paderborn have lately made of a coadjutor. M. Furstemberg has been elected. Vienna caballed exceedingly in favor of the Archduke Maximilian. It appears that the Duke wishes to promote peace, since he endeavors, by every means, to strengthen the Germanic confederation, which certainly has that only for its end, though the means may give room for reflection. I have my reasons for being of that opinion, which I shall explain on some other occasion. To-day I am at the mercy of the courier.

Parties are very busy at Berlin; especially that of Prince Henry, who is eternally eager, without well knowing what he wishes. But all is silence in the King's presence; he still is King, and so will remain to the last moment.

As the immediate death of the King is not expected, I shall continue at Brunswick some days, in order to prepare him for my return (much more premature than I had announced) and that I may more nearly study the Duke.

The coinage continues to be an object of contention, and exaggerated discredit. I think it would be of use to publish apologetic reasons concerning the gold coin, confessing its too high rate (for wherefore deny that which is demonstrated?); and justificatory proofs, relative to the silver, the crowns of sixty-nine, and those since 1784, still remaining prohibited.

You no doubt know that the Duke, Louis of Brunswick, has quitted Aix-la-Chapelle, and is retired to Eisenach. The troubles of that petty republic may perhaps explain his retreat; but these do not seem to me sufficient motives for his new abode, and for this single reason, that the Duchess of Weymar is his niece.

LETTER III

July 14th, 1786.

I DINED and supped yesterday with the Duke. When we rose from table, after dinner, he took me aside to the window, where we conversed for about two hours, with much reserve at first, on his part, afterward with more openness, and at last with an evident desire to be thought sincere.

An expression of esteem for the Comte de Vergennes, and fear for his approaching retreat, gave occasion to this private conversation. The expression alluded to was immediately followed by the question (which was asked in a tone of affected indifference, and betrayed a very strong degree of curiosity), " No doubt M. de Breteuil will be his successor? " The Duchess was of our party. I answered, lowering my voice, but articulating with great firmness, " I hope and believe not." It was after I had said this that he led me to the window, at the far end of the apartment. He presently began to converse, with all the energy which his slowness and native dignity admit, of the inquietude which the Germanic body could not avoid feeling, should M. de Breteuil, who was at the head of the Austrian party, and who has long been a servant and friend of the Cabinet of Vienna, succeed to the place of first Minister.

I replied (speaking of the Comte de Vergennes with every respect, and of the generous and pacific intentions of the King with great confidence) that, should the Comte de Vergennes retire, it would probably be of his own free will; and that no one would have greater influence than himself in the choice of his successor; that consequently, whether he remained in office or went out, the first Minister would not be of the Austrian party; and, though most assuredly the probity of the King, and the *morale* of his politics, would continue to render the connections between the Courts of Vienna and Versailles respected, as they would all others, yet, that the interest of Europe, and of France in particular, was so intimately united to the continuance of peace, that these connections, far from inciting war, could but contribute to render peace durable; that France was sufficiently puissant, from innate strength and from the state of her affairs, honorably to own that she dreaded war, which she would take every care to shun; that I did not think sudden war probable, especially when, studying the administration of the Duke of Brunswick, I perceived that he had performed his duties, of Prince and father, with so much assiduity and success; that, however natural it might be for man to seek that career, in which he was indubitably the first, I could not believe he (the Duke) would sacrifice to the desire of military renown, so much of which he had already acquired, his favorite work, his real enjoyments, and the inheritance of his children; that all circumstances called him to supreme influence over the affairs of Prussia after the death of the great King, and that, Prussia being at this time the pivot on which continental war or peace were balanced, he (the Duke of Brunswick) would almost singly decide which was to ensue; that he had formerly sufficiently shone the hero of war, and that I was convinced he would hereafter remain the angel of peace.

He then forcibly denied ever having been fond of war; even at the time when he had been most fortunate. He showed, independent of his principles, how ardently his family and personal interest would induce him to beware of war. "And if it were necessary," added he, "in an affair so important, to consult nothing further than the despicable gratification of self-love, do I not know how much war is the sport of chance? I have formerly not been unfortunate. I might hereafter be a better general, and yet might not have the same success. No prudent man, especially one who is advanced in life, will risk his reputation in so hazardous a pursuit, if it may be avoided."

This part of his discourse, which was long, animated, energetic, and evidently sincere, was preceded by a phrase of etiquette and remonstrance, in which he assured me that he never should possess, and was far from desiring to possess, any influence in Prussia. To this phrase I reverted; and, by a rapid sketch, proving to him that I was well acquainted with Berlin, the principal actors there, and the present state of men and things, I demonstrated (which he most certainly knows better than I do) that his interest, the interest of his house, of Germany, and of Europe, made it a duty in him to take the helm of State in Prussia; to preserve that kingdom from the hurricane most fatal to States, the strength of which principally depends upon opinion. I mean from petty intrigues. petty passions, and want of stability and consistency of system. " Your personal dignity," added I, "which is truly immense, and a thousand times more elevated than your rank, however eminent that may be, no doubt forbids you to tender your services; but it is your duty, I will not say not to refuse, no, I repeat, it is your duty to take measures, and employ all your abilities, all your powers, to gain an ascendency over the successor, and to seize the direction of affairs."

This mode of treatment greatly developed the man. He spoke with truth, and consequently with a degree of confidence, of Berlin. He told me Count Hertzberg had not let him remain ignorant of our intimacy; he depicted many of the persons who have influence,

such as I know them to be. I clearly saw that there
was a coolness, founded on some unknown subject,
between him and the Prince of Prussia; that he (the
Duke of Brunswick) neither loved nor esteemed
Prince Henry; and that his (the Duke's) party was
as powerfully formed as it could be, in a country hitherto little in the habit of cabal, but which, perhaps, will
presently be initiated.   I purposely assumed much
faith in the warlike dispositions of the Cabinet of
Berlin.   The Duke gave good proofs that, independent
of the Heir Apparent, who, though personally brave,
was not warlike, as well because of his manners and
habits as of his prodigious stature, it would be madness to begin; that the moment of acquisition by arms,
which, perhaps, still was necessary to Prussia, was not
yet come; and that it was necessary to consolidate,
etc., etc.   All this was very serious, very sensible, and
very circumstantial.

The Oriental system, Russia, Poland, Courland, all
passed in review.

They still have their fears concerning the Oriental
system; that is to say, concerning the part that we
might take.   They seem to believe that Russia will
never powerfully second the Emperor, except in support of the Oriental system, and whatever may contribute to its success.   Poland is to reconstruct.   We
remitted speaking of it, as well as of Courland.   Suddenly, and by a very abrupt transition (it seems to me
he employs transitions to surprise the secrets of those
with whom he converses, and on whom he earnestly
fixes his eyes while he listens), he asked what I meant
to do at Berlin.   "Complete my knowledge of the
North," answered I, "which I have had little opportunity of studying, except at that city; since Vienna
and Petersburg are to me forbidden places.   And who
knows?   We always presume on our own powers.

It may be hoped that, the subject being so grand, the soul may elevate the genius. I, perhaps, shall dare to snatch the portrait of Cæsar from the daubers who are so eager to besmear." This answer seemed satisfactory. I found it easy to interlard my discourse with agreeable compliments. I told him he had rather conquered than vanquished us; that we regarded the fate of Germany as resting on his shoulders, etc., etc.; and that, therefore, the design of writing the most brilliant history of the age in which I lived had placed me, even before I was acquainted with him, in the rank of one of his most ardent admirers. I know not whether he did or did not believe that I solely occupied myself with literature; but the supposition that I shall write history will perhaps render him more accessible to me, and acquire me more of his confidence; for he appears to possess the love, and even the jealousy, of fame to the utmost degree.

I am pressed by the courier because, not having quitted the Court all yesterday, I could not write before this morning; and the courier departs at eleven o'clock. Writing in cipher is very tedious; I therefore omit a thousand particulars which lead me to believe—

1. That the English will not, by any means, be so quickly successful in their artifices in the North as might be feared; if the Court of Berlin may at all depend on the Court of Versailles.

2. That it is time to speak a little more openly to the former; and not to confound mystery and secrecy, finesse and prudence, ambiguity and policy.

3. That the Duke of Brunswick, whom I believe to be by much the most able Prince of Germany, is sincerely desirous of peace; and that he will inspire the Cabinet of Berlin with the same sentiments, if but the least restraint be laid on the Emperor; who, said he to me, has spoken in outrageous terms, in the presence

of seven or eight witnesses besides myself, of the Prince of Prussia.

4. That the intention of the Duke is to govern Prussia, and to obtain great confidence and superior influence in Europe; that he would dread lest these would not be augmented by war, which he is convinced ought to be avoided, at Berlin; and that war is not really to be feared, except as far as France shall encourage the Emperor, who without us will not be anything.

I have not time to-day to give more than a sketch of the Duke such as he appears to me, who certainly will not be thought a common man even among men of merit. His person bespeaks depth and penetration, a desire to please tempered by fortitude, nay by severity. He is polite to affectation; speaks with precision, and with a degree of elegance; but he is somewhat too careful to speak thus, and the proper word sometimes escapes him. He understands the art of listening, and of interrogating according to the very spirit of reply. Praise, gracefully embellished and artfully concealed, he finds agreeable. He is prodigiously laborious, well informed, and perspicuous. However able his first Minister Feronce may be, the Duke superintends all affairs, and generally decides for himself. His correspondence is immense, for which he can only be indebted to his personal consideration; because he cannot be sufficiently wealthy to keep so many correspondents in pay; and few great Courts are so well informed as he is. All his affairs are in excellent order. He became the reigning Duke of Brunswick in 1780, and found his principality loaded with debts, to the amount of forty millions of livres. His administration has been such that, with a revenue of about one hundred thousand louis, and a sinking fund in which he has deposited the savings of the English sub-

sidies, he will, in 1790, not only have perfectly liqui-
dated the debts of the sovereignty, but, also, those of
the State. His country is as free as it can be; and is
happy and contented, except that the trading class
regret the prodigality of his father. Not that the
reigning Duke is less sensible to elegant pleasures
than another; but, severely observant of decency, and
religiously faithful to his duty as a Prince, he has
perceived that economy was his only resource. His
mistress, Madame Hartfield, is the most reasonable
woman at Court; and so proper is this attachment that,
having a short time since discovered an inclination for
another woman, the Duchess leagued with Madame
Hartfield to keep her at a distance. Truly an Alci-
biades, he delights in the pleasures and the graces;
but these never subtract anything from his labors or
his duties, not even those of prudence. When he is
to act as a Prussian general, no one is so early, so
active, so minute as himself. It is a mark of superior
character and understanding, in my opinion, that the
labor of the day can be less properly said to be sufficient for him than he is for the labor of the day; his
first ambition is that of executing it well. Intoxicated
by military success, and universally pointed out as a
great general (especially since the campaign of 1778,
during which he all the winter maintained the feeble
post of Troppau, to which the King of Prussia annexed a kind of vanity, against every effort of the
Austrians), he appears effectually to have quitted
military glory, to betake himself to the cares of government. Everywhere made welcome, possessed of
unbounded curiosity, he still is capable of assiduously
confining himself to Brunswick, and attaching himself
to business. He is, in fine, a man of an uncommon
stamp, but too wise to be formidable to the wise. He
delights much in France, with which he is exceedingly

well acquainted, and appears to be very fond of whatever comes from that country. His eldest son, returning from Lausanne, has passed through Franche-Comté, Languedoc, and Provence, and is very desirous to return to France. I shall soon know if he is to be sent back. In my opinion the son cannot be treated with too much respect there, so as to testify confidence in the father; which it seems to me would give the latter pleasure, by which he would certainly be sufficiently confirmed and flattered, to keep this treatment in memory.

I cannot at present speak of the supper, when the Duke removed me from the place of honor, opposite the Duchess, where I sat at dinner, to seat me beside himself, which is always at the far end of the table. The conversation was lively, and absolutely individual, but not political. (We had listeners.) He questioned me much concerning France. I am to dine with him to-day, and to sup with the Duchess Dowager, at Antoinetten-Ruh. I could not avoid this tax on propriety, which deprives me of an opportunity of supping with the Duke,—a favor he rarely grants, and which appeared to be much remarked here, yesterday, where I am observed with anxiety. Perhaps I am supposed a place hunter.

The continuance of Zimmermann at Potsdam is prolonged, more than it was supposed it would have been. He writes that the dropsy is not confirmed, and he again talks of an asthma. This is medical cant. He is the creature of the King, not of the public. Certain it is that he has gained no victory over eel pies and *polenta;* that there are no longer any wrinkles in the face; and that the parts are all inflated and œdematous.

Prince Henry, however, is returned to Rheinsberg, where the youthful and handsome R——, as it is said, occasions rain and fair weather.

I can warrant it as a fact that a Scotchman who is first physician to Catherine II. of Russia, being lately at Vienna, dined at the table of the Emperor, and was seated by his side. Indeed, this was avowed in the Gazettes; but it was not there avowed that, while this physician remained at Vienna, Cobenzl (the Austrian Ambassador to the Court of Petersburg, but then at Vienna) having been ordered to show the physician a pleasure house in the vicinity of the metropolis, the Emperor on horseback HAPPENED to meet the doctor on the road, and continued in conversation with him, at the coach window, for the space of more than two leagues.

LETTER IV

July 16th, 1786.

TO-DAY I was three hours alone with the Duke, after rising from dinner. The conversation was animated, frank, and almost confidential: it confirmed me in most of the opinions I gave in my last letter (Number III.), but it has inspired me with much fear, concerning the situation of Prussia after the death of the King. The successor seems to have every symptom of the most incurable weakness; the most corrupt among the persons by whom he is surrounded, of whom the gloomy and visionary Bishopswerder may be ranked as first, daily increase in power. There is a coolness said to prevail between the Heir Apparent and his uncles. The coadjutorship of the Order of St. John, bestowed with great solemnity on Prince Henry, the eldest son of Prince Ferdinand, which deprives the successor of more than fifty thousand crowns per annum, is the most recent cause of this coolness. It should seem that there have been very powerful in-

trigues for the establishment of these two young
Princes, whom both city and Court regard as the children of Count Schmettau. The measures taken to
effect this were strengthened at the very moment when
the King was supposed to be expiring, so as to bind
the successor, of whom they consequently have testified
their suspicion. To the King's brother, Prince Henry,
the half at least of all this appertains; nor has the
Heir Apparent attempted to conceal his dissatisfaction.
Thence it results that all the subaltern parties, and
their dirty cabals, become more active; so that the respect in which the Court of Berlin has been held, and
in which consists its greatest power, depends, perhaps,
but too much on the life of the King; unless the Duke
of Brunswick should seize the reins of government, the
burden of which he seriously appears to dread. In
effect, a kingdom like this, which has no constituent
foundation, will be cruelly agitated, should the winds
of Court begin to blow; and should the Duke, who has
formed himself without having studied in the school
of adversity, and whose reason and sagacity it is impossible to speak too highly of, fear to reverse the
whole system of his mode of life. But he does not
start at difficulties; and he is too much interested in the
prosperity of Prussia not to seek to obtain influence
there.

It does not appear to me probable that the first six
months, or even the first year, should produce any
change, or do more than prepare for change. The
Duke has repeatedly assured me that all the Protestant
powers of Germany, and a great part of the Catholic,
would incontrovertibly be in the interest of France,
whenever the latter should fully convince the Germanic body of her amicable intentions; and when I
asked what pledges should be given us that the high
part with which the Elector of Hanover was invested,

in the confederation of the Princes, should not sway
the Cabinet of Berlin to the side of the English, and
should not become an invincible impediment to any
sincere union between Versailles and Prussia, he
clearly showed me, so as not to admit of reply, that
the Germanic league would never have existed, or at
least would never have assumed its present form, had
it not been for the ambiguity of our conduct, relative
to the Schelde, to Bavaria, and to the Oriental system. He added that the Elector of Hanover, and the
King of England, were two very distinct persons:
and that the English and the Germans were great
strangers to each other.

Here I ought to observe that, in my opinion, the
Duke overacts his part, whenever he speaks of depress-
ing England, which I well know he loves; and that
perhaps because he feels his family connections may,
in this respect, render him more liable to suspicion.
In a word, I cannot too often repeat that they do not
appear to have confidence in us, but that such confidence is very sincerely desired; and that the more because the Emperor, unsupported by France, is not
held in the least dread, and that there is a reigning conviction he will not dare to take a single step, when the
Cabinet of Versailles shall say, " We will not suffer
any infraction."

Be it however remarked that the incoherent conduct of the Emperor, and his abrupt vagaries, often
unhinge all the combinations of reason. The Duke
has to-day learned a fact of this kind, which may well
incite meditation.

The Baron of Gemmingen, some time since, wrote a
very violent pamphlet against the German confederacy.
Dohm, an excellent Prussian civilian, answered in a
strong and victorious manner. The Ministry of
Vienna, in consequence, requested our Ministry to

entreat the Court of Berlin to suffer wordy hostilities to cease. The latter consented; but there has just appeared (printed indeed at Munich, but indubitably coming from Vienna) a satirical and bitter reply to Dohm. Verbal wars are rarely insignificant at Vienna, where they are never begun but under the auspices of Government.

The following is another fact of serious import, if true. The Duke has received advice, from Vienna, that between four and five thousand Russians have entered Poland, where the Diet threatens to be very turbulent. The Duke is desirous we should take a decisive part concerning and against all new arrangements tending to the further dissolution or dismemberment of Poland. I have not knowledge sufficient of this country to enter into any circumstantial detail; but I spoke to him on the subject of Courland, explaining my ideas, relative to the late proceedings of Russia in this country, such as they will be found in my Memorial; and I introduced my discourse as if arising out of the conversation. He was ardently attentive to what I said, and promised to write according to my sense of the danger to Count Hertzberg. I well comprehend that the circumstances of the moment are nothing less than favorable; and the assent which was warmly given by a most excellent politician emboldens me to entreat that my Memorial may be taken into consideration, though it should only be practicable in future, and that some instructions may be sent me, on the manner in which I may sound the Duke of Courland on this head, whom I shall meet at Berlin, and the principal persons of Courland, with whom I may easily correspond; my trade of traveler being known, and my desire to collect facts and to deduce consequences giving great opportunities to inquire and speak concerning all subjects.

MEMORIAL

Sent to the Court of France, Concerning the Declaration Made by Russia to Courland, and Published in the "Leyden Gazettes," from the 20th of May to the 3rd of June, 1786.

COURLAND has lately been officially menaced with the indignation of the Sovereign of all the Russias, on the supposition that the report, relative to the abdication of the Duke of Courland in favor of the Prince of Wurtemberg, a general in the Prussian service, should be true.

The reigning Duke, Ernest John, a ferocious man, so much abhorred in his own country as not to be able to remain there, although he should not dread any violence from the Ministry of Petersburg, is known to be the son of the famous Biron, who was reinstated Duke of Courland, in 1760, by the influence, or rather through the fear of Russia, which power, with the aid of forty thousand men, expelled Prince Charles of Saxony, the uncle of the Elector and the legitimate Duke, to restore the former favorite of Elizabeth, whom a court faction had lately recalled from Siberia.

It is also known that this Ernest John has more than once felt the whole weight of the resentment of Catherine II.; that he has been near twenty years banished into Siberia; that he has no influence whatever in Courland; and that his abdication is universally wished.

But it is not known, or rather it is kept secret, that he was enjoined, by a Ukase (or edict) six years ago, to resign his duchy to Prince Potemkin; and that, by the advice of the Chancellor Taubè, and of the Chamberlain Howen, he averted the storm by remitting to Prince Potemkin (whose affairs ever were and are in disorder) two hundred thousand ducats. Rason, the ministerial secretary of the Duke, was intrusted to carry him this sum.

Whether it be that Potemkin, while waiting for the execution of his grand projects, which perhaps relate. to the Oriental system, or to circumstances that are yet immature, wishes to acquire this accession of power; whether it be that he is in want of money; or more especially whether it be that the Duke of Courland, since his situation has been so precarious is known in consequence of his avarice to have become one of the richest princes in Europe, and that, rendered effeminate by adversity, old age, and the daily importunities of his last wife, who has acquired some influence over him, he is endeavoring to place himself beyond the reach of ill fortune; be it which of these causes it may, a similar crisis is again returned.

The Cabinet of Petersburg is ignorant of none of these things. It doubtless fears that the Court of Berlin is speculating concerning the provinces of Courland; hoping, by the aid of a new Duke, to have it entirely at its disposal. The conditions which gave Poland a right of protection over Courland having ceased, when power became law, and at the moment the oppressed republic found it impossible to fulfill those conditions, it is not absurd to apprehend that Prussia will surreptitiously take the place of Poland, and thus to its own profit confirm the right by the deed.

Courland is in reality far from a contemptible country. Its climate, being in the 57th degree of latitude, though sufficiently is not insupportably cold. Its extent in length is eighty leagues, and in breadth fifty. Its soil is fertile, and its natural products are very necessary for all the commercial and maritime powers. Two principal and navigable rivers divide it, from east to west, the Aa and the Windau; several brooks and canals intersect it in every direction. It has two ports, Windau and Liebau on the Baltic. In its present important and indolent state its commerce, active and passive, does not employ less than from six to seven hundred vessels, of three, four, and as far as eight hundred tons burden. It contains seven or eight small towns, and its population is estimated at more than a million and a half of inhabitants. The landholders may be supposed not to be in a state of wretchedness, since the revenues of the reigning Duke, whose influence in the republic is so small, annually amount to two hundred thousand pounds sterling. Such is the outline of the situation of Courland.

It would be of little use to prove in this place that the republic being a free State, the Prince of which is purely elective, so that though he may abdicate he cannot transfer his privileges, Russia cannot legally interfere in the affairs of Courland, which ought to be as independent as are its rights. This word RIGHTS is totally stripped of meaning when opposed to the word POWER. Russia has long been in the habit of vexing Courland, internally and externally; of dictating the choice of its Governors; of laying its suffrages under restraint; and of extorting or forcibly seizing on its money, its produce and its men. The Monarchs of Petersburg have always made it a principle to familiarize the Courts of Europe to the supposition that Courland has no political existence except such as Russia shall please to bestow. All this is well known.

The points I should wish briefly here to examine are:

1. Whether it is not evidently our interest to introduce a new order of affairs; and—

2. Whether we have not the means so to do.

Courland, kept back and oppressed by every kind of exterior and interior tyranny, possesses no one species of manufacture. It abounds in naval stores; stores for which reason there is an affinity, resulting from circumstances, between Courland and France, which latter holds the first rank among industrial nations, or an affinity between their mutual products, the direct barter of which would give birth to the most advantageous kind of trade.

In reality, there exists at present a species of barter between Courland and France; but in so indirect a manner that it is carried on at second or third hand, by the intervention of the English, the Dutch, the Swedes, the Danes, the Prussians, the Hanse Towns, etc.

This intervention absorbs and destroys all the benefit which a trade so advantageous would be of to France, and which certainly ought abundantly to procure us, and at a moderate price, a price unknown in our dockyards and markets, ship timber, masts, spokes, fellies, veneering wood, etc., grain, ship beef, saltfish, vegetables, etc. The natural returns for these would be the produce of our industry, from the coarsest to the finest articles (for nothing is manufactured in Courland), which the Courlanders (whose consumption is great, and who are very desirous of articles of luxury, and even of finery) would then obtain from us at a moderate price, still infinitely lucrative to our traders.

The advantage of this direct trade would not be confined merely to money; for, besides the influence which such intimate connections with Courland would give us in the Baltic and the North, where we should become the mediators between Prussia, Russia, and Poland, which last State must necessarily soon undergo some new change, France, by a commercial treaty with Courland, would acquire two ports on the Baltic, which would at least remain neuter and almost exclusive to herself. These would be useful to us, both in war and peace, as depository places for stores, and most of the materials which are requisite for the royal and mercantile marine; and would highly compensate the disadvantage which continually increases, and which is preparing for us in the North, relative to our marine, in consequence of the strict connections between England and Russia.

To the attentive observer, England presents every symptom which can menace the possessions of the Dutch in the East, and which can forebode the desire of revenge. Russia can at any time rob France of a great part of the naval supplies of war in the European seas.

This order of affairs cannot too soon be reversed.

Let it be attentively observed that there is no question here of a new treaty, but the revival of an ancient one; for the Cardinal de Richelieu made a treaty with Courland, in 1643, which was registered by the Parliament of Paris, in 1647; so that, should we at present treat with Courland, we can decisively affirm, and demonstrate, we are committing no innovation.

This seems to me to be a very important remark, which ought not a little to influence the resolution that may be taken, and the form given to that resolution, when once it is taken.

The States of Courland desire this political affinity between the two countries. The Chamberlain Howen, of whom I have spoken, is a man of the greatest influence in the republic, and, of all the Courlanders, the most anti-Russian; because that, while an envoy from Courland to the Court of Warsaw, he was carried off, by order of the Empress, and banished into Siberia. His nephew was indirectly, but formally, charged to question the Government of France on this subject. I positively know he has spoken to the Comte de Vergennes, and that the only answer he received from the Minister was:

1. That, he being Minister for Foreign Affairs, this was a subject that did not appertain to his department.

2. That it was requisite that the Duke of Courland

and the States, conjointly and officially, should make a proposition to the King, concerning a treaty of commerce.

To this I reply:

1. That, most certainly, the Minister for Foreign Affairs ought to consult with the Minister of Finance, on whatever relates to commercial treaties, but that this does not therefore appear to me a sufficient reason to reject either the project or the proposal.

2. That it would be absurd to suppose that Courland, bowed as it is under the iron rod of present circumstances, would expose itself, by taking any open step, without first being certain its propositions should be favourably received, and that the country should be protected against that power which, possessed of strength and in the habit of taking its will for law, should make every effort to counteract and prevent whatever might tend to impart solidity to the constitution of Courland, and to render its political independence respectable.

I see no hope that any power, except Prussia, should interest itself in the affairs of this province. And this is the second point which it is my intention to prove, in this Memorial.

1. Because the situation of the Prussian States is such that the stability and prosperity of Courland ought no less to influence the King of Prussia than if this country was one of his own provinces.

2. Because he cannot prudently covet Courland, which Russia would never leave him in peaceable possession of, and which would but increase the length of his provinces, already too much extended, without rendering the power more real or more compact.

This latter point is self-demonstrative; and, as to the advantages which Prussia might derive from the future stability of Courland, and from the increase of its energy and industry, these are evident from a mere view of the map. Between the States of Brandenburg and Russia there is only the dismemberment of Poland, which at present forms part of Prussian Lithuania and of Courland, of which the King of Prussia, politely speaking, would become the useful proprietor that very day on which he should become its guardian and protector. Russia, therefore, necessarily and indubitably is formidable to none of the powers of Europe, Prussia excepted, on which kingdom she can bring evil, and which can do her no injury.

On the other part, it is known that there is only a very narrow slip of Polish Lithuania between the States of Prussia and Courland, which barely extends from five to six leagues. Here Prussia might easily make legal and amicable acquisitions, sufficient to open a very advantageous transport trade on the Memel, and the canals that might be cut between that river and the rivers of Courland, descending to the ports of the Baltic, of which I have spoken.

Either I am much deceived or the Ministry of Berlin might easily be made to comprehend that, instead of forming projects of ambition on this republic, its real interest would be to declare, in some manner, Prussia to be the representative of Poland in her engagements toward Courland, as stipulated by the *pacta conventa* and the *pacta subjectionis,* which have been actually and necessarily destroyed. Prussia might find a hundred reasons of public right to allege, independent of her dignity and safety. This proposition, and that of acceding to our treaty of commerce with Courland, would therefore contain nothing imprudent; it would perhaps be a good means of depriving the House of Brandenburg of all fears relative to our Northern politics. Nor does it seem to be impossible but that the King of Prussia would, on this condition, support

the declaration we might make to the Court of Petersburg, that it was our determination to protect Courland; and not to suffer a free country, allied to France
by ancient treaties, to be humbled, over which we
would not permit any direct and legislative influence
to be exerted by any Court.

Such a declaration, softened by every diplomatic
formality, which is so easily practiced, would at that
time be sufficient, in my opinion, especially if made in
concert with the Court of Berlin, to repel the projects
of usurpation conceived by Russia over Courland.

Be these things as they may, this small country, too
little known, together with Poland and the Germanic
body, claims the serious attention of the King of
France; who, if my opinion be right, has no other
general interest, on the continent, than that of maintaining peace and the reciprocal safety of States.

LETTER V

July 19th, 1786.

YESTERDAY morning, before my departure, the Duke
granted me an audience for the space of about three
hours; or rather, personally indicated a conference,
under the pretense of remitting letters to Berlin, and
which, indeed, he committed to my care. We again
spoke of general affairs, and of the particular situation
of Prussia; of the suspicions which he pretends it is
impossible to avoid entertaining, concerning our intentions and our system (how should I answer him
such is the disorder of our finances that it is impossible
we should have any system?) ; of the dread that daily
increases, which the Emperor necessarily inspires, who
does good awkwardly, but who does enough to acquire
great power, the basis of which is magnificent, and

highly disproportionate to that of any other monarchy, France excepted; of the impossibility of finding any counterpoise to this power, except in the prudence of the Cabinet of Versailles; of the little hope that the new regulations of Prussia should be wise; of the various directions which the various factions that were fermenting at Berlin might take; of the military vigor and the ambitious fumes which intoxicate the Duke of Weymar, who aspires to enter into the service of Prussia, and to embroil parties; of the necessity which there was that the Cabinet of Versailles should send a man of merit to Berlin, there to inspire awe and give advice, keep watch over the factious and the turbulent, etc., etc., etc.

At length, questioning me with an air of fearing what he was going to say was an absurdity, he asked whether I should think the project of an alliance between France, England, and Prussia an impracticable chimera; the end of which, solemnly avowed, should be to guarantee, throughout Europe, to each Prince his respective possessions; a measure in itself noble, and worthy of the two first powers, which should command all others to remain at peace; founded on the evident and combined interest of the two rivals, and the greatest obstacle to which would be that no one would dare to put it in execution.

The idea, on which I have for these seven years been ruminating, is too sublime not to be seductive. It would infallibly immortalize the Sovereign by whom it should be realized, and the Minister by whom it should be promoted. It would change the face of Europe, and totally to our advantage; for, once again, commercial treaties, however advantageous to England, would never make the English anything more than our carriers and our most useful factors.

The Duke has permitted me to correspond with

him; he even desired me so to do, and I find I have
obtained almost that very place in his opinion which
I myself could have wished.

July 21st, 1786.

FIRST POSTSCRIPT.—I am arrived, and perhaps I
shall learn but little to-day. The dropsy is in the
stomach; nay, in the lungs. He was informed of it
on Thursday. He heard it with great magnanimity,
say some; others affirm he treated the physician, who
was too sincere, very ill. He might drag on life, if
he would take advice, Doctor Baylies says, another
year; but I suspect he will never give up eel pies.
Count Hertzberg has been at Sans Souci this week
past; he had never before been sent for. Two days
previous to that on which the King made him this
kind of honorable reparation, if, however, it be anything else than the necessity of giving breath to those
who are obliged to converse with him, and of enliven-
ing his conversation, the Heir Apparent dined with
the Count at his country seat, and passed the best part
of the evening with him and the Prince of Dessau.
This has bewildered the parties that are hotly animated
against this estimable Minister, in and for whom, according to my opinion, our embassy has always testified too little confidence and respect.

SECOND POSTSCRIPT.—I have intelligence, from
what I believe to be a very certain and profound
source, wholly independent of the Cabinet of Berlin,
that the Emperor has made preparations which greatly
menace those parts of Moldavia and Wallachia that
would be convenient to him to possess; that he is immediately expected to repair to those frontiers in person; and that such motions cannot otherwise be
explained than by reacting the conquest of the Crimea

in those countries. This information, combined with the ultimatum which Russia has delivered in to the Porte, seems to me to be of sovereign importance. I do not know the precise intentions of the Court of France; but if the indefinite aggrandizement of the Emperor, and particularly the execution of the Oriental system, are as formidable to us as I suppose them to be, I entreat deliberations may be held whether it befits the dignity of the King to suffer the tragedy of Poland to recommence, the interest of the State to lose the Levant trade, or prudent policy to temporize, when the match is putting to the touch-hole. I cannot for my part doubt but that our inactivity, in such a case, must be gratuitous; because the Emperor would most certainly not brave us; and fatal also, since we are precisely the only power who have at once the interest and the strength to impede such attempts. England will trouble herself little concerning them, and without us Prussia is nothing.

LETTER VI

July 21st, 1786.

.   .   .   .

An odd incident has happened to me. I am just re-turned from the French Ambassador's who sent me word he could not have the honour of receiving my visit, because he was busy. To feel the whole import of this act, it is necessary to know that there has lately appeared an article in the "Hamburg Gazette," affirm-ing in express terms I had received orders to quit France. You will further recollect that, in general, the Ambassador of France is eagerly desirous of re-ceiving the visits of French travelers. Such is the present combination of circumstances that this, which

would only, on any other occasion, be an affair of
rather serious impoliteness, is at this moment a very
embarrassing affectation. I believe I have no need to
tell you I am far superior to punctilio; but this is not
mere form. The natural preponderance of France
is such that the respect in which a native of that
country is held cannot be wholly independent of the
reception he shall meet from the Ambassador. What,
then, must be thought when he shall be envied, suspected, and watched, and when pretenses are sought
to render his character equivocal? And what must
be his situation, when, far from seeking to quarrel
with the Ambassador it is his duty and his wish, on all
occasions, to preserve appearances, and to protect him
from becoming instead of making him ridiculous?

You will have no difficulty in comprehending that it
is an intricate affair, and that I must well reflect on
the part I have to take. At present I must dissemble,
and expose myself to a new refusal to-morrow; but
it will be impossible to suffer this new refusal to remain unnoticed. I write you word of this in order
that, in any case, and rather too soon than too late,
you should inform M. d'Esterno it is not the intention of Government that I should be treated in a
disrespectful manner, and still less as a proscribed
person. He is so much of a timid trembler, that he
may have been imposed upon by the Hamburg para-
graph. I do not think him sufficiently cunning to have
written it himself. He certainly appeared ridiculously
disturbed at my return, and entirely departed from
his silent circumspection, that he might discover, by
questioning those whom he supposed intimate with me,
what were my intentions. Some of the numerous persons who do not love him, especially among the *corps
diplomatique,* have amused themselves with inventing
tales relative to my views, similar to those of the

"Thousand and One Nights." His brain is in a state of fermentation upon the subject; and the more so as he is acting out of character. I may in consequence of this be very ill-situated here. To prevent this you will take proper measures. I shall tell you more before I seal this letter; he is not a person who will oppose the least ministerial insinuation.

LETTER VII

July 23d, 1786.

THERE is nobody here, consequently I shall for some days lead an inactive life. There is no Court, except that of Prince Ferdinand, which is always insignificant; he is at present on the recovery. Prince Frederick of Brunswick knows nothing. The English Embassy caress and suspect me. Count Hertzberg still remains at Sans Souci; I must, therefore, satisfy myself with the sterility of the moment. I imagine I have discovered that the real occasion of the threatening declaration of Russia respecting Courland, was a secret proposal of marriage between the Countess of Wurtemberg, the natural daughter of the Duke, and a Prussian; and the increasing intimacy of the Duke with the Heir Apparent, who has found in the purse of this savage Scythian that pecuniary aid with which he ought long since to have been supplied by France. The Duke of Courland departed, soon after the menace of Petersburg appeared, with his wife, who is said to be pregnant, to drink the Pyrmont waters. According to all appearances, instead of remaining at Berlin on his return, he will go to Mittau. He still continues to make acquisitions in the Prussian dominions; he has lately bought the county of Sagan, in Silesia; and the King, who was not a little vexed to see the Prince of Lobkowitz spend the revenues of this fine estate at Vienna, treats the Duke of Courland with great favour. Besides remitting the manor fees, he consented to alienate or at least to entail the fief on female descendants, which before was revertible to the Crown on the want of male heirs; so that the Duke, who has no son, found that, by his carelessness, or a very strange kind of ignorance, he had risked six hundred thousand German crowns on a chance the most hazardous.

It is indubitable that Prince Potemkin is, or appears to be, more in favor than ever. It has been found necessary to approve his disobedience. There are reports that he has sought a reconciliation with the Grand Duke, which he has accomplished.

The new Minister of Petersburg (the son of Field-marshal Romanzow) is not successful here; intelligent people, however, affirm he possesses understanding and information. I know he has strong prejudices against me, which I shall endeavor to remove, and to gain his intimacy; for he is of such a nature that much may be derived from his acquaintance. But you must feel I stand in need of some instructions, or at least of a series of questions, which shall serve me as a compass, and by which I may obtain the customary intelligence. General politics have for some years been very incoherent, for want of possessing some fixed system. Which of the two alliances, that of the House of Austria, or that between the two Imperial Courts, Austria and Russia, ought to be regarded as stable, sacred, and subordinate to the other? Is France resolved to quit her natural train, I mean to say her continental system, for the maritime? If so, whether wisely or not, this will at least explain our extreme cautiousness, in what relates to the projects of the Court of Vienna.

The man who wants this knowledge can do little more than wander at a venture; he may, with more or less intelligence, write a gazette, but, not having a sufficient basis to build on, cannot be a negotiator. I entreat it may not be supposed I have the presumption to interrogate; I only mean to explain, in very few words, such of the reasons which, exclusive of my own want of capacity, and of the few means my situation affords me, infinitely circumscribe that utility which I wish and labor to be of to my country.

I hope I shall not be suspected of supposing any importance annexed to those extracts from the German newspapers, which I shall in future send by every courier. It is purely an object of curiosity, but which I thought might be agreeable in a country where, I believe, not a single German gazette is received; and into which so many ambassadors send no other dispatches than those obtained on the authority of these gazettes. I shall only speak in my extracts of the news of the North.

FIRST POSTSCRIPT.—Advice yesterday arrived commanding Lord Dalrymple to depart, and bear the Order of the Garter to the Landgrave of Hesse Cassel.

SECOND POSTSCRIPT.—I have received a very friendly letter from Sans Souci. The King seems to hope he shall still live long; he appears, however, to be much more occupied concerning himself and his pineapples than by foreign affairs. Astonishment is testified (this is a surprising affair!) though in a very obliging manner, that the son of the Comte de Vergennes should pass through Hamburg, Dresden, Vienna, etc., without any hope of seeing him at Berlin. I have answered I was very grateful, in behalf of my nation, for the importance annexed to the topographical peregrination of the son of our Minister for Foreign Affairs, and that I imagined nothing could be more flattering to his father; but that, for my own part, I was wholly uninformed on the subject; though I was persuaded that, if the Court of Berlin was reserved as the last place to be visited, it would only be from a love of the *Crescendo*. I said the same to Count Goertz, by whom I was warmly questioned.

LETTER VIII

BERLIN, *July 26th,* 1786.

THE fine weather supports the life of the King, but he is ill. On Wednesday he was for some minutes wheeled about in his chair, by which he was much incommoded, and suffered greatly during and after the exercise. His pains increased on Thursday, and yesterday he was no better. I persist in my opinion that the period of his existence will be toward the month of September.

The Heir Apparent does not quit Potsdam, where he keeps on the watch. Still the same respectful passion for Mademoiselle Voss. During a short journey that she lately made with her brother, a confidential *valet de chambre* followed her carriage at a distance, and if the beauty, who in my opinion is very ordinary, testified the least desire (to eat white bread, for example), before she had proceeded half a league she found everything she wished. It appears indubitable that she has not yet yielded. No great use can be made either of her uncle or her brothers. Frenchwomen arrive daily; but I doubt much whether there will be any great advantage derived from them, except to innkeepers and milliners.

The Duke of Courland has lent the Heir Apparent

money to pay his debts at Berlin; they are supposed to be all discharged, except those of his Princess, which they are not very anxious to liquidate, from the fear of giving her bad habits.

I have spoken at large with Struensee. He supposes the project of the bank to be a grand and superb operation, which cannot but succeed. He asks timely information, and promises to place and cause to be placed in it a considerable sum; but the secret must only be known to him, and the subject treated only between ourselves.

LETTER IX

July 31st, 1786.

. . . .

I SUPPOSE in reality that, in this commencement of correspondence, my letters are waited for, in order to write to me; however, if my letter of the 23d of July (Number V.) has been well deciphered and considered, it cannot be disowned that I stand in need of instructions. Politics are at a crisis. I repeat, politics are at a crisis. It is impossible they should continue as they are, whether it be from endeavors to accelerate or efforts to retard. Everything denotes the Oriental system to increase in vigor. I have no doubt but that, soon or late, it will be destructive of that of the West; and the danger is immediate, is instantaneous. If Turkey in Europe, speaking in political and commercial language, be one of our colonies, if we are not resolved to leave it to its fate, is it not time to pay it some attention? and because that it is so, is the general system of Europe out of the question? Were the King of Prussia ten years younger, he would well know how to restore the equilibrium, for he would

take as much from Poland as others might take elsewhere; but he dies and has no successor. For my own
part, it is easy to conceive, I shall consume my time
in barren efforts; and, after taking much more trouble,
shall be much less useful than if I knew what track to
follow, and where to gain information.

The King is in daily danger of death, though he
may live some months. I persist in my autumnal prognostics. Prince Henry having sent for me to Rheinsberg by a very formal and friendly letter, it would
appear affectation in me not to go; and I shall set off
on Wednesday, after the departure of the courier. I
shall not remain there longer than a week, where I
shall have good opportunities of intelligence concerning the state of the King, and of gaining information
on various matters.

POSTSCRIPT.—The King is sensibly worse; he has
had a fever these two days; this may kill him, or prolong his life. Nature has continually done so much for
this extraordinary man, that nothing more is wanting
to restore him than a hemorrhoidal eruption. The
muscular powers are very great.

The English Embassy has received advice from
Vienna that the Emperor is in Transylvania, and that
the world is ignorant of what he is doing, what he
intends, or even to what place he is gone.

All the boats on the Danube are taken into his service.

The maritime company wishes to monopolize the
sale of snuff and tobacco in Sweden, offering to pay
half a million annually to the King; but the Swedish
States have totally refused to forbid the cultivation
of tobacco in the kingdom, and this was the condition,
sine quâ non. The actions of this Monarch decline
greatly, on all occasions; another Diet like the present,

and monarchical power would once more fail in Sweden. It appears to be undoubted that the rumor of his having turned Catholic, on his journey to Rome, has alienated the whole nation. But are we to impute nothing to the intrigues of Russia, in the present fermentation?

Struensee repeats that, if the bank be established, he and his friends are ready; that is to say, the most moneyed men in the kingdom, and probably, under a new reign, the Government itself. The man ought to be cherished. It would be of importance were I often empowered to give him good information respecting the state of the place. Meditate on this. His resources are in himself, and will probably survive his administration. He has gained immensely by speculating in the English funds. He ought to be weaned of this, to which he is self-inclined, for he feels and owns that chances in the English funds are exhausted for the remainder of his life.

LETTER X

August 2d, 1786.

Written before my departure for Rheinsberg.

. . . .

THE King is evidently better, at least with respect to pain, when he does not move; he has even left off the use of the *taraxicum*, or dandelion, the only thing Zimmermann prescribed, who, consequently, is in despair. He simply takes a tincture of rhubarb mixed with diarrhœtics, which gives him copious evacuations. His appetite is very good, which he indulges without restraint. The most unhealthy dishes are his greatest favorites. If indigestion be the consequence, as it frequently is, he takes a double aperitive dose.

Frese, his physician of Potsdam, still continues in disgrace, for having dared to whisper the word dropsy on the question being asked him, and an appeal made to his conscience, what was the name and character of the disease. The King is exceedingly chilly, and is continually enveloped in furs, and covered by feather beds. He has not entered his bed these six weeks, but is removed from one armchair to another, in which he takes tolerably long sleeps, turned on his right side. Inflation augments; the scrotum is exceedingly tumid. He perceives this, but will not persuade himself, or appear to believe, that it is anything more than the inflated of convalescence, and the result of great feebleness.

This information is minutely exact, and very recent. There is no doubt of his unwillingness to die. The people best informed think that, as soon as he believes himself really dropsical and at the point of death, he will submit to be tapped, and to the most violent remedies, rather than peaceably resign himself to sleep with his fathers. He even desired, some time since, incisions might be made in his hams and thighs; but the physician feared to risk them. With respect to his understanding, it is still sound; and he even continues his labors.

LETTER XI

August 8th, 1786.

THE King is dangerously ill; some affirm he has not many hours to live, but this probably partakes of exaggeration. On the fourth, the erysipelas with blisters on the legs made their appearance; this prognosticates bursting, and soon after gangrene. At present there is suffocation, and a most infectious smell. The smallest fever—and the curtain must drop.

LETTER XII

August 12th, 1786.

THE King is apparently much better. The evacuation, which was the consequence of the apertures in his legs, has caused the swelling to abate, and given ease; but has been followed by a dangerous excess of appetite. He cannot continue in this state. You may expect to receive a grand packet at my return from Rheinsberg.

LETTER XIII

August 15th, 1786.

I AM just returned from Rheinsberg, where I have lived in the utmost familiarity with Prince Henry. I have numerous modes of communication, which will develop themselves as time and opportunity shall serve; at present I shall only state consequences.

Prince Henry is in the utmost incertitude, concerning what he shall or shall not be under the new reign. He greatly dreads, and more than he wishes to appear to dread, though his fears are very visible, the influence of Count Hertzberg, who is still detained at Sans Souci, but, as I think, only for the sake of his conversation,—at least, as far as respects the old King. This Count Hertzberg has openly espoused the English system; but, though the flatteries of Ewart and his secret arts have much profited by the long contempt in which the French Embassy have held this Minister, I believe his principal reason for attaching himself to England is because Prince Henry, his implacable enemy, is the avowed and fanatical protector of the French system; and because the Count imagines he cannot otherwise make himself indispensably necessary to the opposite party; for which reason he clothes himself in the uniform of the Stadtholder.

In consequence of this, and persuaded as I am that Prince Henry has not sufficient influence over the successor (who is weary of avuncular despotism) to displace Hertzberg, who will continually batter his enemy in breach, by boasting, by meannesses, by a faithful portrait of the Prince's creatures, and by the jealousy with which he will inspire the new King against Prince Henry, who, if he be anything, will be master; convinced also that he (Hertzberg) is useful to France, which is influenced by the uncle because he holds the English system in abhorrence I have exerted every effort to induce Prince Henry (who wants nothing but dissimulation) to reconcile himself with Count Hertzberg, and thus put his nephew out of fear. This he might with the greater security do, because Hertzberg, relative to him, could be nothing more than a first clerk, who, if he should act uprightly, would make as good a clerk as another; and who, should he endeavor to deceive, might be the more easily crushed after having been admitted a colleague.

I have had much difficulty in persuading him, for Baron Knyphausen, the brother-in-law of Hertzberg, and his irreconcilable enemy, because that their interests clash, is possessed of the entire political confidence of the Prince, of which he is worthy, for he is a very able man, and perhaps the only able man in Prussia; but as he is in danger of a confirmed palsy as his mind and body both decay, and as the Prince himself perceives they do, I was able to effect my purpose by dwelling on all these circumstances, while I heaped exaggerated praise on Baron Knyphausen, and expressed infinite regret for his situation; so that I have prevailed on the Prince, and have personally received a commission to negotiate an accommodation between him and Hertzberg; for which purpose I shall go the day after to-morrow to Potsdam.

What may I augur from all this? Weakness only and incoherency. It appears indubitable that petty cabals, the fine arts, the blues, the subalterns, the wardrobe, and particularly the mystics, will engross the new. King. I have anecdotes innumerable on the subject by which I shall endeavor to profit, and which I shall communicate in good time. Has he any system? I believe not. Any understanding? Of that I doubt. Any character? I cannot tell; my present opinion is that no conclusions, for or against, ought yet to be drawn.

To memorials exceedingly well drawn up by Prince Henry and Baron Knyphausen, all tending to demonstrate that, should Prussia attach itself to the English system, fifteen years hence Frederick William will be the Marquis of Brandenburg, he gives replies which are slow, vague, laconic, and hieroglyphic. He wrote the other day, for example (I saw the letter), "THE PRINCE OF THE ASTURIAS IS ALL ENGLISH." Baron Boden, however, who is his confidential correspondent, and who has lately remained shut up with him a whole week in his garden at Potsdam, has protested that the dispositions of the successor are wholly French, and that he had charged him to endeavor to convert Hertzberg. Remark this. Remark, still further, that Boden is a man of low cunning, who may wish to deceive Prince Henry, in whose service he formerly was, with whom he quarreled, and to whom he is

now reconciled,—Heaven knows by what means.
Observe, once again, that the Prince of Salm-Kirburg
has also been (nearly about the same time) a week
concealed at Potsdam. What inconsistency?

It is the advice of Prince Henry that Boden, who is
returned to Paris, should be tampered with. He also
wishes (for your great men do not disdain little
means) that a lady should be sent hither, of a fair complexion, rather fat, and with some musical talents, who
should pretend to come from Italy, or anywhere but
France; who shall have had no public amour; who
should appear rather disposed to grant favors than
to display her poverty, etc., etc. Some elegant trifles
would not be amiss, but take care not to forget the
man is avaricious. The French letters, at least those
which I shall show, ought to speak well of him, and to
report that the King has spoken favorably of him;
particularly that he has said: "This Prince, like me,
will be a worthy man." Repetition might be made of
the success of Prince Henry in France; but in this I
would advise moderation, for I believe Prince Henry
has spoken too much himself on that subject; he has
pretended to prophesy concerning the new reign, and
predictions are disagreeable. Let me add it is affirmed
that, could the new King be gained, he would become
the most faithful and the most fervent of allies; to
this uncle Henry pledges his honor and his head;
and, indeed, the Prince of Prussia has never for-
feited his word. It is added, as you may well believe,
that it is neither possible nor proper to require more,
for in fine we are suspected, and with good reason, etc.,
etc.

You will imagine France has not been thus treated
without any pleadings in the behalf of Prussia; and
the advocates have pretended to prove (the map on the
table), alike by military and political details, that the

alliance of Prussia would be much more effectual to France, against England, than that of Austria. If it be requested, I will draw up a memorial, according to the grounds that have been given me. Nor is it at all required that we should quarrel with Vienna; nothing more is asked than a treaty of confraternity, agreeable to the guarantee of the treaty of Westphalia; a treaty well known at all Courts, and with this only secret article that, should there be any infringement of the peace, we then should go further; and if at the present a treaty should be refused, reciprocal letters between the two Kings, sealed and so left till some event should happen, would be deemed satisfactory. In short, a pledge is demanded against the Austrian system; and the written word of honor of the King of France will be accepted. No subsidies are or will in any case be asked; perhaps even Prussia will pay subsidies to Brunswick and Hesse. Great complaints are made of France for having permitted and even favored the German confederation. "For must not Germany, soon or late, assume some consistent form? Must not Prussia acquire a frontier? And what other means are there than those of secularization, which by this confederacy are interdicted? How otherwise arrange the affairs of Saxony than by Westphalia and Liège?" This latter phrase appeared to me very remarkable.

I do not nor cannot at present mean to send anything more than the great outlines. Prince Henry is French, and so will live and die. Will he have any influence? I know not. He is too pompous; and the Duke of Brunswick, of a very different complexion, is the man necessary to the King and the country, though he is not loved by the former. However, I am supplied with the secret means of correspondence, inquiry, and success; and it could not be more made a common cause between us. I am promised that my services to my country shall be amply repaid on the day an alliance is concluded with France, etc., etc.

I forgot a curious fact. The Heir Apparent wrote to Boden, before his journey to Berlin, to inquire what the people of Paris thought of him. " That you will be feeble, indolent, and governed," was the substance of Boden's reply. The Prince, as he read the letter, stamped with his foot, and exclaimed: "I have suffered by myself and I will reign by myself."

POSTSCRIPT.—By the natural discharge of the water from the legs, which may be calculated at a pint *per diem,* the swelling of the scrotum has disappeared; the patient imagines the general inflation is diminished. It is probable he is feverish every night; but of this he endeavors to remain ignorant. His appetite is so extraordinary that he generally eats ten or twelve of the highest dishes. His supper and breakfast consist of smoked tongues, bread, butter, and a large quantity of pepper. If he feels his stomach oppressed by its load, which is usually the case, he has recourse an hour or two after dinner to a dose of *anima rhei.* He wishes to have six or seven motions in the twenty-four hours, exclusive of clysters. From all this you may gather the result, which is that we are incontestibly at the last scene, more or less protracted.

LETTER XIV

August 17th, 1786.

ALL is over!—Frederick William reigns—and one of the grandest characters that ever occupied the throne has burst one of the finest molds that nature ever organized!

The vanity of friendship was highly interested that you should be the first informed of this event; and my measures were all most carefully taken. On Wednesday, at eight in the morning, I knew he was as ill as possible; that the preceding day the hour of appointment for the day following was noon, instead of eleven o'clock, as was before customary; that he had not spoken to his secretaries till midday, who had been waiting from five in the morning; that, however, the dispatches had been clear and precise; and that he still had eaten excessively, and particularly a lobster. I further knew that the prodigious foulness of the sick chamber, and the damp clothes of the patient, which he wore without changing, appeared to have brought on a species of putrid fever; that the slumbers of this Wednesday approached lethargy; that every symptom foreboded an apoplectic dropsy, a dissolution of the brain; and that, in fine, the scene must close in a few hours.

At one o'clock I took an airing on horseback, on the road to Potsdam, impelled by I know not what foreboding, and also to observe the meanderings of the river, which is on the right, when a groom, riding full speed, came for the physician Zelle, who received orders to make all haste, and who instantly departed. I soon was informed that the groom had killed a horse.

I was thrown into some perplexity. That the city gates would be shut was certain; it was even possible that the drawbridges of the island of Potsdam would be raised the moment death should take place, and should this happen my uncertainty would continue as long as it should please the new King. On the first supposition—how send off a courier? There were no means of scaling the ramparts or the palisades, without being exposed to a fray, for there are sentinels at every forty paces behind the palisades, and at every fifty behind the wall. What was to be done? I had not received, could not receive any orders; I could only use my own resources. And ought I to expose myself to ridicule, by sending intelligence already known, or concerning an event so well foreseen? Was the loss or gain of a week worth the expense of a courier? Had I been Ambassador, the certain symptoms of mortality would have determined me to have sent off an express before death. For what addition was the word death? How was I to act in my present situation? It certainly was most important to serve, and not merely to appear to have served. I hastened to the French Ambassador. He was not at home; he dined at Charlottenburg. No means of joining him at Berlin. I dressed myself, hurried to Schoenhausen, and arrived at the palace of the Queen as soon as the Ambassador. He had not been informed of particulars, and did not imagine the King was so ill; not a Minister believed it; the Queen had no suspicion of it; she only spoke to me of my dress, of Rheinsberg, and of the happiness she had there enjoyed when Princess Royal. Lord Dalrymple, with whom I was too intimate to admit of dissembling what my opinion was, assured me I was deceived. "That may be," replied I; but I whispered to our Ambassador that I had my intelligence from the sick couch, and that he ought to believe stock-jobbers had as good information as the diplomatic body. I know not whether he believed me; but, like me, he would not sit down to play, and left the company soon enough to send news of the approach of death.

I still had great reason to be diffident of the activity of our Embassy. How did I act? I sent a man, on whom I could depend, with a strong and swift horse to a farm, four miles from Berlin, from the master of which I had some days before received two pairs of pigeons, an experiment on the flight of which had been made; so that, unless the bridges of the isle of Potsdam were raised, I acted with certainty; and, that I might not have a single chance against me, for I thought the news tardy in arriving, I sent M. de Noldé by the daily stage, with orders to wait at the bridge of the island. He was acquainted with the station of my other man; the raising of the bridges would speak plainly enough; he had money sufficient to push forward; there was no human power apparently that could counteract me, for my gentry had not a single Prussian post to pass, and were to proceed to Saxony, taking care not to go through any fortified place; and they had their route ready traced.

M. de Noldé was departing at half past six in the morning, with the stage, when General Goertiz, aide-de-camp to the late King, arriving full speed, called aloud: "In the King's name, lower the portcullis," and M. de Noldé was obliged to turn back! Five minutes after, I was on horseback; my horses had passed the night saddled; and, that I might omit nothing, I hastened to the French Ambassador. He was asleep. I wrote to him immediately that I knew a certain mode of conveyance, if he had anything to send. He answered, and I keep his note as a curious proof if, which, however, to me appears impossible, the Comte de Vergennes keeps no courier,—"The Comte d'Esterno has the honor to return thanks to Mirabeau, but cannot profit by his obliging offer."

I then reflected, either he had sent off a courier, who only could convey the news of the King's extreme danger, consequently there must be something to add, or he had received orders not to send any; otherwise his apathy was wholly inconceivable. I, moreover, knew that the Saxon envoy had sent off his chasseur on the eve, so that he was twenty hours and forty leagues in advance with me; it therefore was wholly improbable that M. de Vibraye at Dresden should not hear of the King's danger. The same might be conjectured of the aide-de-camp Whittinkoff, who bore the news to the Duchess Dowager of Brunswick, and would certainly spread it, so that nothing was left for me till absolute death should happen. After considering, I did not find we were rich enough to throw a hundred guineas away; I therefore renounced all my fine projects, which had cost me some thought, some trouble, and some guineas; and I let fly my pigeons to my man with the word RETURN.

Have I done well, or ill? Of this I am ignorant; but I had no express orders, and sometimes works of supererogation gain but little applause. I have thought it my duty to send you this account; first, because it may be of service (observe that several prizes have thus been gained); and secondly, to prove that I wanted neither zeal or activity, but effrontery.

The new King remained all Thursday at Sans Souci, in the apartment of General Moellendorf. His first act of sovereignty was to bestow the order of the Black Eagle on Count Hertzberg. At five in the morning, his Majesty was busy with the secretaries of the late King. This morning he was on horseback in the streets of Berlin, accompanied by his eldest son. Thursday presented a spectacle worthy of observation.

There were many wet eyes, even among the foreign Ambassadors; for they were all present, the French excepted, when the troops took the oath of allegiance.

The ceremony is awful, and would be more so if the oath, which the soldiers repeat word by word, were not so long. Yet this vast military paraphernalia, that multitude of soldiers, who all the morning swarmed in the streets, and the precipitate administering of the legionary oath, seem but to me too exclusively to proclaim the military power; seem but to SAY: I AM MORE ESPECIALLY THE KING OF THE SOLDIERS. I COMMIT MYSELF TO MY ARMY, BECAUSE I AM NOT CERTAIN OF POSSESSING A KINGDOM. I am persuaded these military forms will be mitigated under the new reign.

LETTER XV

August 18*th,* 1786.

PRINCE HENRY received information of the decease somewhat late; not till yesterday, the seventeenth, at midnight. But this, perhaps, was occasioned by their desire to send him one of his favorite officers, who was a very bad horseman. The letter of the King was a page and a half in length, written by his own hand, and inviting the Prince to come, who arrived to-day at three in the afternoon. As soon as it was dark, his aide-de-camp came for me; and what follows is the substance of the Prince's narrative.

He has had an interview of an hour and a half with the King, but is no further advanced in the knowledge of what he shall hereafter be. The King was devoid of ostentation in his behavior to his family; and was very much moved with the Prince, says the latter, but no way communicative. The uncle only attempted to speak of foreign politics. His request in behalf of his favorite, Tauensien, captain and aide-de-camp to his Royal Highness, was immediately granted.

"Resolved on the French system, but desirous of seeing—" "Why?" "Dignity, prudence, the alarming discontents of Holland." "Are you brother or King? as brother interest yourself; as King do not

interfere, you will but have the greater influence."
"Your father, whose name you cannot pronounce
without weeping, was as much French as I am; this
I will demonstrate by his letters." " Oh, I have seen
proofs of that," replied the King, " in those of the
Queen of Sweden."

" Vienna." " Advances it is supposed will be made;
they will be accepted; the war of peace will actually
be concluded."

" The English system?" " God preserve me from
it!" " Russia?" " It has scarcely been thought on."

The whole day passed in well-managed artifice.
The King was on horseback with his eldest son; he
addressed his generals with caresses of every kind:
" If you serve less faithfully than formerly, I, by
being obliged to punish, shall be the person punished."
He spoke a little more seriously to the Ministers, with
whom, notwithstanding, he dined. Severely to the
secretaries—" I well know you have been guilty of
indiscretions; I would advise you to change your
behavior."

Hertzberg hitherto preserves all his consequence.
The King has not once pronounced his name to Prince
Henry, nor the Prince to the King. His Majesty,
however, tenderly embraced Count Finckenstein, a
true French knight-errant, and the only person, after
Knyphausen, in whom Prince Henry confides; that is
to say, willingly. " I thank you," said the King, " for
the eminent services you have been so indefatigable
in rendering my uncle; and I request you will act in
the same manner for my interest." It is to be noted
that Count Finckenstein is the implacable enemy of
Hertzberg, but the uncle of the dearly beloved Mademoiselle Voss.

The will is to be opened to-morrow, in presence of
those interested. The King will not attempt to alter

a single line, one article excepted, the necessity of
erasing which he will submit to his uncles. The old
Monarch has been generous. He has bequeathed
Prince Henry two hundred thousand crowns and a
handsome ring, exclusive of what will revert to him
by the family agreement. The rest are likewise well
treated, but not so magnificently.

The funeral ceremony afforded Prince Henry a
proper excuse for remaining; it is to be performed at
Potsdam. The King will depart thence to receive
homage in Prussia and Silesia; this is an old custom
of the country. Prince Henry will come to an explanation previous to his journey; but he is determined
to wait as long as possible, that the King may begin
the subject himself.

Speaking of me, his Majesty said: " I suspect he is
ordered to observe me; his love for the Emperor probably will not expose him to the temptation of speaking
ill of me, when there is nothing ill to be spoken."

Prince Henry fears that, the mode of life excepted,
the method and especially the ceremonies of Government will be continued. He has charged me to mention that Comte d'Esterno is much too cold, too distant, too entirely an Ambassador, for the new King.
He entreats our Ministry not to be tedious in bargain-
ing concerning the pledges of confidence.

It is said, and I forgot to ask Prince Henry, who
perhaps does not know, whether it be or be not true,
that the King has sent for the Duke of Brunswick.
The Minister, Schulemburg, is in danger. Prince
Henry, by whom he has so long been hated and de-
cried, is resolved to give him support. Schulemburg
returned only this morning. He has composed, or
rather made Struensee compose, an apologetic memorial, adroit and sophistical, in which he has imputed
to the late King that order of affairs which he pro-

poses to remedy. He declaims against monopolies,—
he, who is himself at the head of all the monopolies;
but he endeavors to prove they cannot be suddenly
reformed, especially that of the maritime company.

LETTER XVI

August 22d, 1786.

PRINCE HENRY is singularly well satisfied with the
new King, who the day before yesterday (Sunday)
spent the greatest part of the afternoon with his uncle.
The latter went to him in the morning to know the
watchword. He pretends his nephew indicates an
entire confidence in him; but I fear he interprets compliments into pledges of trust. He affirms the downfall of Hertzberg approaches; this I do not believe.
" I and my nephew," said the Prince, " have been very
explicit;" but I doubt the nephew has deceived the
uncle. The conciliating temper of the King, and his
good-nature, which induce him to receive all with
kindness, may likewise lead to error, without intending deception; and these rather prove he possesses
sensibility than strength of mind.

Prince Henry affirms that the King is entirely
French. He requests that no attention may be paid to
the sending of Colonel or Major Geysau to London,
with accession compliments; these, he affirms, relate
only to the family. The King has besides been deceived; he was told that the Court of St. James had
sent compliments at the death of King George, which
is not true. This, it is added, is an artifice of Count
Hertzberg. Prince Henry did not arrive soon enough
to prevent the thing being done; were it to do again
it should be otherwise. (Remark, it is the Prince himself who speaks.) No one has been sent either to

Vienna or to Petersburg. (Not to Vienna, to the chief of the Empire, who is almost as near a relation as the King of England. And as to Petersburg, Romanzow has made such bitter complaints that Count Finckenstein, moderate as he is, demanded whether he had received orders from his Court to speak in that style.) But it is singular enough that envoys have been sent everywhere else; and particularly Count Charles Podewils (brother to him who is at Vienna) is gone to bear the news to Sweden. This is departing from the old system, to which, it is said, the King means, in other respects, to adhere; for the King of Sweden was held in aversion by the late King; nor is he less hated by Prince Henry. Count Stein, a kind of domestic favorite, is gone to Saxony, Weymar, Deux-Ponts, etc.

Prince Henry wishes the Minister for Foreign Affairs should write, and immediately, that the Court of France hopes the new King will confirm the friendship his predecessor began; and should give it to be understood that all the Prussian Ministers are not supposed to mean as well, toward France, as the King himself (I am not at all of this opinion; for this would be to distinguish Hertzberg, and to render the war against our Cabinet more inveterate. If the downfall of this Minister be necessary, it can be effected only by taxing him with governing the King), and that the reciprocity of good will and good offices may, and ought to, produce a more intimate connection. He wishes M. de Calonne might write soon to him (Prince Henry) a friendly and ostensible letter, but which ought to be sent by safe hands; that it should be recommended to Comte d'Esterno to smooth his brow; and he is particularly desirous a mode of somewhat calming the affairs of Holland should be found, and that this act should be much praised and insisted on.

The Duke of Brunswick has been sent for, and is to arrive on Thursday. It is said he brings another will, which was deposited in his hands. The first was not read before the family, but only in presence of the two uncles and the two Ministers. The legatees have all received their bequests. The date of this will is 1769. It is in a pompous style, and is written with labor and declamation. The King has been exceedingly attentive to specify that his legacies are made from the savings of his privy purse.

The following is a sketch of his donations: The Queen has an annual augmentation to her income of ten thousand crowns. Prince Henry has the gross sum of two hundred thousand crowns, a large green diamond, a luster of rock crystal estimated at fifteen thousand crowns, a set of eight coach horses, two led horses richly caparisoned, and fifty *anteaux,* or small casks of Hungarian wine. Prince Ferdinand the gross sum of fifty thousand crowns, and some Hungarian wine. Princess Ferdinand ten thousand crowns annually (the reason of this was that, in 1769, she was the only Princess of her house who had any children), and a box. Princess Henry six thousand crowns annually. The Duchess Dowager of Brunswick ten thousand crowns annually. The Princess Amelia ten thousand crowns annually, and all the personal plate of the late King. The Princess of Wurtemberg the gross sum of twenty thousand crowns. The Duke of Wurtemberg a ring. The Landgrave of Hesse the gross sum of ten thousand crowns. Prince Frederick of Brunswick the same. The reigning Duke of Brunswick the same, with eight horses (among others, the last that Frederick mounted) and a diamond ring, estimated at twenty-two thousand crowns, etc., etc., etc.

The King has confirmed all this with a very good grace. The only article that he will not agree to was a strange whim of the late King, relative to the interment of his body; he wished to be buried beside his dogs. Such is the last mark of contempt which he thought proper to cast upon mankind. I know not whether the will that is coming will be equally respected with that already opened, even though they should not be contradictory.

As to the situation of the Court, I believe the truth to be that Prince Henry exaggerates his ascendency; and that he is in absolute ignorance of the King's intentions. They prattle much together, but there is no single point on which they have yet come to any stipulation. True it is that five days are scarcely yet elapsed. But wherefore presume? The Prince supports the Minister, Schulemburg; and I know that Schulemburg found the King dry and cold. He had one choice for the French Embassy; and I know the King has another, which he has not even concealed from the Prince. The Monarch hears all, but is in nothing explicit. Bishopswerder himself perhaps does not know what he is to be, and if he be prudent, will not be in too great haste.

I have twice seen Count Hertzberg, and found him still the same, a small portion of dissimulation excepted. He very positively denied being English. He does not seem to me to think he has the least need of Prince Henry, whom he has not been to visit (which is very marked, or rather indecent behavior) since his promotion to the Order of the Black Eagle. I wished to insinuate to him that it would be easy to consult the uncle by the aid of the nephew; this he declined, but gave me an apologetic memorial for Prince Henry, relative to his personal discussions with Baron Knyphausen. Either Prince Henry or Hertzberg, or both, are much deceived. Hertzberg certainly sups almost every night with the King; and the opinion of some well-informed people is that this Minister, and General Moellendorf, will be appointed to educate the Prince of Prussia.

The Marquis of Luchesini is continued in his place by the present King; but hitherto he has only been desired to write the poem for the funeral. The secretary of Prince Henry, it is said, is to compose the music; and this is one of the things which turn the uncle's brain.

I have sent the King my grand Memorial; he has only acknowledge having received it, adding that I might remain persuaded whatever should come from me would give him pleasure; and that, of all the obliging things that were said to him, none flattered him more highly than mine.

P. S.—The Ministers took the oath of allegiance yesterday, about three o'clock; hence, no probable changes for some time to come. Count Arnim Boytzemburg, sent for by the King, arrived with all haste, and passed the evening with his Majesty. I believe him proper for nothing but a place about Court; it may, however, have relation to the Embassy to France, but more probably to the place of Grand Marshal, or that of Minister of the Landschafft, a kind of president of the provinces, who greatly influences the assessments of the taxes, and other internal arrangements.

LETTER XVII

August 26th, 1786.

I FEAR my prophecies will be accomplished. Prince Henry appears to me to have gained nothing but bows from his nephew. One article of the will of the King's grandfather disposed of the succession of certain *bailliages,* so as to bequeath an accession of income, of about forty or fifty thousand crowns, to Prince Henry, including an augmentation of the revenue of Prince Ferdinand. Circumstances not being exactly the same now as supposed by the testator, the Ministers (that is to say, Hertzberg) have pretended that this bequest no longer was legal; and the King, eluding to grant the legacy, has made a proposal to his uncle to have the suit determined either in Germany, France or Italy. The Prince has written an ingenious and noble letter to him, but in which he indicates the enemy. The King has redoubled his outward caresses for his uncle, and has submitted to three judges, who have been nominated by the Prince. I hence conclude that the uncle will gain the suit of the *bailliages,* but never that of the regency.

Hertzberg, however, has commissioned me to make some advances from himself to the Prince, and this I think is a sign that he is not in perfect security. I never could prevail on the Prince to comply; sometimes inflated, sometimes agitated, he neither could command his countenance nor his first emotions. He is deceitful, yet knows not how to dissemble; endowed with ideas, wit, and even a portion of understanding, but has not a single opinion of his own. Petty means, petty councils, petty passions, petty prospects; all is diminutive in the soul of that man. While he makes gigantic pretensions, he has a mind without method; is as haughty as an upstart, and as vain as a man who had no claim to respect; he can neither lead nor be led. He is one of too frequent examples that insignificance of character may stifle the greatest qualities.

The thing the new King fears the most is being thought to be governed; and in this respect Prince Henry, of all men, is the least adapted to the Monarch; who I believe would consent not to reign, provided he might only be supposed to reign.

Remarkable change! The general directory is restored to the footing on which it was under Frederick William I. This is a wise act. The result of the madness of innovation, under Frederick II., was that, of all the Kings in Europe, he was the most deceived. The mania of expediting the whole affairs of a kingdom in one hour and a half was the cause that the Ministers were each of them absolute in their departments. At present, all must be determined in a committee; each will have occasion of the consent and sanction of all the rest. In a word, it is a kind of Council. This, no doubt, will have its inconveniences; but how are inconveniences to be avoided?

The edict for suppressing the Lotto is signed, as I am assured. I shall at least have done this much good to the country. But the King has permitted the last drawing, which is wrong; there ought to have been none under his reign. Perhaps it is only popular report.

The Duke of Brunswick arrived this evening. M. Ardenberg-Reventlau, a man of merit and his favorite Minister—though M. Feronce is the principal—preceded him, and was here at a quarter after four. The Duke was admitted to see his Majesty, who rises at four o'clock; at half after six he was on the parade. The King received him with neither distance nor ardor. Perhaps nothing more is meant by this journey than politeness. Necessity only could make such a man Prime Minister, who will not trouble himself with fruitless efforts, but who will be very tenacious in his grasp. I shall not converse with him till to-morrow. The will he brings will probably be burned; it is said to be of a much earlier date than the other, and as far back as 1755.

The Landgrave of Hesse Cassel, it is affirmed, is coming; also the Duke of Weymar, the Prince de Deux-Ponts, and even the Duke of York. Of the latter I doubt.

Hertzberg pretends that the King, by becoming the pledge of the Stadtholder, ought to make us easy concerning Holland, but he has not told us who shall make the pledge respected.

Prince Henry wishes advice should be sent that Count Hertzberg, who has not the good word of the world, appears to have gained the entire confidence of the King, and even to act the master. This last imputation is probably the most effectual method to procure the downfall of any man, under the present sign.

There are many small Court favors granted, but no considerable place bestowed. I have attempted to reconcile Hertzberg and Knyphausen, which I was in a train to accomplish, by demonstrating to them that their coalition would erect a throne which could not be shaken. Knyphausen refused, because, alleged he, Hertzberg is so deceitful it can never be known whether the reconciliation is or is not sincere; "and it is better," said the Baron, "to be the open enemy than the equivocal friend of a man whose credit is superior to our own."

I am inclined to think Hertzberg must be displaced, if we wish the Prussians should become French. Three months are necessary to draw any conclusions that should be at all reasonable. I again repeat, if you have any grand political views, relative to this country and Germany, put an end to the democratical quarrels of Holland; which are only the disputes of cunning, profitable to those who have their fortunes to make, but not to those whose fortunes are made.

LETTER XVIII

August 29th, 1786.

To PROPHESY here daily becomes more difficult; time only can afford any rational prognostics. The King apparently intends to renounce all his old habits; this is a proud undertaking. He has made three visits to Schoenhausen, nor has he cast one look on Mademoiselle Voss; no semblance of an *orgia;* not one woman's bosom touched since he has sat on the throne. One of his confidants proposed a visit to Charlottenburg. "No," replied he; "all my former allurements are there." He retires before ten in the evening, and rises at four; he works excessively, and certainly with some difficulty. Should he persevere, he will afford a singular example of habits of thirty years being vanquished. This will be an indubitable proof of a grand character, and show how we have all been mistaken. But even, the supposition granted, which is so far from probable, how deficient are his understanding and his means. I say how deficient, since even his most ecstatic panegyrists begin by giving up his understanding. The last day that he exercised the troops he was ridiculously slow, heavy, and monotonous. The men were four times ranged in columns, and concluded with parading. This continued three hours, and in the presence of a general such as is the Duke of Brunswick. Everybody was dissatisfied. Yesterday, the first Court day, he was ill; he forgot some of the foreign Ministers, and uttered nothing but a few commonplace phrases, hasty, embarrassed, and ill-chosen; this scarcely continued five minutes. He immediately left us to go to church; for he does not miss church; and religious zeal, homilies, and pulpit flatteries already begin to be everywhere heard and seen.

Prince Henry has gained his suit, concerning the

bailliages, as I had foreseen; in other respects, he has not advanced a step, consequently has gone backward. He dines every day with the King, and does wrong; he affects to whisper with him, and does wrong; he speaks to him of public affairs incessantly, and does wrong. The King goes alone to visit the Duke of Brunswick; and also goes in company with Hertz-berg, or meets him at the Duke's. The latter pretends to interfere only with the army,—the sole thing which, according to him, he understands. I have never yet seen him in private, but he has appointed me an audi-ence on Wednesday morning.

The English faction continues very active, and this proves there are difficulties to encounter. In reality, it is an alliance so unnatural, when compared to ours, that it seems to me we should not suffer ourselves, though the King should commit blunders, to be routed by his mistakes.

The Monarch becomes very difficult effectually to observe. He reverts to the severe ceremonies of Ger-man etiquette. It is imagined he will not receive for-eigners, at least for some time. I know all that can be learned from subaltern spies; from valets, court-iers, secretaries, and the intemperate tongue of Prince Henry; but there are only two modes of influencing,— which are to give, or rather to give birth to, ideas in the master, or in his Ministers. In the master! How, since he is not to be approached? In the Ministers! It is neither very easy nor very prudent to speak to them on public affairs, I not being in a public char-acter; and the discussions which chance affords are short, vague, and incomplete. If I am supposed ca-pable of business, I ought to be sent to some place where I should have a public character. I am afraid I shall here cost more than I am worth.

Count Goertz goes to Holland; I know not whether

instead of Thulemeyer or *ad tempus*. He is followed
by the son of Count Arnim, who is a young shoot for
the *corps diplomatique*. Goertz is not a man without
talents: when sent into Russia, under every kind of
disadvantage, he obtained a good knowledge of the
country; he is cold, dry, and ungracious; but subtle,
master of his temper, though violent, and a man of
observation. That he is of the English party is certain; he is loyal to Hertzberg, and convinced that the
alliance of Holland and France is so unnatural it must
soon end. I own I think as he does, especially should
we abuse our power.

A new Ambassador is appointed, *in petto,* for
France. I have not yet been able to discover who;
but Hertzberg supports the ridiculous Goltz with all
his power. Schulemburg daily declines in favor. The
maritime company have already lost their monopoly
of coffee, of which there are four millions and a half
pounds' weight consumed in the various provinces of
the Prussian monarchy. Hence we may observe that
the free use of coffee, which daily becomes general in
Germany, is the cause that the consumption of beer
is gradually and much less. The same company may
be deprived of a prodigious profit on sugars; but it
will be in vain to destroy old monopolies only to substitute new, though they should be for the profit of
the King.

The personal debts of his Majesty are paying off by
the Minister, Blumenthal; it is said there are tolerably
great reductions made, but not unjustly, as I imagine,
for there are no complaints on the subject. Exclusive
of the Royal Treasury, Frederick II. has left savings
so great that they will scarcely be absorbed by the
personal debts of Frederick William II. It is said he
will pay off his Italian opera, and everybody believes
there will be a French opera instead. This certainly

would be no trifling means of support to intrigue.

The freedom of scrutiny is restored to the Academy, and the Germans are henceforward to be admitted members. I regard the curatorship of this body as a favor conferred on, and a tolerable resource of power for, Hertzberg, who will be curator by title, and president in reality. The presidency of the Academy is so truly ministerial that the late Frederick exercised it himself, after the decease of the restless and morose de Maupertuis. Count Hertzberg said to me, at Court, " You are a compliment in my debt." " On what occasion?" " I am curator of the Academy; which title gives me greater pleasure and, in my opinion, is more honorable than a ribbon." Forty persons heard our discourse. " Certainly," replied I, " he who is the minister of knowledge may well be called the Prime Minister."

The King will not ruin himself in gifts; he has hitherto bestowed only prebendaries, which cost him nothing except a pension of three hundred crowns, on General Levald. I am informed that he has just granted one of eight hundred crowns—to the poet Rammler. It would perhaps have been more delicate not to have begun by pensioning fame, and her trumpet.

LETTER XIX

September 2d, 1786.

ALL circumstances confirm my predictions. Prince Henry and his nephew have almost quarreled. The uncle is inconsolable, and thinks of retiring to Rheinsberg. He will almost certainly return during the journey of the King, through Prussia and Silesia. Probably we shall have no great changes before the Monarch has performed these journeys, if then.

There is one, however, besides those I have before
spoken of, which is remarkable; and that is, a commission to examine the administration of the customs,
—what is to be abrogated, what preserved, and what
qualified, especially in the excise.

M. Werder, a Minister of State, and the intimate
friend of Hertzberg, the enemy of Schulemburg who
brought him into place, and father-in-law to the secretary of the English Embassy, or perhaps to his wife,
is at the head of this commission. The other members
are ridiculously selected; but the very project of such
a reform is most agreeable to the nation; as much so
as the pension of eight hundred crowns granted to
the poet Rammler, and the promise of admission of
Germans into the Academy, is to the distributors of
renown. It remains to be seen whether the people have
not been led to hope too much; and whether it is not
requisite to be certain of substitutes, previous to the
promise of relief.

The King goes to Prussia attended by Messieurs
Hertzberg (for the King to be attended by a Minister
out of his department is unexampled), Goltz, sur-
named the Tartar, Boulet, a French engineer, General
Goertz, Gaudi, and Bishopswerder.

This Goltz the Tartar is he who, in the last campaign of the Seven Years' War, raised an insurrection
of fifty thousand Tartars, in the Crimea and the
neighboring countries; who were marching to make a
diversion in favor of the King of Prussia, and had
arrived at Bender, when peace was concluded. Notwithstanding this, Goltz can boast of but little abilities;
except that he is a good officer, and ardently active.
He was indebted for his great and singular success
to a Dutchman named Biskamp, whom he met with
in the Crimea. He attached himself to this very
able and enterprising man, who understood the

language, knew the country, and served Frederick II. according to his wishes; by whom, indeed, he was well paid. This Biskamp is at Warsaw, and there forgotten, which is very strange. I have supposed the relating this anecdote, which is but little known, might be interesting.

Boulet is an honest man, for whom the King shows some affection, and to whom he is indebted for all he knows concerning fortification.

General Goertz is the brother of the Goertz who is going to Holland, but not his equal; he is artful and subtle, and his good faith is of a suspicious complexion.

Gaudi is the brother of the celebrated general of the same name; little known hitherto as the Minister of the Prussian department, but capable, well-informed, firm, decided, and indubitably the man most proper to influence interior arrangements in reconstructing the grand directory.

Bishopswerder you are acquainted with; he and Boulet each lately received the commission of lieutenant colonel.

The King has told Schulemburg that, on his return from Prussia, he will determine which of his nine departments he shall be deprived of. He and his wife are the only ministerial family who are not invited to Court. The probabilities all are that Schulemburg will demand leave to resign, should his colleagues continue to humble him, and the King to treat him with contempt. But Struensee probably will keep his place, and he then proposes to act, in concert with us, in our public funds; especially should the King, as is apparent, commit to his charge the four millions of crowns which he means to set apart for the operations of previous finance. Struensee is the only man who understands them. This is a subject not to be neglected, as it hitherto has been, even so far as to render it impossible for me to act with propriety. We might profit by him, during peace; but if unfortunately the news which is whispered be true, concerning the increasing ill health of the Elector of Bavaria, depend upon war, for I then hold it inevitable. Is this a time for us to exist from day to day, as we do, when each month (for there is a probability, at any time, that he should die within a month) menaces all Europe with inextricable confusion?

M. de Larrey, sent from the Stadtholder to compliment the King, openly affirms it is impossible the disputes of Holland should be appeased without effusion of blood; and the speculations of Hertzberg upon this subject are boundless; but the secret is well kept by those who surround the King.

LETTER XX

TO THE DUC DE——

September 2d, 1786.

By what fatality, monseigneur, has it happened that I have not received your letter, dated the sixteenth, till this day? And, still more especially, why was it not written some weeks sooner? The importance of the proposition with which it concludes will never be fully understood; and which, made at any other time, except when the King was dying, would have been willingly accepted. It will never be known, had it been presented soon enough, how much it might have effected, impeded, and indicated, relative to a Prince whose understanding perhaps is not great, but who possesses gratitude, and who will much more certainly be an honest man than a great King; so that his heart rather than his mind ought to have been

appealed to; and that at a time when he was far
otherwise accessible than at present,—walled in, as he
is, by system and intrigue. How does it happen that
you are the only person of the country you inhabit
who conceived this plan? How could the Cabinet of
Versailles give up the merit of offering trifling sums
to Serilly? How could it permit the Duke of Courland
to secure the claim of having hushed the loud cries of
creditors to silence? How impolitic and disastrous
are the sordid views, the confined plans, and short-
sighted prudence of certain persons! In what a situation would such an act have placed us, as it would me
personally, in his opinion! All things then would
have been possible, would have been easy to me. But
of this we must think no more; we must only remember this is a new proof that reason is always on your
side.

Since the death of the King I have sent supplies of
information to your Cabinet, respecting the *Aulic
phases,* and my dispatch of to-day, a great part of
which no doubt our common friend will read to you,
is a statement, according to the best of my abilities, of
present and future contingencies. You will there perceive that Prince Henry has accomplished his own
destiny; that his trifling character has, on this occasion,
weighty as it was, been stranded on the rock of his
excessive vanity, as it has before so often been; that
he has at once displayed an excessive desire of power,
disgusting haughtiness, insupportable pedantry, and a
disdain of intrigue, at the same time that his conduct
was one continuation of petty, low, dirty cabal; that
he has despised the people in power, while he himself is surrounded only by those who are evidently
either foolish, knavish, or contemptible,—one sole
man, Baron Knyphausen, excepted, and he is in daily
danger of being carried off by apoplexy; that, in fine,

no man can be more out of favor, and particularly out
of confidence, or can have put himself into a situation
in which confidence and favor will be more difficult
to regain.

I therefore persist in my opinion that the Duke of
Brunswick, who is master of himself, by no means
ostentatious, and who is possessed of profound talents,
will be the man,—not of the present moment, but of
the moment of necessity. My reasons are numerous,
and so deduced as, in my opinion, not to admit of
contradiction, the order of events and circumstances
which I see and foresee considered. All this does but
render the execution of your project the more necessary, and which I regard as very practicable, with
some small exceptions, if executed by the persons in
whom you ought to confide,—should you, with your
natural dexterity, and irresistible seduction, pursue
the plan of interesting the vanity of the MASTER, so as
to make it his own act, and, as you have so well expressed it, that it shall be he himself who shall inform
his Ministers of his intentions.

I repeat, your project is the more immediately necessary because that England cabals, with great industry,
in her own behalf, under the pretense of the interests
of Holland, which are very much at heart, in the
Cabinet of Berlin. I own that what I have often
insinuated here, namely, that the Prussian power is
not sufficiently consolidated, and that, if opposed to
stand the shock of France and Austria combined, it
must be reduced to powder, is a proposition not so
unanswerable but that, thanks to Russia, there are
many objections to be made; and so there always will
be, even in suppositions the most unfavorable to
Prussia.

1. Because this would but be commencing a deplorable career of sanguinary contentions, under the direc-

tion of the Emperor, who is so little able to direct that he may be affirmed to be the least military of men.

2. That the utmost success would leave a Prince without counterpoise in Europe, who has claims and pretensions of every kind.

Lastly, and more especially, this would be painfully to seek that which the nature of events spontaneously offers; like as spring makes the apparently dry and sapless tree bud and bloom.

There are some errors in ciphering, which are the cause that I do not perfectly understand the grounds of your dissension with me, concerning the maritime system; but I too well know the extreme justness of your mind, which does not remain satisfied with phantoms, to imagine our opinions are very opposite. And, for my own part, I have never pretended to say that we ought not to maintain a navy which should make our commerce respected. The question to determine is, What ought the extent of this commerce to be, which is to be effectually protected? You, like me, perceive that no alliance with England can be solidly established but by a commercial treaty, which should have exact, clear, and distinct lines of demarcation; for, were unlimited freedom of trade permitted, they would be the sufferers. How might they support the rival-ship? And, if we do not cut away the voracious suckers from the root of the tree, how shall we prevent the Indies and Antilles from eternally continuing the apple of discord?

Be this as it may, monseigneur, do not suffer yourself to be discouraged or disgusted by difficulties. Ascend the height with a firm though measured step, and with inflexible constancy. You have found the only unbeaten track which, in these times, can lead to political fame, and which best may tend to the pacification of the earth. How admirable is it to unite the talents of the hero, the principles of the sage, and the projects of the philosopher! By a single diplomatic act to reverse all the obsolete forms, all pitiable rubrics, all the destructive arts of modern politics, would be to gain no vulgar crown; and a prospect so magnificent must be a most powerful support to your fortitude.

I need not repeat how much I am devoted to you, or how entirely you may dispose of me.

LETTER XXI

September 5th, 1786.

IT is impossible that I should send you intelligence more exact, concerning the situation of Prince Henry with the King, than that which my preceding letters contain. The Prince himself no longer conceals the truth, and, like all weak men, passing from one extreme to the other, he clamorously affirms the country is undone, that priests, blockheads, prostitutes, and Englishmen are hastening its destruction; and, by the intemperance of his language, confirms what the indiscretion of Chevalier d'Oraison, and the personal confidence of the uncle to the nephew, when he was only Prince of Prussia, probably before but too certainly told Frederick William II. I repeat, he has completed his disgrace, in the private estimation of the King. It is my opinion that, if he may be permitted, he will either quit this country, in which he has not one friend, one parasite, except in the most subaltern and abject class, or will become insane, or will die; such is my augury.

Not that I am convinced that the administration must always be committed to subalterns. The King has too much dread of seeming to be governed not to

have the necessity of being governed. Why should
he be the first man who should pretend to be what
he is not? Frederick II. who by nature was so perfectly designed to govern, never testified a fear of
being governed; he was certain of the contrary. The
present King fears he shall, and therefore shall be.
While public affairs are transacted separately, he will
not seem to be; for nothing is more easy in this
country than to receive and to pay. The machinery is
so wound up that the surplus of revenue is great indeed. It is easy to pay some attention to detail, to
keep watch over the police, to make some subordinate
changes, and to coquette with the nation. And here
be it said, by the way, there seems a determination of
humbling the vanity of foreigners; so that, as I have
always affirmed, the *gallomania* of Prince Henry has
been very prejudicial to us. Some good will be done;
for it is not here as in other kingdoms, where the passing from evil to good is sometimes worse than the
evil itself, and where there is terror in resistance. All
is here done *ad nutum*. Besides, the cords are so
stretched they cannot but relax; the people have been
so oppressed, have suffered such vexation, such extortion, that they must find ease. All will proceed,
therefore, and almost without aid, while foreign politics shall continue calm and uniform; but, whenever
a gun is fired, or even at the first lowering storm, with
what a petty crash will this scaffolding of mediocrity
come to the ground! How will these subaltern Ministers shrink, from the slave at the oar to the terrified
steersman? How will they call for a pilot's aid?

Who must be this pilot? The Duke of Brunswick.
Of this I have no doubt. Every little accident, in the
day of trouble, is only an additional aptitude to fear.
Besides that, the Prince is, of all men, he who best can
conduct little vanity; he will satisfy himself with ap-

pearing the servant of servants; the most polite, the most humble and indubitably the most adroit of courtiers; while, at the same time, his iron hand will fetter all paltry views, all trifling intrigues, all inferior factions. Such is the horoscope I draw; nor do I think, at present, one more rational can be erected.

Hertzberg is the man who must be managed in the State; and for this Comte d'Esterno is not qualified, because he formerly deserted him too much; and he well perceived it would have been indelicate and stupid to have veered too suddenly. Hertzberg, however, may ruin himself by his boasting, and even by his ostentation. This is a mode of effecting the fall of Ministers which the courtiers will not fail to employ because of the character of the King, and which may succeed.

But Holland and her convulsions are the subject of present consideration. There is a conviction that we can do what we please; and, though I am far from thinking this to be incontrovertible, I still think that, were we to say to the party that has gained so much ground, probably from a conviction that we were ready to march up to their support (for how would they have dared to make themselves responsible if they had possessed no securities for such future contingencies as may be expected?). I repeat, were we to say, YOU MUST GO NO FURTHER, we should be obeyed. It will be supposed, I neither pretend nor wish to give advice. I am too far removed from truth, which I can only inspect through the magnifying glass of passion; and the Comte d'Esterno informs me of nothing; but I can distinctly perceive that that hurricane, which is forming in those marshes, may extend to other countries. The French Embassy of Berlin will not say thus much to you, because they do not see things in the same light, but are persuaded

that the interest of the brother will have no influence
on the connections of the King. Of this I doubt, and
have good reason so to doubt. Hertzberg is wholly
Dutch, for it is the only decent manner in which he
can be English; and he may greatly influence foreign
politics, although he does not understand them. As,
the other day, he was rehearsing his eternal repetition
of—THE KING WILL BE THE PLEDGE OF THE STADT-
HOLDER—I said to him, "I respect the King too
much to ask who shall be the pledge of the pledge;
but I dare venture to ask—HOW WILL THE KING
MAKE HIS PLEDGE RESPECTED? What shall happen
when France shall demonstrate that the Stadtholder
has broken engagements entered into under her sanction? The King is not the brother-in-law of Holland;
and the affair of Naples is sufficient proof that family
interventions may be eluded? What can the King accomplish against Holland? And is he not too equitable to require us, who cannot wish that the Dutch
should become English, to risk our alliance for the
knight-errant of the English?" To all this Hertzberg, who beholds nothing on this sublunary earth
but HERTZBERG and PRUSSIA, made vague replies; but,
at the words, "What can the King accomplish against
Holland?" he muttered, with a gloomy air, "HOL-
LAND WILL NOT DEFY HIM, I BELIEVE." Once again,
beware of Holland; where, by way of parenthesis the
English legation affirms that we have bought the town
of Schiedam; that M. de Calonne, in particular, inun-
dates the country with gold; and, in a word, that he
is personally the brand of discord.

I have reserved the questions with which your letter
begins, to conclude with; first, because they relate to
affairs the least pressing, since it appears impossible
that the Emperor should make any attempts on Turkey
in Europe before the coming spring; and next, it was

necessary I should previously recollect myself; the
concurring circumstances of the death of the King,
and the accession of Frederick William, being the subjects which have almost exclusively demanded my attention, and induced me to defer more distant objects
to future consideration. Still, I fear mine is a barren
harvest, Prussia not having any continued intercourse
with these wide lying countries, which are more than
four hundred leagues distant; for she has neither any
great merchant, nor any system of politics, because
the *corps diplomatique* of Prussia is extremely deficient.

As to those individuals that are met with in society,
they are ignorant, and can afford no information.
Buckholz, the Prussian envoy to Warsaw, a man of
ordinary capacity, but active, and Huttel, who is in
the same capacity at Petersburg, an intelligent person,
write word that Russia is more pacific than Turkey,
and that the internal Ottoman provinces call for war.
The frontier provinces, appertaining to the Tartars,
certainly are not friendly to Russia. Moldavia and
Wallachia are governed by Hospodars, who, being
Greeks, most certainly are sold to whoever will purchase them, consequently to Russia. The Emperor
deceives them, and is hated there, as elsewhere. I
shall speak further of this, and shall endeavor to give
a sketch of a journey along the frontiers of these
countries, which should be undertaken in the disguise
of a trader, and kept rigidly secret, by which the state
of the frontiers, the magazines, the propensities of the
people, etc., etc., might be known, and what is to be
hoped or feared, if it be found necessary to arm (in
which case it is very probable Prussia would voluntarily aid us with all her powers),—that is to say if
the Emperor should determine to pay no respect to our
remonstrances, as he has twice done before.

Perhaps I might be more useful employed in such a journey than at Berlin, where at every step I tread on danger, and shall so continue to do, unless I have credentials, at least as an assistant; which perhaps would be the more proper, because it sometimes happens that such an interlocutor is spoken to with greater freedom than an Ambassador; for the refusals he meets, or the proposals he makes, have no ministerial consequences; and thus each party gains information, without either being offended.

Pay serious attention to this, I request. In vain you recommend me to act privately; permit me to inform you that, in despite of all my efforts, this is impracticable. I have too much celebrity, too much intercourse with Prince Henry, who is a true Joan of Arc, and who has no secrets of any kind. I am made to speak when I am silent; and when I say anything it is unfaithfully repeated. It is impossible to conceive all that has been attributed to me since the King's death; that is to say, since an epoch when I have taken advantage of the interruption of social meetings to keep myself recluse, and to labor only by mining. Comte d'Esterno discredits me all in his power. The English Embassy exclaims: *"Fœnum habet in cornu, longè fuge."* The favorites keep me at a distance; the wits, the priests, and the mystics have formed a league, etc., etc. Each fears an invasion of his domains, because my real business is not known. I cannot remain and be of any utility, unless you shall find means to inform Count Finckenstein that I am only a good citizen and a good observer; but that these I am, and that I am authorized to give my opinion. I cannot doubt but that this Minister is very desirous these few words should be said. I am, however, in conscience obliged to repeat, the part I have to play daily becomes more difficult and more invidious; and that, in order to be truly useful, I must have some character given me, or be employed elsewhere.

Prince Henry at present reads his recantation; he again pretends Hertzberg has received his deathblow, and that his downfall will be instantaneous. He relates miracles of the Duke of Brunswick, and flatters himself that he shall, soon or late, have great influence —"He will be in no haste. He will ply to windward six months." He affirms the English projects are absolutely abortive. Hertzberg, he is confident, acts as if he had lost all understanding, and precisely as if he, Prince Henry, had counseled him, in order to render his fall more headlong, etc., etc., etc. In fine, his discourse is a mixture of enthusiasm and rodomontade, of presumption and anxiety; a flux of words that confirm nothing; or of half phrases without any determinate meaning, except of exaggeration and tumor. Hence, it is difficult to conjecture whether he deceives himself or wishes to deceive; whether he maintains the cause of vanity, feasts on illusion, or if he has recently any ray of hope; for, as I have said, it is not impossible but that Hertzberg, by his boasting, should effect his own ruin. Prince Henry presses me to request the Court to send me some credentials, while the King shall be in Prussia and Silesia; or, at least, to write concerning me to Count Finckenstein, by whom the intelligence may be communicated to the King.

No change in the new habits of the Monarch. Madame Rietz has been but once to see him; but, on Saturday last, he wrote to his natural son by that woman, and directed his letter: "To my son Alexander, Count de la Marche." He has ennobled, and even made a Baroness of the mistress of the Margrave of Schwedt (Baroness of Stoltzenberg, which is the title of a Barony, worth about eight thousand crowns a year, given her by the Margrave), who is nothing more than a tolerably pretty German girl, formerly an actress, by whom the Margrave has a son. It was not thought proper to refuse the only thing this old Prince of seventy-seven wished or could request. Perhaps, too, it was a pretext to do as much for Madame Rietz. The husband of this lady is *erzkaemmerer,* a place nearly corresponding to that of first *valet de chambre,* and treasurer of the privy purse; but it is supposed he will do nothing more than get rich; his wife hitherto has never had any serious influence.

The Court Marshal, Ritwitz, having suddenly become raving mad, after a quarrel with one of the provision officers, Marwitz, who is a totally insignificant person, has been proposed to the King. "He will do as well as another," replied the Monarch. Is this thoughtlessness, or is it fear of importance being annexed to a place which in reality but little merits importance? This question it is impossible to answer.

Lucchesini increases in his pretensions; he demands a place in the finance or commercial department; perhaps the direction of the maritime company, but this would be a very lofty stride. Annexed to wit and information, he has some qualities to which ambition is seldom allied; at most they will entitle him to become a member of the *corps diplomatique,* of which he is capable. I believe this Italian to be one of the most ardent in keeping me at a distance from the King, who will not indeed be easy of access before the winter.

The commission of regulations has hitherto rather appeared a caustic than a healing and paternal remedy. There is much more talk of the sums the employment of which cannot be justified than of easing the excise. Verder, the president, is besides known to be the personal enemy of some of the members of the tax administration. This, perhaps, has occasioned suspicions. Verder, however, was proposed by the Duke

of Brunswick, who, in fact, had need of his aid in
some affairs that relate to his country.

Hertzberg has certainly been in a storm, and the
credit of Count Finckenstein appears to be augmented,
though I confess the shade of increasing favor is
scarcely perceptible. I persist in believing that Hertzberg is immovable, unless by his want of address.

LETTER XXII

September 8th, 1786.

THE sixth, at a review of the artillery, I dismounted
my horse to attend the King, in the front of the ranks.
The Duke of Brunswick joined me; and, as we talked
of mortars, bombs, and batteries, we gradually removed to a distance. As soon as we were alone, he
began to speak to me of the prodigious knowledge I
had of the country; giving me to understand he had
read my memorial to the King. He then reverted to
the new reign, and suddenly afterward to foreign
politics. Having entered at length into the subject,
and spoken more than is necessary here to repeat, he
added, "In God's name, arrange affairs in Holland;
free the King of his fears. Must the Stadtholder
never be other than *ad honores?* You are in full
credit there, and this credit you cannot lose; if you
did, the party by which you obtained it would be too
much exposed to danger. I repeat, put us at our ease,
and I will answer on my head for everything else;
but use dispatch, I conjure you. On Sunday I shall
depart for Brunswick; come and visit me, while the
King is gone to Silesia; we can converse freely there,
and nowhere else. But write to your friends that they
ought to exert all their influence to engage the French

Ministry to use moderation with the Prince of Orange, who cannot be proscribed without State convulsions. Things are not ripe for his abolishment; give him protection. France cannot render a greater service to Europe. What, is your Court yet to learn those forms which effect no change, but which give every support?" Here we separated, because the subject began to be too interesting. But tell me—ought I not to go to Brunswick?

To this I should add that Count Goertz has taken eight chasseurs with him, who are to convey letters to the frontiers of the Prussian States, in order that no dispatches may be sent by land nor pass through foreign hands. The Duke of Brunswick has repeated what Prince Henry had told me, and which I forgot to inform you of, that one of the principal motives for selecting Count Goertz was his former friendship with M. de Veyrac.

From my conversation with the Duke, I conclude that he is or soon will be master of affairs; and this explains the new fit of joy, hope, and presumption which has seized on Prince Henry, who has been persuaded by the cunning Duke that, if he will but have patience, the scepter will devolve on him; and that he, the Duke, will be no more than high constable. It is said Koenigsberg will be appointed Field Marshal. This, added to the smooth turn which the Duke has given discussions and pecuniary matters, has turned the Prince's brain, who told me the other day that " the Duke was the most loyal of men, and his best friend; that he owned a fortnight ago he was of a different opinion; but that," etc. So that the metamorphosis has been produced within this fortnight. In truth, there is no real difference between a fool and a man of understanding who thus can suffer himself to be deceived; as little is there between a fool and a man

of understanding who can be persuaded that a fool is
a man of understanding.   Both these things daily
happen to Prince Henry.   On the thirteenth he departs for Rheinsberg and is to return the day before
the King.

The fervor of the novice appears somewhat to abate.
I have good reason to believe that Mademoiselle Voss
is ready to capitulate,—ogling, frequent conversations
(for the present assiduity at Schoenhausen is not paid
to the Queen Dowager), presents accepted (a canon-
icate for her brother), and an attempt at influence.
(It is she who placed Mademoiselle Vierey in the
service of the Princess Frederica of Prussia.)   To
ask is to grant.   Since the accession all circumstances
denote how dazzling is the luster of a diadem; but so
much the better, for her fall only can render her but
little dangerous.   She is wholly English, and is not
incapable of intrigue.   When we reflect that the credit
of a Madame du Troussel had the power, under a
Frederick II., to bestow places of importance, we may
imagine what may happen under another King, as soon
as it shall be discovered that intrigue may be employed
at the Court of Berlin, as well as at other Courts.

Madame Rietz yesterday received a diamond worth
four thousand crowns; she will probably be put on the
invalid list, with some money, and perhaps a title.

Her son, at present, has publicly the title of Count
de la Marche (or Count Brandenburg), and has a
separate establishment.

General Kalckstein, disgraced by the late King, and
regretted by everybody, has received a regiment.

At present, and till I hear other news relative to
Berlin, accept the following important anecdote, which
I think it necessary to send in the now doubtful state
of the health of the Empress of Russia: About six
years ago, a young foreigner, and a gentleman, in the

service of France, was presented to the Grand Duchess, by a lady who had been educated with her, and who has remained her intimate friend. It was the intention of this young gentleman to enter into the Russian service. He was presented to the Grand Duke by the Grand Duchess, who warmly solicited, and while he was present, a place for the youth in the service of her husband.

The young favorite, well-formed and handsome, often visited the Grand Duchess. Invited to her palace, feasted, distinguished, and continually receiving new favors, he fell in love; of which the Grand Duchess was informed by his extreme confusion. One grand Court day, at a masked ball, in the evening, she had him conducted by one of her women into an obscure apartment, and sufficiently distant from those where the Court was held. In a little time the conductress quitted him, and advised him to wait, and the Grand Duchess arrived in a black domino. She removed her mask, took the youth by the hand, led him to a sofa, and made him sit down by her side. The Grand Duchess then told him this was the moment for him to choose between the service of France and the service of Russia. A certain time, however, was allowed him to come to a decision. Coquetry and even caresses succeeded. Wavering, taken by surprise, distracted between love and fear, the youth behaved with excessive awkwardness at the beginning of the interview. The Grand Duchess, however, encouraged him, inspired him with audacity, and made him every advance, till at length he vanquished his timidity and indeed became very daring.

To this scene of transports, adieus suddenly succeeded, which partook as much of terror, and of despotism, as of love. The Grand Duchess commanded the youth, in the most tender but the most absolute tone, to inform the Grand Duke that he could not accept the rank of captain, which was intended to be given him. She added that he must depart, instantly depart; and that his head must answer should the least circumstance transpire. She, at the same time, pressed him to demand some mark of remembrance. The terrified youth, confused and trembling, requested a black ribbon, which she took from her domino. He received the pledge, and so totally lost all recollection that he left the ball, and quitted Petersburg, without contriving any means of correspondence, arrangements for the future, or precautions of any kind, in favor of his fortune. In a few days he left Russia, travelling day and night, and did not write to the Grand Duke till he had passed the frontiers. He received a very gracious answer; and here the affair ended.

This person is returned to, and is now in, the service of France. He has little firmness, but does not want understanding. Were he guided he might certainly be useful; at least, attempts might be made after so extraordinary an incident. But for this it would be necessary he should go to Russia before there is any change of monarch, and should tempt his fortune, now that the Grand Duchess has not so much fear. I am not personally acquainted with him, but I can dispose of his most intimate friend, in whom every dependence may be placed. I have not thought proper to name the hero of the romance, whom it is not necessary to know, unless it should be intended to afford him employment. If, on the contrary, it should be thought proper for him to pursue any such plan, I will name him instantly.

The Elector of Bavaria is certainly not in good health; he may not live to see winter; and it is scarcely probable he will reach the spring. I shall go from hence to Dresden, that I may not appear to absent myself purposely for the Duke of Brunswick. I shall remain there seven or eight days, as long at Brunswick, and three or four weeks in the whole. My journey will be exactly of the same duration as that of the King, in whose absence there is nothing to be learned, and I shall certainly profit by my peregrinations, and learn more at Brunswick in a week than I should here divine in three months.

My letter is too long to speak of Turkey in Europe. I doubt the Emperor cannot be prevented, if he is not destitute of all capacity, from marching any day he shall please to the mouth of the Danube; but on the same day he must become the natural enemy of Russia, who will find in his presence one too many on the Black Sea, and this may render the combined projects abortive. I am assured that Moldavia and Wallachia desire to be under the Emperor's Government. This I cannot believe, since his own peasants fly their country, and even go to Poland, rather than remain in his power. But the before-mentioned provinces are absolutely unprotected, and I think no opposition can be made, except in Roumelia and Bulgaria. In fine, I believe we only, by promises or threats, are able to prevent the Emperor from laboring at this grand demolition. If we believe the rodomontades of Petersburg, Russia is singly capable of the work. But, were she to attempt it, what would she be on the succeeding day? You are not ignorant she has received some check; that Prince Heraclius has been obliged to desert her cause; that she is once again reduced to defend Mount Caucasus as a frontier; that she cannot at present march into the heart of the Ottoman territories; and that perhaps this would be the best moment for recovering the Crimea. Should all these particulars be true, and these conjectures well founded, it is impossible that I should know any one of them so perfectly as you do yourself.

The dispute, relative to the *bailliage* of Wusterhausen, has been very nobly ended by the King. He has retaken it, but has made an annual grant of fifty thousand crowns to Prince Henry, seventeen thousand of which the latter is obliged to pay Prince Ferdinand. The *bailliage* does not produce more than about forty-three thousand.

Prince Ferdinand at present recants the renunciation to the Margraviate of Anspach. As it is known that Prince Ferdinand has no will of his own, it is evident he receives his impulse from Prince Henry, and the more so, because this is the *manet altâ mente repostum* against Count Hertzberg. It would be difficult to imagine anything more silly, or better calculated eternally to embroil him with the King.

I have always regarded the singularity of Romanzow, of not going into mourning, and his violence with Count Finckenstein concerning not sending a complimentary envoy to Petersburg, which occasioned the Count to demand whether he had orders from his Court to speak in such a style, as the effervescence of a young man; especially since Baron Reeden, the Dutch envoy, did not likewise go into mourning from economy, which shows it was not considered as a matter of any great importance. As these debates very ridiculously occupied the *corps diplomatique* for a week; and as the Comte d'Esterno, who has conducted himself well on the occasion, must have mentioned it, I thought it to no purpose to write on the subject. But as Romanzow, of all the foreign Ambassadors, did not attend the funeral at Potsdam, this mark, either of thoughtlessness or dissatisfaction, was felt; and, the time necessary to receive orders being past, I send information of the fact, to which I do not,

however, pay so much attention as the good people in
the pit, though it has greatly displeased the boxes.
The Cabinet of Berlin must long have known that
friendship, on the part of Russia, is hopeless till the
accession of the Grand Duke; but it is impossible to
butt with more force, or greater disrespect, than
Romanzow has done.

LETTER XXIII

September 10th, 1786.

THE following are some particulars concerning what
happened, on the day of interment, at Potsdam.

The King arrived at seven o'clock. At half-past
seven he went with the Princesses Frederica and Lou-
isa of Brunswick, the young ladies Knisbec, Voss, etc.,
to see the chamber of Frederick. It was small, hung
with violet-colored cloth, and loaded with ornaments
of black and silver. At the far end was an alcove, in
which the coffin was placed, under the portrait of the
hero. This coffin was richly ornamented with cloth
of silver, laced with gold. Toward the head was a
casque of gold, the sword that Frederick wore, his
military staff, the ribbon of the Black Eagle, and gold
spurs. Round the coffin were eight stools, on which
were placed eight golden cushions, meant to sustain:

1. The crown.
2. The golden globe and cross.
3. The gold box containing the seal.
4. The electoral cap.
5. The scepter.
6. The Order of the Golden Eagle, of diamonds
and other precious stones.
7. The royal sword.
8. The royal hand.

The balustrade was hung with violet-colored velvet. A splendid glass chandelier was in the center, and on each side was a mutilated pyramid of white marble veined with black; that is to say, of white cloth, marbled with great art. The chamber appeared to me to want light.

His Majesty afterward passed into the canopy *salon*, hung with black, and adorned with plates of silver from the Berlin palace; and next into the grand hall, hung with black. Eight artificial black columns had been added to this immense hall. Its only embellishments were garlands of cypress, and here again there was too little light.

In about half an hour the King returned to his apartments; and, at half past eight, Prince Henry, Prince Ferdinand, and the Duke of Brunswick came to see the same apartments, where they only remained five minutes.

At a quarter past nine the King went to Prince Henry. The regiments of guards formed under their windows. The canopy was brought; it was of black velvet, surrounded by cloth of gold, and laced with a crape fringe. On the cloth of gold were black eagles. Twelve posts, covered with velvet, supported the canopy; and over them were twelve silver eagles, each a foot high, which produced a good effect.

After the canopy came the state coach; very large, very low, hung with white satin edged with gold fringe, and drawn by eight horses covered with black velvet.

To the state coach succeeded a chariot, in black velvet, on which was a black crown, drawn by eight cream-colored horses, in black velvet harness, on which were fixed black eagles, embroidered in gold. The livery servants, chamber lackeys, heydukes, running footmen, huntsmen, and pages followed.

The Grand Duchess pressing her suit with the young Frenchman.
—p. 93

From the painting by Vogler.

The Princesses, ushered by Messieurs Goertz and Bishopswerder, were at church.

At ten o'clock the procession began. The place of assembly was the grand hall with the eight columns. A gentle descent had been made from the grand canopy to the door, to which the state coach was drawn up to receive the coffin. The road from the palace to the church was planked, and covered with black cloth. The procession was truly superb, and conducted with great order. The troops formed two lines.

The church was illuminated with wax candles and small lamps; and the coffin was deposited under a cupola, supported by six pillars of white marble. The organ began to play and the funeral service was performed, which continued half an hour. The return was not disorderly, but it was not made in procession.

When the guests came back to the palace, the tables were ready spread, and the courses were served up at noon. The guests rose from table at half past one. The King, Prince Henry, the Duke of Brunswick, and the Princesses, went to Sans Souci. Such was the manner in which the morning was spent.

There was no comparison to be drawn between this and the funerals of the Church of Notre Dame with respect to magnificence, taste, or splendor; but they did everything that could be done, the country and the time considered.

There was much order from the commencement to the close. The music was indifferent, had no effect, no energy, no charm, and was ill executed,—not one good voice, Concialini excepted, who did not sing well.

The tables were well supplied, the viands abundant and select, the servants numerous and orderly. Each of the aides-de-camp general did the honors of a table.

French, Rhenish, and Hungarian wines were served in profusion.

The King, going to table, led Prince Henry. On every occasion his Majesty saluted with dignity. His countenance was neither serious nor too cheerful.

He testified his satisfaction to Reck, who replied that Captain Gonthard had regulated the whole; and that he had no other merit except that of having procured him everything of which he stood in need.

The King wore the grand uniform of the guards. The Princes were booted. Prince Goethen had mourning spurs, which was remarked.

The King went and returned in company only with the Duke of Brunswick.

LETTER XXIV

September 12th, 1786.

THE King departs to-morrow. The order of his journey has undergone no change. He will be back on the 28th, and again set out on the 2d for Silesia. I shall probably have a good opportunity, on his return, to speak of finance and of substitutes. Previous to this Panchaud must absolutely unite with me to form a good plan of speculating in our funds,—good for the finances, and in particular good for the King who is to be allured. Remember the importance of this Monarch.

Bishopswerder increases in credit, which he carefully conceals. Welner, a subaltern creature, endowed with understanding, management, and knowledge of interior affairs,—a mystic when mysticism was necessary to please, and cured of his visions since the King has required these should be kept secret,—active, industrious, and, what is more, sufficiently obscure to be employed without creating jealousy,—Welner, I say, appears to gain prodigious influence. He has the qualities necessary to succeed, and even to outwit all his competitors.

I again repeat, Boden ought not to be neglected, by the way of insinuation. He is vain, and should be capable of corruption; for, always suspected of the most insatiable avarice and the basest means, he has lost a place of eight thousand German crowns by the death of the Landgrave of Hesse Cassel, and, it is said, is driven to expedients. He corresponds with the King, and rather intimately; that which he should often repeat must produce an effect. He is the hero to slay Hertzberg, who, I may add, has not been successful concerning Holland, and, in despite of whom, Thulemer may still be recalled.

Prince Henry still feeds on hopes. I have no doubt that he is cajoled by the Duke of Brunswick. But he is exactly at the same point, except that Hertzberg is not so powerful. The King intends Alvensleben for the French Embassy; a man of high birth, sense, and wisdom, as it is affirmed. He is at Dresden. I shall endeavor to study him and shall take him letters.

No person is satisfied; civil and military, courtiers and Ministers, all pout. I imagine they expected it would rain gold. I have nothing to add to my prognostics, which may be reduced to this alternative: the nation sacrificed, while affairs continue tranquil, that we may persuade ourselves we govern; the Duke of Brunswick, should perils intervene, and the storm begin to blow.

In the name of business and of friendship, do not forget a plan of operations for finance. Schulemburg is supported, and I have reasons to believe he will not be dismissed. Should I acquire influence in finance I would not be his enemy. He will be more serviceable than any other, Baron Knyphausen only excepted, who will never be anything while Hertzberg is in power.

Remember that you have an incapable envoy in Bavaria, and that this will become an embassy of importance at the death of the Elector. If it be meant to place me, which must be meant if I am to serve, had not I best make my first appearance here?

LETTER XXV

DRESDEN, *September* 16th, 1786.

I SHALL say nothing particular to you yet of this country, as you may suppose, for who can run and read? Besides, I find the inconvenience of having no credentials, and, consequently, have not been able to speak with propriety on affairs, except in very general and metaphorical terms.

Stuterheim, the Minister for Foreign Affairs, with whom I have dined, is said to be a very well, a labyrinth of secrecy, and it follows that his subalterns are exceedingly reserved. The Ministers here rather give in their REPORTS than act. " Give in their reports " is the consecrated phrase. But I have been so well convinced by what I have seen under Frederick II., that the King, who governs most himself, is so little the master, and is so infinitely deceived, that I am perfectly aware of the degree of credit which these Court *dicta* deserve.

I have seen Alvensleben. Should he go to France, I do not think he will live long. He is worn out, and only keeps himself alive by extreme abstinence, and an almost total sequestration from society. He is well acquainted with Germany, is said to act with prudence and propriety, is successful in what he undertakes, and has a good moral character. He is not, however, without art, and, perhaps, he wishes to be cunning. He is not precisely the man for France, but he is a specimen of the fruit of the country, and, for any other use, is some of the best it produces. I imagine you will find him agreeable.

I shall endeavor to get into the currency of the country, but, I repeat, while I shall have no credentials, and am left so much in ignorance concerning home affairs, I shall be much more proper to collect literary and written opinions than for any other business; and the thoughts of men are not written in their faces. Nor do you, for example, find in any book that a Prime Minister has confided his eldest son, on his travels, to such a blockhead as G——, or to a Chevalier du Vivier, who never utters a word that he does not utter an absurdity, and, perhaps, some that are dangerous. But why has he related that he waited at Hamburg five weeks for permission to take the Vicomte de Vergennes to Berlin, on occasion of the accession of the King, and that this was refused? Is he afraid that they should be insensible at Berlin of the affectation of having avoided that Court? I should never finish were I to cite all the incoherencies he utters, the least of which is ridiculous in the extreme.

In reality, if I am to commence as a subaltern in the diplomatic corps, I have no objection to Hamburg, where, exclusive of the great intercourse of the commerce of the North, with which we are unacquainted, and in which we do not sufficiently participate, since we wish to have an envoy there, we ought to have an active person, instead of one from whom nothing is so desirable as that he should be deaf and dumb.

The vast connections that are between the grand

emporiums of trade are such that these posts are never things of indifference. Why do not they bestow a sinecure on M. du Vivier?

LETTER XXVI

DRESDEN, *September 19th*, 1786.

THERE are few MEN here, yet is the machine tolerably well regulated; nothing can better prove that order and constancy are more necessary for good government than great talents.

The extreme credit of Marcolini is to be regarded as a popular rumor. He is a favorite without ascendency (as without merit) at least in the Cabinet; his influence does not extend beyond the Court. At present he is in Italy, and the routine of affairs is the same. Probably some favors which pass through his hands, and which the excessive devotion of the Elector rather bestows on Catholics than on Lutherans, are the real cause of these murmurs; which, however, are sufficiently believed to occasion the Emperor to make a stupid blunder. He has sent here one of the silliest of Ambassadors—one O'Kelly, an Irishman—because Marcolini had married his niece. He thought by this means to have governed everything; but the trap was so palpably gross that no one has taken the trouble to remove the bait.

The Ministers who have real influence are Stuterheim and Gudschmidt. The first is very infirm, but prudent, sage, and with understanding enough to know on what subjects he is ignorant, to ask information, and to consult others. He, however, draws near his end. The second does not show himself to the world. It is affirmed that he is a man of the greatest merit;

that he has infinite knowledge; that not a single pamphlet in any language throughout Europe escapes him; that his judgment is sound, his understanding perspicuous and penetrating, and his temper communicative; which last quality is in him the more compatible with discretion because he possesses its piety without its superstitions. He ranks first in the confidence of the Elector; but it must be added he is sixty years of age, and has ill health.

Among the Ministers we must also enumerate M. Worm, a well-informed man, who possesses some principles of political economy, with information not very common on the general relations of commerce, together with industry, activity, and great quickness of apprehension; but, as it is said, rarely with much justness of understanding. His moral character is suspected. He is accused of not keeping his hands pure from bribery; but it is not the less true that he is of great service to internal government. He appeared to me to be artful, communicative, ironical, satirical, and crafty, but very proper for business in all countries.

Of all the foreign Ambassadors, I believe M. Saftzing, from Sweden, to be the only one above, or rather not below, mediocrity. I except the English envoy, who has the character of being an able man, but whom I have not yet any proper opportunity for examining. He is open and complaisant, even to affectation, considering that his character is English. If we except Alvensleben, not one of the remainder deserves the honor of being mentioned.

The Elector is a man distinct from Princes in general, yet he appears to partake of the character of the King of England. The consistency of his mind, which is entire, has a small alloy of obstinacy. I spoke but little to him, because of the confusion of the dinner.

Etiquette is observed at the table of the Elector; consequently I paid every care and attention to seat M. de Vergennes near the Prince. He speaks with intelligence and precision, but his voice is harsh, sharp, and shrill. His dress and countenance seemed to indicate devout and wheedling, but acute and implacable, jealousy. The very ill education of the Electress, her noisy mode of speech, and her unreserved freedom, greatly occupy this Prince to his disadvantage; for, besides that such kind of vigilance ever bears somewhat of the stamp of ridicule, his crabbed figure, rendered more disagreeable by a paralytic affection of the eyes, becomes at such moments restless, disturbed, and hideous.

Such, and so ungracious, as he is here depicted, he is a Prince who, from many considerations, is worthy esteem and respect. Since the year 1763, his desire to do good, his economy, his indefatigable labors, his innumerable privations, his perseverance, and his industry, have not for a moment relaxed. He has paid all the personal debts of the Electors; and is advanced in the liquidation of the debts of the State. He pursues his plans with inflexible punctuality. Slow, but not irresolute, difficult in accomplishing, but intelligent, with few resources at a first view, but possessed of aptitude and the gift of meditation, his only weakness arises from his religion, which yet does not occasion him to exaggerate his rights, or to neglect his duties. One step further and he would have been a bigot, and one step backward and he would no longer be a devotee. It is much to be doubted whether his confessor, Hertz, has the least influence except in the distribution of some footmen's places. The Elector supports his Ministers with uncommon firmness, against all, and to all. In a word, but for him the country had been undone; and, should he have the good fortune to see a duration of peace, he will render it very flourishing. Population visibly increases; the annual surplus of births over deaths amounts to twenty thousand; and the number of the people is less than two millions. Trade, which might be better, is not bad. The army imitates that of Prussia, over which it has the advantage of being purely national; but, to say the truth, Saxony is the least military of all the provinces of Germany. Credit is good, and even great. The paper currency is at par, or nearly; and the interest of money at four per cent. The Cabinet of Dresden is the only one in Europe which has adopted the true principles of coinage. Agriculture is in a state of passable respectability. Manufactures are free; the rights of the people are unfringed; justice is impartially administered; in a word, all things considered, it is the, most happy country in Germany. Yet this is a remarkable circumstance, and excites admiration when we recollect the terrible scourges which have successively, and sometimes collectively, laid this fine, but ill-situated country, desolate.

They are persuaded here that we instigate the Turk; that there is a coolness between the two imperial Courts; and that Russia is in want of men, money, and horses. It must be frankly owned that her bank operations have a gloomy appearance. It is supposed we shall endeavor, should it be absolutely necessary, to effect a diversion in Germany, without interfering, except by coming to the aid of those who should be too much exposed to danger. For no one imagines we shall suffer Germany to devolve on one single head, nor even to be divided between two. And, with respect to Turkey in Europe, it is thought that our interest, conjointly with that of England, will, by one means or other, avert the destruction with which it is menaced.

On inquiry, I find the Elector of Bavaria has not properly had an attack. He has only changed his mistress; and when he does so, he alters his regimen to excite venery. It happens on these occasions that he has nervous affections, which resemble false attacks, and which will some day bring on a paralytic stroke. His life is not depended upon.

The hostilities of the Stadtholder have produced an effect here greatly to his disadvantage. For my part, I do not think his affairs in so disastrous a state as they seem to be believed. Should we embroil province with province, we shall lose our advantages; it will in vain be urged that the Stadtholder is master of Guelderland; the nobility is numerous in that province, and they form A PUBLIC opinion.

I send you the state of the military in the Electorate of Saxony, which is no secret; but I shall also add, by the next courier, that of the public stores, which I procured by a singular accident, the particulars of which it would be useless here to relate. I shall only remark that the custom which the Elector has for several years adopted in his offices, of employing supernumeraries without salaries, might give place to discovery, however well secrets may here be kept.

I shall commit to M. de Vibraye, who is returning to Paris, all the minutes of my ciphers, well and duly sealed, and addressed to you.

He does not expect to return hither, and has hopes of the Swedish Embassy.

May not the changes which will take place in the *corps diplomatique,* by the vacancy of M. d'Adhémard, afford an opportunity of giving me something more agreeable and less precarious than a secret commission, which must end of course, with the life of a Minister who is hastening toward the grave? I hope your friendship will not slumber. You must own others might act with less diligence. If you will take the trouble again to read my dispatches as they are here sent, not in ciphers but correct, and will at the same time consider all the difficulties of various kinds that I have had to surmount, and a few means which my cloudy situation can afford, you will not be dissatisfied with my correspondence. Since, for example, Zelle has published the history of the King's disease, I have the satisfaction to perceive the information I sent you was exact. True it is that, under the late King, at the conclusion of so long a reign, a man knew to whom to address himself; whereas at present it is necessary to discover which are the doors at which you must knock. Yet I think I have given a passable picture of men and things. And what could I not effect of this kind, what could I not discover, had I credentials?

LETTER XXVII

DRESDEN, *September 21st,* 1786.

I HAVE several times mentioned, and particularly in Numbers XI. and XIX., this Boden; I can only refer you to the circumstances you will there find.

As to the person named Dufour, whose real name is Chauvier, and who was a journeyman barber in France, had I thought it of any importance I should have spoken before and given his character at full; for he is one of the circuitous paths pointed out to me by Prince Henry. He certainly had influence over the Heir Apparent, which he obtained:

1. Because he was persecuted by the late King, by whom he had been expelled; so that, in order to return, he was obliged to take the name of Dufour,

which is that of a family of the French colonists.
And—

2. That he might aid to banish the spleen. He
often dined in private with the Prince, who was so
familiar with him, some time before his accession,
that when wearied with his discourse he would dryly
bid him hold his tongue. Dufour was one of those
with whom I should have made myself intimate, had
the King continued to live some time longer; and he
was among the persons and things that occasioned
me to project a journey to Potsdam. But death suddenly interposed, and I should have sought his intimacy too abruptly; not to mention that subaltern
influence has, on the King's accession, totally disappeared.

The person named Chapuis is a man who is not deficient in understanding and address. He was born in
French Switzerland. He is the governor of the natural son of the King, and the well-beloved of Madame
Rietz. Thinking his acquaintance might be valuable
in many respects, I consequently sought it, under the
pretense of literature only; but at present Chapuis has
not in himself any one point of contact. To run after
such people, so circumstanced, would but be to render
myself suspicious to no purpose. I mentioned to you,
on my return from Rheinsberg (Number XI.), " I
have numerous modes of communication, which will
develop themselves as time and opportunity shall
serve." But these have been retarded by the accession.
Applications of this secret kind can only be made in
the depth of winter, and during the Carnival, with
utility and safety.

These, generally, are rather TOOLS proper for a spy
to work with than the engines of influence. Should
such people ever have power over foreign politics, the
puissance of Prussia must draw to a conclusion. This

country must not be estimated by France; there is not here the same margin in which to insert follies, or to correct. And as in general man remains at that point where it is necessary he should be fixed, the King of Prussia will act with circumspection in what relates to foreign affairs.

Not that this should prevent us from recollecting that we ought to guard, with extreme caution, against a coalition between Prussia and Austria, for this system also is capable of defense. It is even the easiest of execution, and the most splendid; nor would Prince Henry be so averse to it as he himself supposes, should he perceive the least glimmering of hope. Hitherto, indeed, I have not noticed anything that could give suspicion, but I shall more carefully examine whatever might occasion such an event, on my return to Berlin. There can be little danger that I should become languid in the pursuit of this object, having four years ago published my fears of such an event, and having begun to send my static tables of Austria, only that you might attentively consider the immense basis of power which the Emperor possesses, and whose alliance with France I cannot but consider as the masterpiece of Prince Kaunitz, and the type of our indelible levity.

It may be that this power of the Emperor is as much overrated elsewhere as it is the reverse in France; but even this is a reason which may lead to prefer, instead of the perilous honor of being the champion of the Germanic liberties, the easy and deceptive advantage of dividing the spoils. Therefore, delay appears to me more unseasonable than it has been, for it is probable that the King of Prussia, having once pledged himself, will not recede, which seems to be warranted by his personal probity, his hatred of the Emperor, the antipathy that exists between the two nations, and the universal opinion which prevails that the chief of the empire is a perfidious Prince.

Your project concerning Brunswick is certainly excellent, and I shall spare no labor that may tend to give it success. But the man is very circumspect, Hertzberg very vehement, and the crisis equally urgent.

I have conversed with several of the English who are returned from the Emperor's reviews; he behaved there with great affability, and was very talkative. He particularly distinguished a French officer, who had traveled on horseback, that not a single military position might escape him on his route. The Austrian troops, in general, manœuver well by companies, and even tolerably by regiments, but, collectively, their inferiority to the Prussian army is prodigious. Opinions on this point are unanimous. They were not capable of keeping their distances, even when filing off in the presence of the Emperor. This grand pivot, on which tactics turn, is unknown to the Austrians, whereas the Prussians so habitually, so religiously, observe their distances, that any failure of this kind is an error unheard of.

The inferiority of the Austrian army compared to the Prussian, is attributed:

1. To the want of a sufficient number of officers and subalterns, compared to the number of soldiers.

2. To the economy, totally anti-military, of the Emperor, who, while the companies nominally consist of two hundred men, does not maintain more than fifty or sixty under arms, and sends the others home, even against their will, so that three-fourths of the soldiers are never disciplined.

3. To the troops being dispersed, kept in petty detachments, and never exercised as a whole, except when they are encamped, where, even then, they are disciplined by detail.

4. To the very great inferiority of the officers. The corps of captains forms the soul of the Prussian army, and, at the same time, is the disgrace of the Austrian, etc.

It is generally affirmed that, should the two nations go to war, there is little doubt concerning which would have the advantage; that there is no equality between them, even supposing their generals to be equal; and that the contest most certainly would be favorable to the Prussians, during the first campaign. But this equality of generals is not true. Laudon, though still vigorous, cannot wear much longer. Besides that, he has often said he never would command an army, unless at the distance of four hundred miles from the Emperor. The abilities of Lacy are suspected, though he enjoys the entire confidence of Joseph II., and, it is rumored, has rendered himself singularly necessary, by the complication of the military machine. No commander in the Austrian army can contend against the Duke of Brunswick, nor even against Kalcreuth, or Moellendorf.

Persons who have come very lately from Russia affirm that the Empress is in good health and that ERMENOW has obliterated her long sorrows for the death of LANSKOI. It is also said that Belsborotko gains ground upon Potemkin, but of this I more than doubt.

I have no belief in the facility with which the fifth dispatch may be deciphered. I think that, in general, the ciphers have rather been conjectured than divined. The way by which they are commonly known is the official communication of writings, which is made from one Court to another, and, which the Minister has sometimes the ill address to send without his accustomed cipher, on a known day. This is a quicksand of which I am not in danger. It is necessary, however, to have a variety of ciphers, and I entreat you will not neglect any occasion of sending me some that are new and more complete.

LETTER XXVIII

DRESDEN, *September 24th,* 1786.

YOUR letter of the fourth of September, which, by mistake, your secretaries have dated the fourth of August, came to hand very late, and I shall reply without written references and solely from memory, in the annexed sheet, to the principal points. I had, indeed, previously answered them; nor do I believe that anything has escaped me which it was in my power to learn, or that I have any reason to repent having sacrificed too much to respect and to probabilities, at the time of the death of the King. Had I pursued my plan, I should have been four days sooner than any of the diplomatic couriers; but I request you will answer me whether it was possible to divine the conduct of our embassy. I disregarded the minute circumstances of death, as I had done that of the news itself; nor could I divine that these, being no longer secret, and having become so easy to examine and describe, should yet have remained secrets to you. I suspect it the less because certain Ambassadors (indeed, most of them) appeared to me so embarrassed by the completing of their dispatches that I should not have imagined they would have disdained a supply which was to be obtained with so much facility. Satisfied also with having informed you, thanks to lucky circumstances, of the progress of the disease, in such a manner as few Ministers were informed, I despised those particulars that were become public. But there were some that were sufficiently interesting, relative to the last two days of the King, from which a banquet might be prepared at an easy expense; and the poignancy of which not death itself could destroy,—relating as they did to a mortal so extraordinary, both in body and mind.

His disease, which would have killed ten men, was of eleven months' continuance, without interruption, and almost without relaxation, after his first fit of an asphyxic apoplexy, from which he was recovered by emetics, and after which the first word he uttered, with an imperious gesture, was SILENCE. Nature made four different efforts to save this her rare composition,—twice by diarrhœas, and twice again by cuticular eruptions. Hence it might be said, by the worshipers of a God, that this his image was broken by the Creator himself; and that nature did not abandon one of the most beauteous of her works till the total destruction of the organs, exhausted by age, had been effected; nor till after a continual warfare between body and mind during forty-six years; till after fatigues and agitations of every kind which signalized this fairy reign, and after the most ruinous disease.

This man died on the seventeenth of August, at twenty minutes past two in the morning; and on the fifteenth, when, contrary to his constant custom, he slept till eleven o'clock, he transacted his Cabinet business, though his feebleness was excessive, without any want of attention; and even with a conciseness scarcely perhaps to be found in any other Prince in good health. Thus when, on the sixteenth, the reigning Monarch sent orders to Zelle to repair instantaneously to Potsdam, because the King had remained insensible almost since the noon of the day before, and because he was in a lethargic sleep, the physician, arriving at three o'clock, and finding Frederick II., with animation in his eyes, sensibility in his organs, and so much recollection, not being called, dared not make his appearance. Zelle judged he was past recovery less from the cadaverous odor which exhaled from his wound than because he, for the first time during the whole course of his reign, did not recollect that he had not expedited the affairs of the Cabinet. The conclusion was sagely drawn: dying only could he forget his duty. . . . Two-thirds of Berlin at present are violently declaiming in order to prove that Frederick II. was a man of common, and almost of mean capacity. Ah! could his large eyes, which obedient to his wishes seduced or terrified the human heart, could they but for a moment open, where would these idiot parasites find courage sufficient to expire with shame?

LETTER XXIX

DRESDEN, *September 26th*, 1786.

CONVERSING with a well-informed man who is returned from Russia, I learned a fact totally strange to me, though no doubt known to the Comte de Vergennes; but, whether or no, one which appeared to me proper to make you acquainted with; and more especially because the project is pursued with greater ardor than ever.

When Hyder Ali, having advanced beyond the Orixa, was at the height of his prosperous success, the inhabitants of the north of Bengal, interrupted in their customary commerce by the conflict between the English and their enemies, brought their iron as far as the frontiers of Siberia, there to find a market. This extraordinary fact was the cause of a remarkable attempt made by Russia, in 1783. She sent a fleet to Astracan, to seize on Astrabat, there to form an establishment, on the northern coast of the Caspian Sea, and thence to penetrate into the interior parts of India. The enterprise failed; but is so far from being abandoned that, at this moment, a plan may be seen in relief at Petersburg, of the works by which it is intended to fortify Astrabat.

Of all the gigantic projects of Russia this is, perhaps, the least unreasonable; since it is pointed out by the nature of things, and since there is already an inland navigation completely carried on from Astracan, on the Volga, the Mita, the Lake Jemen, the Wologda, the Canal of Ladoga, and the Neva, to Petersburg. Should this plan ever be pursued with activity and success, it must either happen that England will seriously think of an alliance with us, against the system of the North, or she must suffer every sort of an advantage to be obtained over her at Petersburg; for the interest of the Russians must then become totally opposite to those of the English; and hence may arise dreadful hurricanes, that may sweep away their puissance in the East.

How many revolutions, how much strife between men and things, shall be occasioned by the development of the destiny of that empire which successively overawes and enslaves all surrounding nations? It must, indeed, be owned that her influence in each place ought to decrease in an inverse proportion to the multiplicity of these places. But how great is the influence of these augmenting points of contact, relative to Europe! And, without prematurely divining the fate of Turkey in Europe, with an intent to overcharge the picture, should Russia seize on the Polish Ukraine, as the manner in which she is arming on the Black Sea, and disposing of her commerce, seem to indicate and to threaten, how much greater shall they still be? What species of understanding must the Emperor possess, if it be impossible to make him perceive that the Turks and the Poles are less dangerous neighbors than those strange people; who are susceptible of all, capable of all, who become the best soldiers in the world, and who, of all the men that inhabit the globe, are the most malleable?

The various ideas I have acquired here, where I have made a tolerable harvest, will be comprised in a particular memorial. They are not immediately necessary, and are too numerous to be inserted in my dispatches. But there was one temptation, which was rather expensive, that I could not resist. The Elector has employed his engineers in the topography of Saxony. Twenty-four maps have already been laid down; they are kept in great secrecy, and yet, by paying some louis for each map, I can have them copied. True it is I recollected that, since I COULD, M. de Vibraye perhaps HAS—but, as we rarely do all we may, or even all we ought to do, it is excedingly possible this should not be so; and then I should have lost an opportunity that nevermore could be recovered. This reflection determined me, in the hope that the intent of the act would be its apology; and, as I have not put the Government to the least fruitless expense, or which did not appertain to the better execution of the office I have undertaken, my surplus accounts, I suppose, will be passed.

The Elector of Bavaria is not ill. His new mistress seems only to have been the whim of a day, and his favor again reverts to his former, Madame von Torring Seefeld, originally Minuzzi.

LETTER XXX

DRESDEN, *September 30th, 1786.*

You have been informed, no doubt, by the courier of Tuesday, of what happened on Monday, at the first Court held by the Queen; but, as I think it is proper I should add some reflections on this subject, I shall begin by relating what passed.

The Princess Frederica of Prussia, who imagined that, according to the very sensible custom of the country, the Queen would sit down to play with natives, and not with foreign ambassadors, had placed the Comte d'Esterno at her table; for it was she who arranged the parties. She asked the Queen whom she appointed for her own table. The Queen named Prince Reuss, the Austrian Ambassador, and the Prince of Goethe; but, this species of infantine elephant having, after some consideration, declared that he did not know any one game, the Queen substituted Romanzow, the Russian Ambassador. The Princess Frederica was exceedingly surprised, but either dared not, or would not make any remonstrances; and the Queen's party sitting down to play, the Comte d'Esterno, with great positiveness, energy, and emphasis, refused to sit down at the table of the Princess; declaring he certainly would not play. He immediately withdrew.

Everybody blames the Queen and the Count. The first for having committed an unexampled blunder, and the second, say the people of Berlin, ought not to have refused the daughter of the King. Perhaps this judgment is severe; though I own I should not myself have refused; because, in my opinion, we should not show we are insulted, except when we wish to be supposed insulted. And, as I think, it would have been very thoughtless to have taken serious notice of the absurd mistake of a Princess who is the most awkward of all the Princesses in Europe. Neither had Comte d'Esterno, rigorously speaking, any greater cause for complaint than any other of the royal ambassadors, among whom there is no claim of precedency. Perhaps, too, it would be imprudent to endeavor to establish any such claim; for this would be very certainly to call that in question which tradition and universal tolerance have granted to us. And here let me observe that, as soon as Lord Dalrymple knew Comte d'Esterno had been to complain to Count Finckenstein, he declared he made no demand of precedency whatever; but neither would he suffer precedency from anyone. I should, therefore, have accepted the party of the Princess; but should have said aloud, and, pointing to the table of the Queen, " I see we are all here without distinction of persons; and certainly fortune could not have been more favorable to me." (The Princess may really be called handsome.) Had I thought I still owed more to my Sovereign, I should, on the next Court day, have refused the nomination of the Queen; though it must have been a violent and hazardous step, and reparation must have become a public topic; instead of which it is the insult only that is talked of, and that considerably, in the world.

Will the Comte d'Esterno, or will he not, at present, accept the first invitation he shall receive? Should he comply, it will remain on record that, having resented the procedure, he has acknowledged himself second. Yet how may he refuse? I have proposed to Prince Henry, who is the *mezzo termine,* that there should be a Court held by the Queen Dowager, who, from her circumspection and native dignity, is more respected than the reigning Queen; and that Comte d'Esterno should be of her party, with the Emperor's ambassador; which distinction would be the more marked because that this Queen never yet played with foreign ministers. If her mourning for her husband does not counteract this project, it seems to me the best under the present circumstances. The Queen has written a letter to Count Finckenstein, which must have been read to Comte d'Esterno, in which is inserted the word EXCUSE, and wherein she requires the King should not be informed of the affair. But it is answered the offense was public, and excuses are wished to be kept secret, since silence is required.

The most important and incontestably certain fact is, that there was no premeditation in the matter; that it was the silly giddiness of the Queen in which it originated; that Count Finckenstein and the whole Court are vexed at the affair; that should the King hear of it he will be very much offended with the Queen, whom he has not seen for these six weeks, and whom he thwarts on all occasions; that he has reversed all the arrangements, which in the rapture of accession, she has made with the Master of the Household; and that, in fine, never had Queen of Prussia, that is to say, the most insignificant of queens, less influence.

If, therefore, it be true, on the one part, that the place of every man in this world is that which he himself shall assign to himself, that our rank, already much on the decline in the public opinion, has no need to sink lower, and that Russian insolence, which takes indefatigable strides, has need of being watched and traversed, it is perfectly certain on the other, also, that the proceeding of Monday was distinct and unmeaning, which ought not to be regarded with a lowering brow, under circumstances which may lead from lowering to cold distance, and from the latter to great changes; or, at least, to decisively false steps, to which the Courts of Vienna and London are desirous of giving birth, and by which they will not fail to profit.

Such is my advice, since I have had the honor to have this advice asked. Permit me to add, that Berlin is not any longer an indifferent embassy, but that it is necessary there to be active, yet cautious; amiable, yet dignified; firm, yet pliant; faithful, yet subtle; in a word, to unite qualities which do not often meet. M. de Vibraye means to ask this embassy, should Comte d'Esterno retire, or be sent elsewhere. I speak uninterestedly, since I have no reason to presume that, should it be determined to send me on an embassy, I should begin by one of so much consequence; but it is my duty to say that M. de Vibraye, and particularly his lady, are not the proper persons. His understanding is heavy and confined; rather turbulent than active; and timid than prudent. He is more the giver of dinners than the representative of monarchy; he has neither manners, elocution, nor eyes. Madame de Vibraye, who does not want understanding, would be too gay even for Paris, and, to speak plainly, she has little propriety, and less decency. But as she is enterprising, she makes pretensions to dignity with all the behavior of thoughtlessness; and, as she molds her husband as she pleases, by suffering him to believe he is absolute master, she renders him morose, uncivil, and rule. Besides which, she sequesters him from the world; and such sequestration must everywhere, and particularly at Berlin, be totally disadvantageous to an Ambassador of France. This is one of the errors of Comte d'Esterno.

The following is the chief intelligence I hear concerning the King and his administration, relative either to his absence or his return. He is exceedingly dissatisfied with the Stadtholder. It is affirmed you ought to accept the declaration of Count Goertz. I repeat incessantly, that this is the very time when our intentions ought no longer to be suspected; since assuredly, if we wish the destruction of the Stadtholdership, the Prince of Orange has given us a fine opportunity. Prince Henry affirms that, provided he was restored to the right of maintaining order, and not of giving order, at the Hague, and was in possession of a little money, the King would be contented. I believe he, the King, feels the necessity of not making a false step at the beginning of his political career. One fact, I can assure you, is certain, which is that it was the advice of Hertzberg to march ten thousand men into Holland; and that there was on this occasion a very warm contention between him and General Moellendorf, in the King's presence. By this you may judge of what is to be expected from the violence of such a Minister. Still, however, this has not prevented him from being created a Count in Prussia; and, if I am not mistaken, his influence continues.

With respect to domestic affairs, whatever Prince Henry may say to the contrary, the credit of Schulemburg is on the decline; were it only that he no longer appears in the transaction of public business. It is, however, affirmed that he, with many others, is soon to be made a Count, for they are not economists of their titles. The commission for the regulation of the customs begins to strike bold strokes; but they alight on individuals, and are not aimed at general reformation. Launay has received information that the King henceforth can give him only six thousand crowns per annum, in lieu of twenty thousand, the sum he before had; and that he must accept this or resign. Launay, enraged, and the more so because he has long since demanded his dismissal, loudly declares he will print an estimate, which will prove not only that, in justification of each of his acts, he has a letter from the late King, the fiscal temper of whom he has moderated much oftener than he has provoked, but that he likewise has refused twenty bargains, offered him by Frederick II., which would have acquired him tons of gold. The scandal of this estimate, should he dare to publish it, will be very great; and the analyzing of it will rather be a commission of inquiry into the conduct of the late King than of the present state of the customs, which might easily have been foreseen were thus regulated. The commissioners have dismissed Roux, the only able man among the collectors, with a pension of five hundred crowns; and Groddard, a person of insignificance, with a like sum. They have bestowed their places on Koepke and Beyer, with a salary of three thousand crowns, neither of whom know anything,—with this difference, that the last is exact, assiduous, and laborious; but both of them are without information, and devoid of principles. Generally speaking, the commissioners themselves have none; nor have they the least knowledge of how they ought to act. Commissions here will all be the same; for, exclusive of the inconveniences that are annexed to them in every country, there is in this the additional one that men of knowledge are very scarce, and they must, therefore, long continue ill-sorted. But the King wishes to satisfy some, bestow places on those who have protectors, and particularly not to have any Prime Minister. There must be an embargo on business while it remains in this state; and I have many reasons for supposing that no person will, for some months to come, have found his true place, or that which he is destined to keep; we must not, therefore, be in haste to judge.

But we may affirm that the King has exceedingly

displeased the people,—less in refusing to partake of the festival prepared for his return than in avoiding the street where the citizens had assembled to see him pass. " He treats us as his uncle did, on his return from the Seven Years' War," say the mob; " but, before imitating him in this, he ought to have imitated the great actions of his uncle." It must be owned good sense is sometimes on the side of the multitude.

With respect to the domestic affairs of the palace, anyone may remark at the first glance that they are totally in disorder. No master, no one to give directions, no funds assigned; footmen and the household officers govern all. Dufour, or Chauvier (I before explained to you that this was one and the same person), like all the other subordinate confidants without any influence whatever, is rather ill, than well treated. Colonel Vartensleben, formerly banished into Prussia because of his intimacy with the hereditary Prince, is supposed to increase in favor. But the two men to be observed are—Welner, to whom it is affirmed are communicated all ministerial papers, the reports on all projects, and the revisal of all decisions; and Bishopswerder, who, besides universal suspicion, talks with too much affectation of having no influence over the King not to betray himself, in a country where people are not artful enough to say they do not possess a thing which they really do not possess in order that it may be supposed they do.

With respect to pleasures, they are improved upon. One very remarkable arrangement is, that a cook has been appointed for the Princess Frederica of Prussia, the King's daughter by his first Queen; thus she is to have a kind of household; which, if I am not mistaken, is nothing more than a mode, and none of the most moral, of procuring frequent and decent interviews with Mademoiselle Voss, who is capitulating; for she has declared that no hopes of success must be entertained as long as Madame Rietz shall continue to be visited. The latter went to meet the King on his return; then, passing through the city with an arrow's speed, she flew to Charlottenburg, whither the King came, and where she lives. She acts the prudent part of taking charge herself of the pleasures of his Majesty; who apparently sets a great price on any new enjoyment, be it of what kind it may.

It is secretly rumored, though I cannot warrant its truth, that England is prodigal in caresses, and reiterated offers of a treaty of commerce, on the most advantageous terms; and that Russia itself spares no advances. Certain it is that our enemies and their partisans loudly proclaim that we have lately disbanded ten thousand men; which is sufficient proof, say they, that we have no thoughts of holding the two imperial Courts in awe.

I can also certify that the Grand Duke and the Grand Duchess, who long had afforded no signs of existence to Prince Henry, have lately written him very charming letters, but these are no impediments to the licentious discourse of Romanzow, who, on the eve of the King's funeral, asked, in a public company, whether there would not be rejoicings on the morrow; and who has bestowed the epithet of THE ILLUMINATION OF THE FIVE CANDLES on the night of the second, on which homage was paid to the new King, and when a general illumination was ordered. Apropos of homage, Prince Henry is permitted to make written oath, and this favor has not a little redoubled his fumes; he still wagers that Hertzberg will be disgraced. This Hertzberg yesterday read a pompous account to the Academy of his journey into Prussia, and he was suffocated with incense by all the candidates.   Nothing could be more completely silly.

I shall conclude with a word concerning Saxony. I do not believe the health of the Elector to be good, he withers visibly; and this is promoted by the violent exercise which he takes, from system, and in which he perseveres with all his invincible obstinacy.   He will leave no sons, and there is no imagining the hypocritic imbecility of his brothers, who are not married; the result of which is that this fine country is dangerously menaced by future contingencies.   Marcolini, as I have said, is on his journey through Italy; and it is supposed that one of his commissions is to seek a wife for Prince Anthony.   Prince Henry, who fears lest choice should be made of a Tuscan Princess, or some other of the Austrian alliances, has conceived the project of bestowing the hand of the Princess de Condé on him, by which we should secure the Electorate and the Elector.   I give this as I received it.

First Postscript.—Let me add that, with respect to the map I determined to have secretly copied, it is the map of the most important part of Saxony; and one which all the foreign ambassadors, without exception, with M. de Vibraye at their head, are convinced the Elector will not permit his brother to see.   I have had a windfall much more valuable,—that of the land survey of 1783, made with great exactitude, and containing a circumstantial division of territorial wealth. I shall have it copied in haste, for which I do not imagine I shall be blamed.   M. de Vibraye is quitting Dresden, whither he does not wish to return.   It is a pleasant post, and a very excellent one from which to observe the Emperor and the King of Prussia.

Boden is on the road hither; he is imagined to be presumptuous enough to solicit the French Embassy.

Either he will be disappointed or the Court of Berlin will act improperly. The King still continues in the intention of sending you Alvensleben. I spoke to you of him when at Dresden, where I conversed much with him; he is certainly a man of information and understanding. M. d'Entragues was intimately acquainted with him, and this friendship has continued. It would be very easy to send for M. d'Entragues, who is at Montpellier; whether it were to conduct or to watch his entrance on the scene of action.

SECOND POSTSCRIPT.—Prince Henry was sent for by the King this morning, on business, and invited to go and dine at Charlottenburg. This he has acquainted me with, and desired me to come to him at five o'clock. I can add nothing to this enormous length of ciphering, except that I wish to repeat that the intelligence of the ten thousand men proposed by Hertzberg is fact. It has appeared so important to me, when combined with the affairs of Hattem and Elburg, which seemed to give invincible demonstration that Count Hertzberg had long promised, in the secret correspondence of which I have spoken, the aid of the army of the new King. I say this information appeared so important that I thought it my duty to make it known to the Comte d'Esterno, by a channel which he cannot suspect is derived from me.

With respect to Court intrigues here, I have proof that Prince Henry tells everything to Prince Ferdinand, who tells everything to his wife, who, lured by the tempting bribes she receives in ready money, betrays Prince Henry. Luckily, the excessive stupidity of this Princess deadens her influence, and congeals the good-will which the King wishes to entertain for her.

LETTER XXXI

DRESDEN, *October* 3*d*, 1786.

I HAVE had very little time for the courier of to-day, having spent all day yesterday, from six o'clock in the morning till night, at, and in the affairs of, the Court. The ceremony of rendering homage was awful, notwithstanding the narrowness of the place in which the States were received. As moral ideas have a great influence, even unperceived by us, on our physical sensations, this tribute of respect, paid by armed despotism to the nation it governs, this species of paternal colloquy between the Monarch and the deputies, here called the States, establishing in some manner a correlative engagement,—to which only a little more dignity on the part of the deputies, and at least the appearance of deliberation, are wanting to give pleasure to the heart,—fill the mind with sublime and affecting reveries. To a Prince capable of reflection, I would only wish this ceremony to be contrasted with the military oath, and the different emotions they excite to be analyzed, in order to lead him to examine whether it be true that a monarchy depends wholly upon force, and whether the pyramid ought to rest upon its basis or upon its point.

After the discourse of the Minister of Justice (Reek) to the States, after the harangue of the first order (the ecclesiastics), conducted by Prince Frederick of Brunswick, Provost of the Chapter of Brandenburg, and after the oath of the nobility, the declaration and confirmation of privileges, the enumeration of titles to be bestowed, made by the Minister Hertzberg (the Minister Schulemburg is one among the number of new Counts), the King advanced, on a projecting balcony, over which a very fine canopy had been raised, to receive the oaths and the homage of the people. The citizens were assembled, by companies, wards, and trades, in the square opposite the palace. The symptoms of tumultuous joy are here, as elsewhere, the effects of sympathy (I had almost said contagious) between a great multitude of men, assembled to behold one elevated superior to them all, whom they called their Monarch and their Majesty, and on whom, in reality, depends the greatest part of the blessings or the woes that await them.

It must, however, be remarked that the order was much greater all the day, and at night, than could have been hoped in any other large metropolis. It is true that they distribute here neither wine, *cervelats,* nor money. The largesses are distributed to each quarter, and pass through the hands of the pastor and the magistrate. It is equally true that the passions of this are scarcely so strong as the emotions of other nations.

The King dined upward of six hundred people. All who were noble were invited. When the proposal was made to me to remain, I replied that, apparently, only the national nobility was meant; and that, had it been intended to admit foreigners to that favor, they no doubt would have had the honor of receiving such an intimation. All the English, and almost all the French, like me, and with me, retired.

The illuminations were not very great. One was remarked where all the small lamps were covered over by crape, so that the light appeared dim, gloomy, and truly funereal. This was the invention of a Jew, and it was in the front of his own house that it took place. It calls to my mind a beautiful passage in the sermon which preceded the ceremony, and which was preached in the Lutheran church. The minister of the prevailing religion long invoked, and with considerable pathos and energy, the blessings of toleration,—" That happy and holy harvest, for which the Prussian provinces are indebted to the family by which they are governed."

I send you the best medals that were struck on the occasion. They are your own. Others are to be distributed among the foreign ambassadors, who, no doubt, will send them home. There are some in gold, but I thought them too dear, the workmanship considered. Each general in the service was presented with a large medal, the price of which is forty crowns. Each commander of a regiment received a small one, of the price of six ducats. The large are good, the small very indifferent. I speak of those that were distributed yesterday; and only of the likeness.

October 4th, 1786.

THE day of homage and its preparations have wholly consumed the time, and obstructed all society, since the last courier; for which reason I have at present little to say. Prince Henry was invited, the other day, principally, as I believe, let him say what he will, because M. de Custine, the father, dined with the King. However, his Majesty, before dinner, spoke to the Prince concerning Holland, and complained that the discourse of M. de Veyrac, who had informed Goertz he could not interfere, was in exact contradiction to the promises of the Cabinet of Versailles. The subject of Holland puts him out of temper, as it naturally must; and yet, as I have incessantly repeated, " When could we find a better opportunity of acting disinterestedly than at present; now that the Stadtholder, contrary to reason and all propriety, has taken a violent and decisive part, a few days before the arrival of the advice which was intended to be sent him by the King?"

I have had a very impassioned scene, concerning Holland, with Count Hertzberg: patience, firmness, and something of cunning, on my part; violence, passion, and want of reason, on his. It is evident to me that he is pursuing some secret project concerning Holland.

Apropos of M. de Custine; he made the King wait an hour for him at dinner. It is a melancholy circumstance for France that she should continually be, in some measure, represented by certain travelers, when political affairs are in a delicate state. Our Duc de la F——, amid an assembly of our enemies, said to the Duke of Brunswick, " Apropos; pray has your Highness ever served? " At Dresden, a ceremonious and circumspect place, where our embassy has given much dissatisfaction, this same pitiable interrogator, having been shown a collection of precious stones, the most magnificent that exists in Europe, said to the Elector at high dinner, " Very good! Yes, indeed, very good! Pray how much did the collection cost your Highness? " A certain M. de P——, a week before the death of the King, dining at Potsdam with the Prince of Prussia, hearing the name of M. de H—— mentioned, exclaimed, " Apropos; I forgot that I have a letter from him, which I am to give you." And this letter he threw to the Prince across the table. He no doubt imagined such familiarity was exceedingly natural—he who, at Prague, taking leave of the Emperor, seized and shook him by the hand, testifying the great satisfaction he had received at having seen his manœuvres, and renewed his acquaintance with him. And, what is better, it is M. de —— who relates this anecdote here; which there are Englishmen enough would take care should not have been forgotten, had he not with so much precaution treasured it up in his memory. Wherefore permit such people to travel, whom, by means of the places they enjoy, it is easy to detain at home? There is no possibility of exaggerating the evil which such ridiculous pasquinades produce, at a moment when the ill-designing are so numerous, and who wish that the nation should be judged by such specimens.

Suffer me further to remark, of Messieurs de Custine, that, foolish as the father is, physically a fool, a fool unmeasurable and disgusting, equally is the son a man of great hopes, and appears in all companies with universal success. Not any man so young, with whom I am acquainted, unites so much modesty, so much reason, and such decent timidity, to so great a talent for observation, or to manners so agreeable and mild, so much caution and wise activity. There is no doubt but that the extravagances of the father display these qualities to advantage in the son, but they exist, and on the most solid basis, for, in all probability, he he has taken an aversion for, by being a continual spectator of, the follies of his father. He is a scion who, of all the young men I have known, is most proper to be transplanted into the diplomatic nursery.

The King, all yesterday, was cold and taciturn; not an emotion, not a gracious word, not a smile. The Minister Reek, who harangued the States in the name of the Sovereign, promised, in his discourse, that no new tax should be imposed during the present reign, but that, on the contrary, those that existed should be diminished. Was he commanded to make this promise, or did he venture to make it uncommanded? Of this I am ignorant, and it is a matter of doubt.

The day before yesterday, the King had some domestic brawls and a scene of jealousy, at Charlottenburg, to support from Madame Rietz. The remembrance perhaps remained with him yesterday; whether or no, the discourse of his Minister of Justice spoke more pleasingly than his countenance, however agreeable it may in reality be. He is to depart on the fourth for Silesia, and does not return till the seventeenth.

A part of the palace is at present furnishing, but in a simple style.

Public notice has been given that those persons who had been promised reversions of fiefs should appear, that their reversions were annulled, and that they were not allowed to solicit till first there should be a vacant fief, and not for the reversion of fiefs.

I have seen a narrative of what passed in Prussia. The person who wrote it has employed very sounding expressions to depict the enthusiasm of the public, and among them, the following phrase of the King: "I have found Prussia very ill, but I will cure her."

Count Katzerling, who had suffered great losses during the Seven Years' War, and met with very ill treatment from the late Monarch, after having been very graciously received by him, had accepted a loan of one hundred and fifty thousand crowns, for thirty years, without interest.

It is said the Bishop of Warmia will be here within three weeks. He is a very amiable man, with the levity of a Pole, and was much in the favor of the Prince of Prussia. The King seems to remember this; he has been treated with much greater kindness than any other person in Prussia.

In November, the King is to balance the statements of expense and receipt.

FIRST POSTSCRIPT.—I forgot to inform you that, for so cloudy a day, Prince Henry was yesterday highly caressed. He dined and supped with his Majesty, and singly attended him to see the illuminations.

SECOND POSTSCRIPT.—I return from Court, the Ambassadors were mingled promiscuously, but, as the Ministers of the two Imperial Courts were together, the King proceeded in rather a singularly retrograde manner. It so happened (because of the number of Englishmen that were to be presented) that Lord Dalrymple was the nearest to the King's door, and preceded the Imperial Ambassadors. The King began with the latter. He then returned to Lord Dalrymple, after which he descended much lower toward Comte d'Esterno, and spoke no further to him than by thanking, in general, the foreign Ambassadors for their illuminations. Should this neglect of customary forms continue, I think it would be right to let it be understood that it gives displeasure, for the rumor of the hatred of the King for the French is daily strengthened, and rumor, sometimes, in reality produces the event it proclaims.

LETTER XXXII

DRESDEN, *October 4th,* 1786.

IT APPEARS extremely probable that habit will be the conqueror, and that Frederick Wililam will never be more than what his penetrating uncle had foreboded. No terms are too hyperbolical to express the excessive negligence of his domestic affairs, their disorder, and his waste of time. The valets dread his violence; but they are the first to turn his incapacity to derision. Not a paper in its place; not a word written at the bottom of any of the memorials; not a letter personally opened; no human power could induce him to read forty lines together. It is at once the tumult of vehemence and the torpor of inanity.

His natural son, the Count of Brandenburg, is the only one who can rouse him from his lethargy; he loves the boy to adoration. His countenance brightens the moment he appears, and he amuses himself, every morning, a considerable time with this child, and this, even of his pleasures, is the only one in which he is regular; for the remaining hours are wasted in inexplicable confusion. His ill humor the other day, for example, which I had supposed was occasioned by the quarrel at Charlottenburg, induced me to inquire into particulars. It was nothing more than a musical dispute. The King would have a chamber concert. He ordered two-and-twenty musicians to be assembled. It was his intention to have performed himself; his violoncello was uncased and tuned. Fourteen musicians only came; and passions, threats, intemperance succeeded. The *valets de chambre* laid the blame on Kalikan, whose business it was to summon the musicians. Kalikan was thrown into prison. Duport, the famous violoncello player, and consequently the favorite musician, came to the aid of Kalikan, and gave the King the letter which the *valets de chambre* had intercepted. His choler then became outrageous; everybody fled, but no further effects have followed this subaltern prevarication. Poor King! Poor country!

I am persuaded by two particulars: the one, that his Majesty has conceived the idea and the hope of becoming a great man, by making himself wholly and purely German, and by hectoring French superiority; the other, that he is already in his heart determined to resign business to a principal Minister. He has not, perhaps, yet owned the fact to himself; but at least he is inwardly convinced it must be so. In this case his last resource will be to call in the aid of the Duke of Brunswick, or of MY UNCLE.

The first of these plans is the work and the master-piece of Count Hertzberg. He has said, and justly said: "There is only one mode of acquiring reputation; which is to impart an impulse to your nation, that under your reign a new kind of glory may take date. This impulse you can only give by acting determinately. What can you ever effect as the partisan of France? You can only be the feeble imitator of Frederick II. As a German you will be an original, personally revered throughout Germany, adored by your people, vaunted by men of letters, respected by Europe, etc., etc." The explication of the enigma is, that Count Hertzberg imagined this to be the shortest road to make himself Prime Minister.

But the necessities of accident demand, or will soon demand, a different person. Servile as the country is, it is not habituated to ministerial slavery; and Hertzberg, long a subaltern, rather crafty than able, deceitful than cunning, violent than determined, vain than ambitious, old, infirm, and not promising any long duration of life, will not bend the people to this servility. They must have (though this Welner, who is so much attended to at present, and whose influence near spectators only can discover, may push his pretensions), I repeat, they must have a man whose rank can quell subordinate candidates; and the number of such men is not great. I can discover but two men of this kind,—Prince Henry and the Duke of Brunswick. To the disadvantage of not living in the country, the latter adds that of being necessarily formidable to a feeble and indolent, but vain and jealous, Prince; who may imagine that Prince Henry will not commit the same injury on his, the Sovereign's, reputation as a Prince who cannot leave his own country, and reside here constantly as Prime Minister, without being undoubtedly and conspicuously such. For which reason the credit of Prince Henry daily strengthens, in spite of his ill address. However, he has boasted less within some few weeks; and, instead of not returning from Rheinsberg, whither he again goes during the absence of the King, till the middle of December, as was his intention, he will be here on the same day as his nephew.

Yet, exclusive of the personal defects of Prince Henry, and the errors of which he will indubitably be guilty, how shall we reconcile the German system and the Monarch's hatred of the French to the confidence granted this Prince? The symptoms of such hatred, whether systematic or natural, continually increase and correspond. The King, when he dismissed Roux and Groddart, said: *"Voilà donc de ces B——dont je me suis défait."* The real crime of Roux, perhaps, was that he kept a Jewess whom the Prince of Russia wished to possess, and obstinately refused to listen to any kind of accommodation. A French merchant brought some toys to show him, to whom he harshly replied: "I have baubles already of this kind to the amount of seven millions." He then turned his back, and did not utter another word, except to bid him not go to the Queen, for if he did, he should not be paid. The action was far from blamable; it is the manner only that I notice. Boden was passably well received, except that the only consolation he found for his fever was, "Go to Berlin, and keep yourself quiet, for you have a companion that will stay by you these three months." Boden said to him, "I should have had thousands of messages to your Majesty, had I dared to take charge of them." "You did well to refuse," replied the King; and in so rough a tone that Boden dared not even given him the letters of Dusaulx and Bitaubé.

Launay is treated with severity, and even with

tyranny. He was confined to his chamber while his papers were examined, independent of a general prohibition not to leave Berlin. One Délâtre, his personal enemy, has been opposed to him on all occasions, and has been sent for to become an informer against him, —a man devoid of faith or honor; suspected of great crimes; a dissipator of the King's money; an unbridled libelist, and as such denounced by our Court to that of Berlin, which officially returned thanks, two years ago, for our behavior on that subject. I say he was sent for; because owing, as he does, eighty thousand crowns to the King, would he have ventured to come without a passport, or being asked? It is evident that Launay is persecuted as a farmer of the taxes, and as a Frenchman.

It is believed that the collectors and farmers-general will all be dismissed at the festival of the Trinity, the time when those accounts that shall actually be settled are to be examined. This is the grand sacrifice that is to offered up to the nation. But what is to supply the deficiency in the revenue? For in fine, the farmers, last year, paid six millions eight hundred thousand German crowns; and it is not only impossible to replace this immense sum, but, knowing the country, it is easy to foresee that the German farmers of finance will scarcely collect the half of the amount.

Of what will the convocation of the provincial and finance counselors, and the deputies of the merchants, be productive? Of complaints, and not one project which will not be distinct, partial, and in contradiction to the general system,—or such as the nature of things presents as a system; for in reality not any as yet exists.

I return, and say, all these projects are contrary to the personal hopes of Prince Henry. Will he make all his passions subservient to his ambition? (He is far from possessing that degree of fortitude.) Or, does he dissemble that he may obtain power? Of this I do not believe him uniformly capable. I rather fear he is once again the dupe of caresses; which, however, it must be confessed, are more substantial and more marked than they ever had been before. I particularly fear he should be in too great haste, and too eager to gather the harvest before it be ripe; neglecting the care of providing seed for futurity.

The King has given the Minister of Justice, Reek, a box of petrified shells, splendidly enriched with diamonds, estimated to be worth twelve thousand crowns; a similar box to the Minister Gaudi, and ten thousand crowns; another of the same kind to General Moellendorf; a fine solitaire to the Marquis di Luchesini; and a diamond ring to Philippi, the lieutenant of the police. He has further broken up three boxes set with diamonds, of which thirty rings have been made; these he has taken with him to distribute in Silesia.

Take good note, that Launay has not had the alternative of accepting a salary of six thousand crowns, or his dismission; he has merely received information, under the form of an order, that his salary was reduced to six thousand crowns.

Count Hertzberg this day gave a grand dinner to foreigners, to which the new Spanish Ambassador was invited, but neither Comte d'Esterno nor any Frenchman; which affectation was the more remarkable since all the English, Piedmontese, Swedish, and not only foreign Ambassadors but complimentary envoys, were there assembled. Comte d'Esterno takes a proper revenge; he gives a grand dinner to-morrow, to which Count Hertzberg is invited.

POSTSCRIPT.—Mr. Ewart, the secretary of the English Embassy, said to me yesterday, in the presence of fifteen people, Count Hertzberg supporting him with voice and gesture, in these precise terms, "The Stadtholder is, by the constitution, the executive power in Holland; or to speak more intelligibly, he is precisely in Holland what the King is in England." I replied, in the most ironical and dry tone, "It is to be hoped he will not be beheaded by his subjects." The laughers were not with Mr. Ewart.

Boden has sent your packets. The extracts from the pleadings of Linguet, which are excellent (I speak of the extracts), have been perfectly successful. I entreat you will not fail to send me the continuation. You cannot find a better means of procuring me customers than by things of this kind.

There is a demur concerning Alvensleben. It is Hertzberg who supports Goltz.

Number LXXVIII. of the "Courier of the Lower Rhine" is so insolent, relative to the King of France and his Ambassador, that I imagine it would be proper to make a formal complaint. This might somewhat curb Hertzberg, who is the accomplice of Manson, and who may do us many other favors of a like nature, should this pass with impunity. You are not aware of the influence these gazettes have in Germany.

LETTER XXXIII

MAGDEBURG, *October 9th,* 1786.

LEAVING Berlin, I by chance discovered the person who has remained four days shut up in the apartment of the Prince of Hesse (of Rothembourg), who is no other than that Croisy, formerly St. Huberty, and once the husband of our celebrated St. Huberty, whose marriage was annulled, Counselor Bonneau of the Prince of Prussia, and relative to his own wife a bankrupt, a forger,—in a word, a knight of industry, of the most despicable order, and concerning whom all foreigners ask, "Is it possible such a man can be an officer in the French service?" I am no longer astonished that the Prince of Hesse should be coldly received by the King. To come expressly to lay the train to the mine of corruption; and to depend upon it as a certainty that the combustibles should catch fire, from a knowledge of the errors of the Sovereign; to found hopes of success on the ill opinion we have of him, and in a manner to proclaim this knowledge, by a rapid journey from Paris to Berlin, destitute of all other pretext, since the Prince of Hesse and his minion have stayed only five days, and are already gone back to Paris,—this is at once to display foolish cunning and contemptible conduct. I imagine it is of importance that we should tell the King aloud, and with the strongly marked, ironical tone of disdain, which shall make him feel, without debasing ourselves to speak more openly, that this manœuvre was totally unknown to our Cabinet; for I am persuaded, from some half-phrases which I have heard those who wish us ill drop, that they do not desire anything better than to fix this blot upon us.

I have traveled through Brandenburg to Magdeburg with Count Hatzfeldt, who had been sent by the Elector of Mayence to compliment the King on his accession, and Baron Geilling, sent for the same purpose by the Duc de Deux-Ponts. The latter, formerly a captain of hussars in our service, is a handsome blockhead, who could only have been chosen because he is the brother of Madame Eixbeck, the Duke's mistress. Count Hatzfeldt is a man of great urbanity, and whose knowledge and understanding are deserving of esteem. It seems he will remain some time at Berlin, that he may discover what shall be created out of the chaos. I conversed much on Mayence; the Elector is better, but does not promise any length of life. The two persons who, in all appearance, are most likely to succeed him are Feckenberg and Alberg. The first is wholly Austrian, the latter a man of abilities, of whom the highest opinion is entertained, whose political inclinations are little known, and who dissembles, like Sixtus V., while yet a monk.

That Court at present seems to be exceedingly averse to the Emperor, who every day, indeed, by a multitude of traits, both private and public, and which are really inconceivable, increases universal hatred. It is impossible to depict the effect which his answer to the request of the Hungarians produced—(*Pueri sunt pueri: pueri puerilia tractant*)—together with the violent abolition of all their privileges. But, on the one hand, the great landholders are at Vienna, there enchained by their places, and almost kept under a guard, so that they are in truth the hostages of the slavery of the Hungarians; and, on the other, the aristocracy being excessively odious to the people, there is in this superb and formidable country neither unity of interest, nor center of concord. The regular troops are, besides, posted, and provided with artillery, supported by veterans, colonists, etc., etc.

An Englishman, very much my friend, and a man of excellent observation, whom I have happened to meet with here, and who has visited all the camps of the Emperor, while speaking in raptures of those formidable pillars of his power, Hungary, Moravia, Bohemia, Galicia, etc., confesses that the inferiority of his troops, compared with the Prussian army, has infinitely surpassed his expectation. He affirms it is impossible, either relative to the individual or collective information of the officers or to the military talents of the Emperor, which are in reality null, insomuch that he appears incapable of conceiving such complicated evolutions,—he affirms, I say, it is impossible to compare the two nations: with this difference, that the Emperor, like Cadmus, can make men spring out of the earth; and that the Prussian army, once annihilated, will be incapable of renovation, except from its treasury. Should A MAN once be seated upon the Austrian throne, there will be an end to the liberties of Europe. The health of the Emperor is supposed not to be good; his activity gradually decreases; he still, however, surpasses his real strength, but his projects seem like the wishes of an expiring patient who raves on recovery. He is supposed at present to be on very cool terms with the Empress of Russia.

LETTER XXXIV

BRUNSWICK, *October 14th,* 1786.

THOUGH I ride post, you perceive it is not in the spirit of dissipation. Alas! what mode of life in reality less corresponds with my natural inclination than that indolent activity, if so I may call it, which hurries me into every tumult, and among the proud and fastidious, to the utter loss of time! For such is the general consequence of the confusion of society among the Germans, who converse as they call it AMONG THEMSELVES although thirty persons should be present. Thus am I robbed of study, deprived of my favorite pursuits, my own thoughts, and forced incessantly to comply with forms so foreign, not to say odious, to my nature. You yourself, who lead a life so full of hurry, but who, however, associate with the chosen few, in despite of all the gifts of nature, you must feel how difficult it is abruptly to pass from the buzz of men to the meditations of the closet. Yet is

this indispensably necessary, in order to manage the
ASIDE speeches, by which the current news of the day
is acquired and consequences are divined. We must
gallop five days with the Prince, and pursue all the
physical and moral meanderings of the man, in public
and in private, before we can obtain the right, or the
opportunity, to ask him a question; or, which is better, to catch a word, which may be equivalent both to
question and answer.

But who knows this better than you? I only wish
you to understand my excursions are not the effect
of chance, and still less of whim. Let me add that
each of my journeys improves my local knowledge, a
subject on which I have made it a law not to be easily
satisfied. I hope that, among others, you will perceive
by my memorial on Saxony, and by that on the Prussian States, which are, in reality, works of labor, and
which you will not have a sight of for months to come,
that I have profoundly studied the countries which I
wished to understand, and as ardently in men as in
books; with this difference, however, that I scarcely
dare confide in the mere assertion of the best-informed
man, unless he brings written proofs. The necessity
of that species of superstitious conscientiousness, with
which I am almost mechanically impressed, whenever
I take up the pen, has been demonstrated to my own
mind too often for it ever to forsake me.

Yet whither am I traveling in this painful road? If
I may depend on the few reports which your friendship has deigned to make me of the sensation which
my dispatches have produced, when corrected, arranged, and embellished by you (for how is it possible
for me to correct that which I write at the moment,
by snatches, with lightning-like rapidity, and without
having time to read?), they have given satisfaction.
If I judge by the reiterated symptoms of the extreme

inattention which long silence supposes, on questions the most important, on requests the most instantaneous, and sometimes of absolute forgetfulness of the greatest part of these things, I should be induced to believe that my letters are read, at the most, with as much interest as a packet would be, the materials of which are tolerably clear and orderly, and that the reading produces not the least ultimate effect. Should this be so, is it worth the trouble (I put the question to you, whose energetic sentiments and high thoughts so often escape, notwithstanding all the contagion of levity, carelessness, egotism and inconsistency which exhale out of every door in the country which you inhabit), is it right, I say, that I should sacrifice, to an interest so subordinate as that of curiosity, my inclinations, my talents, my time and my powers? I believe you know me to be no quack, you know it is not my custom to speak of my pains, and of my labors, in fustian terms. Permit me, then, my good and dear friend, to protest that they both are great. I keep three men totally occupied in mechanically copying the materials I have arranged. I am assisted by the labor and the knowledge of several; all my moments, all my thoughts are there, thence depart, and thither return. Should the product be no greater (and I may say to you that you cannot yet estimate the whole product, for the greatest of my labors are still in my desk), it must either be the fault of my own incapacity or of my situation; perhaps of both, and perhaps also of the latter only. But here I am wholly, and, as a man of thirty-seven, ought not to be wholly, devoted to nullities; for nullities they are if nothing be produced, nothing effected, either in behalf of myself or others.

If, therefore, anything BE produced, afford me some proof of it; and when, for example, I ask any question, for the purpose of more effectually executing my trust, let it be answered. When I say it is necessary I should have a plan of operations of such a kind to propose, because I shall be immediately questioned on the subject, and shall lose an opportunity which probably may never be recovered should I be caught unprovided, let such a plan of operations be sent me.

If all this is to have any good effect in my favor, let me be told so; for in my present situation I have great need of encouragement, if it were but to empower me to yield without madness to the impulses of my zeal. I say without madness; for, to speak only of the vilest, but, notwithstanding, the most palpable of wants, when I perceive that I am very unable to make my accounts balance with the present appointments, ought I not to clog the down-hill wheel? And what have I to hope from these appointments, when I recollect how much they are in arrear; and that a change of Ministry may increase my personal debts with the sums which my friends have advanced me, for the service of those who cannot be ignorant I am myself incapable of making such advances? Yet, should I stop, is there not an end to all utility from what I have hitherto effected? Shall I then have anything remaining except regret for time lost, and the deep, the rankling affliction of having attached people to my fortunes for whom I can do nothing but what must be an ill compensation, and at my own expense, for all which they have done for me?

Pardon these expansions of the heart. To whom may I confide my anxieties, if not to you, my friend, my consolation, my guide, and my support? To whom may I say, what is all this to me, since it does not produce me even money? For that I expend in the business I have undertaken, and not in private gratifications. In truth, I should be susceptible of no other, were the hoped futurity come, and I had no dependents. You well know that money to me is nothing, at least when I have any. Where am I going, whither leading others? Have I made a good bargain by bartering my life, stormy as it was, but so mingled with enjoyments of which it was not in human power to deprive me, for a sterile activity, which snatches me even from the frequent and delightful effusions of your friendship? You are to me but a statesman; you, for the pressure of whose hand I would relinquish all the thrones on earth. Alas, I am much better formed for friendship than for politics.

Post Scriptum, began at Helmstadt, and finished at BRUNSWICK, *October 14th,* 1786.

They write from Silberberg, in Silesia, that the King's carriage has been overturned, and that he has received contusions on the head and on the arm. The coachman, it is added, expired on the place. The news reached me yesterday, at Magdeburg, and the same has been written to General Prittwitz; it probably exceeds the truth, but is not wholly without foundation. The extreme agitation of the Duke of Brunswick, and my own emotions, made me profoundly feel the fortunes that rest on this Monarch's head. The Duke immediately sent off a courier, and, as I shall follow him to Brunswick, where he wishes to speak to me at large concerning Holland, I shall learn more circumstantial intelligence, and such as will be indubitable. I have not time to add a single word; I write while the horses are changed.

From BRUNSWICK, *October 14th,* 1786.

Not having found an opportunity of sending off these few lines, I continue.

I arrived here two hours before the Duke. As soon

as he came to Brunswick, he wrote to me with a pencil, on a slip of paper:

"I spoke yesterday evening, before I departed, with the Minister Count Schulemburg, who had left Berlin on the eleventh. He is in absolute ignorance of the alarming intelligence by which we were so much affected, and, as I have heard nothing on the subject since, I begin to have better hopes. I expect my courier will arrive early in the morning. I write you this, Monsieur le Comte, from my mother's, and I hope you will do me the favor to come to me early to-morrow morning and dine with us."

It appears to be very probable that no material harm has happened to the Sovereign.

The splendor of the talents and urbanity of the Duke appeared perfect at Magdeburg. Nothing could be more awful than his manœuvres, nothing so instructive as his school, nothing so finished, so connected, so perfect, as his conduct in every respect. He was the subject of admiration to a great number of foreigners, who had crowded to Magdeburg, and he certainly stood in no need of the contrast which the Duke of Weimar and the Prince of Dessau afforded, the latter the weakest of men, the former industriously laboring to be something, but ill-provided with requisites, if we are to judge him by appearances. He might and ought to become a Prince of importance. According to all probabilities, however, Saxony will devolve on him for want of children in the Electoral branch, and it is an afflicting perspective to contemplate the destruction of all the labors of the worthy Prince who at present governs the country, and who, tormented in his childhood, unhappy in youth, and truly respectable in manhood, will, perhaps, descend to the tomb with the bitter affliction of feeling that all the good he has done will be rendered ineffectual.

I have learned a fact, which will afford some pleasure to M. de Segur, if he be still living. A foundry has been built at Hanover, at a great expense, which has cost the King of England near one hundred thousand livres. The Duke of Brunswick, not being satisfied with his own foundry, had two cannons cast at Hanover, and they were so ill-cast that they were soon obliged to be laid aside. It is not to be supposed, when we recollect the connections between the Duke and the King of England, that this was occasioned by any trick in the founders; the fact, therefore, is a proof that they are bad workmen.

By the next courier I hope to send you the exact result of the dispositions of Berlin, and the Duke, relative to Holland. He has promised me a precise statement of the propositions which appear to him necessary, and he did not conceal the extreme desire he had that they should be accepted by France. These Dutch disturbances daily present a more threatening aspect for the repose of Europe—if not at the present moment, at least from future contingencies, and the coolness and distrust to which they will give rise.

LETTER XXXV

BRUNSWICK, *October 16th*, 1786.

THE two conversations I have had with the Duke have hitherto been but vague respecting Holland, and indeed almost foreign to the subject. His courier, having brought him the news of hopes of an accommodation, and of the retreat of the person who of all those concerned with M. de Vayrac was supposed to be the chief firebrand, having, in fine, brought him details which led him to imagine that his interference will not be necessary, or not yet wanted in Holland,

he passed rapidly over the country to come to one
which is of infinitely greater importance to him; I
mean to say Prussia. He only discovered himself
to be greatly averse to the party of the Stadtholder,
and well convinced that the right of presentation ought
to remain such as it was in its origin; that the constitution of Gueldres, Frieseland, and Utrecht evidently
was in want of reformation, with respect to the inconceivable regulation of the magistrates, who are re-
vocable *ad nutum;* that, in a word, the Prince, who
from absolute monarchical authority, which he in
reality possessed, was sunken into absolute discredit,
by conduct the most abject, and the folly of having
claimed that as a right, in contempt of all law, all
decency, and all popular prejudice, which he effectually
possessed, was not deserving of the least support; but
that, from respect to Prussia, and particularly to retard commotions, it was requisite to restore him the
decorum of pageantry,—except that watch should be
kept over his connections. And here he explained
himself on the subject of Harris, and even concerning
Prince Louis of Brunswick, nearly in the manner I
should have done myself. In conclusion, however, he
not only did not inform me of anything on the subject,
but he imperceptibly declined that debate which a few
days before he had provoked.

I repeat, there is some news arrived of which I am
ignorant, that has occasioned this change in his proceedings. My information is in general much too confined. Thus, for example, it is very singular, nor is it
less embarrassing, and to speak plainly, it is tolerably
ridiculous, that it should be the Duke who should inform me of the treaty of commerce signed between
France and England, not one of the articles of which
I am acquainted with, and on which occasion I knew
not what face to wear. As my usual method is not to

conceal myself behind any veil of mystery, which hides the insignificance of certain Ambassadors, the part I had to act was not a little difficult. I should learn a thousand times more were I myself better informed. In this, as in everything else, fortune follows the successful.

Returning to Prussia, it was quite a different affair, for of this I know as much as the Duke. His confidence was the less limited, and the more profuse, because I presently set him at his ease with respect to Prince Henry, whom he neither loves nor esteems. I perceived with inquietude that his opinions and fears are similar to my own. He is dissatisfied with most of the proceedings and public acts of the King, with that crowd of titles, and that mass of nobility, which has been added so prodigally; insomuch that it will be henceforward much more difficult to find a man than a nobleman in the Prussian States; with the promise made to the Prince of Dessau (whose only merit is such an excess of enthusiasm for mysticism and visionaries that, when Lavater came to Bremen, he addressed the most earnest supplications to him to come and pay him a visit, in order that he might adore him), and perhaps with that given to the Duke of Weimar (who to the same inclinations, and more lively passions, adds greater understanding; but who is too much in debt for his military projects to be otherwise regarded than as a money speculation), to restore the one and to admit the other into the Prussian service; by which rank in the army will be violated, and the army discouraged and vitiated,—a system very opposite to that of Frederick II., who said of the few grandees who were employed in his time, " In the name of God, my dear Moellendorf, rid me of THESE PRINCES." The Duke is equally dissatisfied with that fluctuation which occasions essays to be made on twenty systems at once; with the most of the persons chosen; with domestic disorder; with nocturnal rites, and with the anecdotes the augury of which from day to day becomes more inauspiciously characteristic, etc., etc. In a word, should I transcribe our conversation, I should but send new copies of old dispatches.

" Believe me," said he, " I may, in a certain degree, serve you as a thermometer, for if I perceive there are no hopes of a firm and noble regimen, and that therefore the day of the House of Brandenburg is come, I shall not be the last to sound a retreat. I never received money from the King of Prussia, and I am well determined never to accept anything from him, though I mean to remain in the service. It has, as you have seen, been a dear service to me. I am independent. I wish to pay a tribute of respect to the memory of the great man who is no more, and am ready to shed my blood, if that might cement his work; but I will not, even by my presence, become the accomplice of its demolition. Our debts never exceed our abilities. I shall provide in the best manner in my power for my country and my children; these I shall leave in great order. I keep up my family connections. We perhaps shall be the last who will be smitten by the overthrow of the Germanic body, because of the confraternity which unites us to the Elector of Hanover. I, therefore, shall no further follow the destiny of the Prussian monarchy than as its Government shall maintain its wisdom, its dignity, etc., etc."

At present the Duke despairs of nothing; and in this he is right. He supposes that no person has yet found his proper place. I think like him, and I perceive he hopes his turn will come; of this neither can I doubt, unless the annihilation of the Prussian power has been decreed by fate.

He has informed me of the very singular fact that M. de Custine, the father, has demanded to be admitted into the service of the King of Prussia, and has pretended to disclose all the hostile plans of the Emperor, whose alliance, nevertheless, this same M. de Custine loudly affirms will terminate, with France, the day that Prince Kaunitz dies.

The Duke is very far from being relieved of all his fears concerning the projects of the Emperor, whose puissance and advisers he holds in infinite dread. True it is that his inconsistency should render his designs and the execution of them abortive; that the irrationality of his personal conduct should hasten his end; that the Archduke Francis appears to be a cipher; that among the persons who have influence there is not one formidable man, especially in the army; and that Alventzy and Kinsky, the one manufacturer for the infantry, and the other for the cavalry, possess only ambiguous abilities, etc. But men start up at the moment when they are least expected; accident only is necessary to rank them in their proper place. Condé, Spinola, and the Duke of Brunswick himself, prove that it is possible to be born a general. There is a Prince of Waldeck in the Austrian army, who, it is said, announces grand talents.

The numerous, trifling anecdotes, which the Duke and I have mutually related to each other, would be too tedious for insertion, and out of their place also here. An anecdote, merely as such, is equally devoid of propriety and information; such will have their turn hereafter; but there is one which relates too much to the Russian system for it to be passed over in silence.

The Czarina has, for some months past, appropriated to herself the possession and the revenues of the posts of Courland, leaving a small part only to the

Duke, in order that this branch of administration might not appear to be wholly in the hands of foreigners. Thus does this same Russia, that maintains an envoy at Courland, although there is none at Courland from Petersburg, and that here, as in Poland, proclaims her will to the Duke and to the States, by her Ambassador, who is the real Sovereign of the country,—this Russia, that for some years past, has unequivocally and openly declared that a certain canton of Courland appertained to her, and without seeking any other pretext than that of giving a more uniform line to her limits, makes no secret of not understanding any other code, any other claims, any other manifestoes, than those which the Gauls alleged to the Etruscans—" Our right exists in our arms.   Whatever the strong can seize upon that is the right of the strong."   She will one of these days declare Courland is hers, that the Polish Ukraine is hers, and that Finland is hers.   And, for example, this latter revolution, which will be a very salutary one to her because she will then truly become unattackable, and almost inaccessible, to all Europe united, will be effected, whenever she shall make the attempt, if we do not take good heed.   Whenever the time may come that I shall be informed of this having taken place, and even of the new system of Sweden being totally overthrown, I shall not feel any surprise.

The Duke also told me that the Emperor is greatly improving his artillery; that his six-pounders are equivalent in force to our former eight-pounders; and to this advantage they add that of lightness, in so great a degree, that only four horses are necessary to draw them, while even in Prussia six are still requisite.   As well as I remember he attributes this double improvement to the CONICAL construction of the chamber.   I only relate this that you may verify the truth of the fact by people who are acquainted with such affairs; the diminution of two horses in eight being a thing of infinite importance, and the more so as there would be a servant the less.

The manner in which I have been received by the Duke was infinitely friendly on his part, though somewhat participating, as far as relates to freedom of conversation, of my equivocal mode of existence at Berlin. I believe I may, without presumption, affirm I am not disagreeable to this Prince, and that, were I accredited by any commission whatever, I should be one of most proper persons to treat with him with efficacy. This able man appears to me to have but one weakness, which is the prodigious dread of having his reputation injured, even by the most contemptible Zoilus. Yet has he lately exposed himself to vexatious blame in deference to his first Minister, M. von Feronce, which I cannot comprehend. This M. von Feronce, and M. von Munchausen, Grand Master of the Court, a man who is reported to have little delicacy concerning money matters, have farmed the lottery,—an action shameful in itself, and which I cannot reconcile to Von Feronce, who is really a man of merit. Two merchants, named Oeltz and Nothnagel, have gained a *quaterne,* which is equivalent to the sum of eighteen thousand crowns. The payment of this has not only been refused, but as it was necessary to act with fraud to effect their purpose, the merchants have undergone numerous oppressions; they have even been imprisoned; all which acts they have lately published in a printed case, which contains nothing but the facts concerning the suit, and have laid an appeal against the Duke, or against his judges, before the tribunal of Wetzlar; I own I do not understand this absence of firmness, or of circumspection.

October 17th, 1786.

POSTSCRIPT.—I have just received authentic intelligence concerning the King of Prussia. It was one of his chasseurs to whom a very serious accident happened; the Monarch himself is in good health, and will arrive on the eighteenth or the nineteenth at Berlin.

I learn, at the same time, that Count Finckenstein is dying of an inflammation of the lungs, with which he was seized after a very warm altercation with Count Hertzberg, on the subject of Holland. His life is despaired of, and his loss to us will be very great; as well because he was absolutely ours, as because that, being a temporizer by nature, he would have acted as the moderator of Prince Henry. He would also have directed the conduct of Mademoiselle Voss, after the fall of virtue; and finally because Hertzberg will no longer have any counterpoise. With respect to the latter point, however, I am not averse to suppose that the time when this presumptuous man shall be in absolute discredit may but be the more quickly accelerated. Yet, not to mention the sterility of subjects by which this epoch may be retarded, who shall answer that a man so violent, and wholly imbued as he is with the hatred which the Germans in general bear the French, will not venture to make some very decisive false steps?

The Duke of York arrived here this evening, and had he been the Emperor he could not have been treated with more respect, especially by the Duchess and the courtiers. She, indeed, is wholly English, as well in her inclinations and her principles as in her manners; insomuch that her almost cynical independence, opposed to the etiquette of the Courts of German Princes, forms the most singular contrast I know. I do not, however, believe that there is any question concerning the marriage of the Princess Caroline, who is a most amiable, lively, playful, witty, and handsome lady; the Duke of York, a puissant hunter, a potent drinker, an indefatigable laugher, destitute of breeding and politeness, and who possesses, at least in appearance, much of the Duke de Lauzun, as well in mind as in person, is inspired with a kind of passion for a woman married to a jealous husband, who torments him, and will not suffer him to fix his quarters. I know not whether he will go to Berlin. The versions relative to him are various. Some affirm that, after having been an unbridled libertine, he feels a returning desire of doing his duty. For my own part, I find in him all the stiffness of a German Prince, with a double dose of English insolence, but wanting the free cordiality of that nation.

LETTER XXXVI

BRUNSWICK, *October 27th,* 1786.

I HERE send you the continuation and conclusion of the preceding dispatch, to which I add the translation of a pamphlet, the singularity of which is increased by its having appeared at Vienna, with the permission of the Emperor; who, to the communication made by the censor, has added these very words, " Let this pass among others."

This is but a trifle compared to that caprice which three days afterwards induced him to release the unfortunate Szekely, whom the most powerful remonstrances could not save, and whose cause is here ill enough defended. For what conclusions might he not have drawn from the confidence with which he imparted to the Emperor the situation of his accounts, from the disorder by which they had been brought into this state, from the ardent supplications he made him to purchase for the public a well-tried chemical secret at such a price as would have completed the deficiency in his accounts (I say completed, for Szekely and his family had paid the greatest part of the deficiencies), and from the answer of the Emperor himself,—" Do you address yourself to me as a friend, or as to the Emperor? If to the former, I cannot be the friend of a man who has not been faithful to his trust. If as Emperor, I would advise you to go in person and make your declaration to the Courts of Justice."

This fact, which I have learned since my arrival at Berlin, attended with most aggravating circumstances, is one of the most odious I can recollect, yet might I relate fifty of the same species.

Free Observations on the Crime and Punishment of Lieutenant-Colonel SZEKELY, *of the Guards, by a Friend of Truth,* 1786.

LET the voice of Truth be heard, let her at present be seen without disguise, without veil, in all her awful nakedness. Hear, ye incorrupt judges. I am about to speak of the crime and punishment of Szekely. My heart melts, but my words shall be impartial. Hear and pronounce sentence on me, on Szekely, and on those who pronounced sentence on him.

Szekely announces a deficiency in the regimental chest of the guards, and the disorder of his accounts; and after some pretended examinations is brought before the Council of War. Ninety-seven thousand florins of the Empire have disappeared; but Szekely had placed his whole confidence in the Sieur Lakner, who is deceased, and who was the only keeper of the keys of the chest. Szekely had more than once declared that he himself was a very improper person to have pecuniary matters committed to his charge, and that he never had revised nor verified the accounts of the regimental chest confided to his care. He therefore cannot be suspected of personal fraud, especially when his regiment renders justice to the goodness of his manners, and unanimously points out the cashier Lakner as a person who was debased by meanness, and rendered suspicious by incurring expenses infinitely above his fortune.

This, it is very true, was an exceedingly culpable negligence, but such was the only crime of Szekely; and it was for this reason that the Council of War condemned him to be imprisoned six years in a fortress. The punishment was doubtless in itself sufficient, since Szekely, in effect, and according to the language of the civilians, was *Nec confessus nec convictus* of any prevarication; yet was it aggravated by the Aulic Council of War, which was commanded to make a revision of the process, and which increased his detention to a duration of eight years. Was this tribunal ignorant, then, that it is a custom with our MOST GRACIOUS Monarch himself to increase the severity of all sentences, pronounced against criminals? Let us, therefore, believe that the judges, on this occasion, were only obedient to the rigor of the laws; but the after decision of the Emperor will most assuredly appear inconceivable. The following is the judgment which this Monarch uttered—Yes! uttered, yet did not blush:

" Szekely must, without hesitation, be broken, declared incapable of military service, and delivered over to the civil officer, who shall convey him to the place where the crime was committed in Vienna, where he shall stand in the pillory for three successive days, and remain two hours each day on a scaffold, in the high market place, that his example may be of public utility. As a favor and in consequence of his age, I limit the eight years' imprisonment to which he is condemned to four, during which he shall be confined at Segedin, a penal prison of the civil power of the Hungarian States, where he shall receive the same allowance for food as is granted to other criminals."

The Court of Justice made remonstrances to the Emperor, in which it proved that the punishment was much too severe, and entirely contrary to law and to equity; but the Emperor continued inflexible, and thus confirmed his sentence.

" All superintendents of military chests might, like Szekely, plead that they knew not what was become of the money, even though it should have been stolen by themselves. Whenever there is a deficiency in any chest, and especially of a sum so considerable as ninety-seven thousand florins, and there is no necessity for the judge to prove that the money has been taken by the accused person, but the accused person must show that it has not been taken by him; and whenever he cannot demonstrate this he himself is the thief. As soon as Szekely shall have been broken, and shall be no longer an officer, the sentence against him shall be put in execution, and a paper shall be fixed round his neck on which shall be written—AN UNFAITHFUL STEWARD."

Let us take an attentive retrospect of these supreme decisions.

Szekely is punishable for having been exceedingly negligent; he is the same for having bestowed his whole confidence on a dishonest cashier, of whose pompous luxury he could not be ignorant, since it gave offense to the whole corps of the guards. It was easy to conclude that such a man could not live at an expense so great on his paternal income. It is even prob-

able that Szekely himself, perceiving the disorder of
his accounts, and the deficiency in his chest, and terrified by the infamy and punishment inflicted on such
crimes, sacrificed much to alchemy and the occult
sciences, in the hope of making gold, and thus freeing
himself from his embarrassments.   This, no doubt,
was a folly at which all men of sense would grieve;
it is not, however, the less possible.   It is certain that
the love of chemistry was the ruling passion of
Szekely, and that he indulged his inclinations the
more because he expected sometime thus to recover
his losses.   To this excuse let us add the extreme ignorance of which he accused himself in all that related to
pecuniary affairs.

True it is that, with such a conviction of his own
incapacity, he never ought to have taken charge of a
regimental chest; but were all those who are in possession of places, the duties of which are far beyond
their abilities, obliged to abdicate them, what vast deserts would our public offices afford!   Rabner en-
courages three different species of men, by saying
" On whom God bestows an office he also bestows a
sufficient degree of understanding for the exercise of
that office."   Szekely would not indubitably have
adopted this opinion, could he have foreseen the evil
consequences of his presumption.

Was not that flattering letter which was addressed
to him by Maria Theresa, of glorious memory, in
which, while she gave the highest praises to his probity
and loyalty, this august Sovereign confided to his care,
without any caution, the regimental chest of the
guards, an authentic testimony in behalf of his honor?
Has it been meant by the forgetfulness of this distinction to add a new outrage to all the ingratitudes with
which some have sullied themselves, relative to this
immortal Empress?   Was it intended to tax her with

that levity, that silly credulity, which blind confidence produces? Alas! in despite of all the defects which envy so gratuitously imputes to her, Maria Theresa never was surrounded by such an army of knaves as those from whom all the rigor of the present Sovereign cannot preserve us. So true is it that gentleness and love, from a Prince toward his subjects, are more efficacious means, to preserve them within the bounds of duty, than all the violent acts tyranny can commit.

I return to Szekely and affirm it is impossible that this letter from the Empress Queen, though in some sort the pledge of the fidelity of Szekely, can serve as an excuse to the Prince of Esterhazy, whose personal negligence cannot be justified. Did not his right, as chief of the guards, impose it on him as a law to examine the regimental chest of Szekely? And is not such an infraction of the duties of his place most reprehensible?

Still less can be offered in defense of the fault committed by the Hungaro-Transylvanian Chancery; since according to its instructions, it was in like manner bound to inspect the administration of Szekely. But none of the acts of this superior Court ought to inspire astonishment, since it is no longer distinguished, except by disorder and ill faith; since its responsibility is no longer anything but a word; and since its ideas of exact calculation, and of receipt and expense, are exactly as just as those of Brambille are on physic.

Judges, ye have condemned Szekely. Be it so. Act worthy of your office. Punish his superintendents also, who have by a non-performance of their duty placed him on the brink of that abyss into which you headlong plunged him; without humanity, and void of shame.

The Kings of Europe have all reserved to themselves the most benevolent of prerogatives; that of pardoning the guilty, or of softening the pains the sentence inflicts by which they are condemned. Joseph alone persists in other principles, more conformable to the feelings of his heart. He aggravates the punishment of the wretched. Alas! this no doubt is but to enjoy the ecstatic pleasure of terrifying his people, by the exercise of the most unlimited despotism. Unfortunate Szekely! Ill-starred man! I pity thee. Thou fallest a victim to the splenetic temper of the Monarch! Perhaps, at the very instant when he pronounced thy doom, a troublesome fly stung his brow, and thy dishonor was his vengeance. Deplorable sacrifice of a tyrannical and barbarous heart, yes, I pity thee. Men of worth, men of justice, what must the Monarch be who can ADD to the rigor of the Judge?—A tyrant! What can the Monarch be who tramples under foot the rights of humanity?—A tyrant!! What can the Monarch be who can make the laws and the justice of his kingdom his sport?—A tyrant!!! What can the Monarch be who in criminal decisions shall act only according to his caprice?—A Joseph!!!!

A Joseph!—Oh, God! Great God! What then is man? A poor and feeble creature, whom an imperious oppressor may at any moment reduce to dust; or may rend his heart, extort his last sight, by the seven thousand raging torments which the Hydras with seven thousand heads in sport inflicts.

Dreadful image! Ignominious to humanity, yet woefully true, woefully exact, woefully confirmed by experience! Does not a Sovereign who increases the rigor of sentences openly proclaim: " Ye Judges, whom I have appointed to judge according to law and equity, ye are prevaricators; ye have betrayed your trust, falsified your consciences, and have endeavored to practice deceit upon me?" Such magistrates, therefore, ought not to be continued in office; for, to suffer them still to be Judges is to approve their conduct, and confirm their judgment. But, destructive as the thunderbolt, the Monarch, addressing them, exclaims: "Your sentence is too mild! It is my will arbitrarily to increase punishment, that I may prove myself the master of life and death!" What language, oh, God! from the mouth of a King whom thou hast appointed to be our protector, and not our tyrant!

Szekely would never have been condemned, had he not been intimately connected with the Freemasons. When the Emperor pronounced sentence against this unfortunate man, he forgot himself so far as to say, "I will let those gentry (the Freemasons) understand there is no efficacy in their protection."

Where, then, is the equity of a Monarch who thus prostitutes the power he is in possession of, to the destruction of one of the members of a society which he detests? Who would not smile contemptuously at the poor malice of a peasant who should go in search of his neighbor, after twilight, that he might unseen give him a fillip on the nose, run away, and divert himself with having played him so cunning a trick. Oh, Justice! Justice! Shalt thou forever have eyes that thou mayst not see?

Yes, debased, corrupted was the mouth which increased the rigor of the sentence of Szekely, who previously had been destined to languish eight years in prison. Joseph has diminished the term of his detention. And are these, then, thy favors, sceptered executioner? Yes, this favor granted to a man of quality, who was for three successive days exposed in the pillory, resembles that which a criminal, condemned to the gallows, should receive from thee, whom thou shouldst permit to be racked upon the wheel, because he was too feeble to mount the ladder.

Couldst thou have survived the shame of such a crime, had not thy people themselves applauded thy fury? The curiosity with which all Vienna enjoyed the spectacle the wretched Szekely afforded, proves that the manners of thy subjects already partake of thine own barbarity. But let them tremble, slaves as they are, bowed beneath the yoke. A new Nero promises new crimes, new horrors!

LETTER XXXVII

BRUNSWICK, *October 18th,* 1786.

I FEAR there are some waverings in the mind of the King, relative to Holland; for the Duke, after the arrival of his courier, and receiving information of the danger of Count Finckenstein, again spoke to me on the subject, with a degree of inquietude which was far from dissembled. The following were his precise words: " Holland will certainly occasion a war, especially should the death of the Elector of Bavaria intervene; do you act, therefore, as mediators to smother the rising flames. Come, come, the Stadtholder must have a council, without which he can perform nothing; and how shall this council be selected? "

I replied to the Duke that I was not sufficiently acquainted with those affairs to give any opinion on the subject, but that I was going to make him a proposition which he must regard as only ideal, and as coming from myself, although it might by no means be impracticable.

" Now that I know how far I can depend upon your prudence and your principles," I continued, " I am certain that you will see the affairs and the conduct of the Stadtholder in their true light; that you will not imagine friendship in politics can have any other basis than interests; or that we ought to renounce our alliance with Holland, in order that the Princess of Orange may nightly enjoy more agreeable dreams; that you cannot but comprehend how much it is impossible for us to place any confidence in Count Hertzberg, who, relative to us, is frantic, and how much our distrust may be increased should our sole counterpoise to this violent Minister disappear by the death of Count Finckenstein. I shall, therefore, thus far, willingly step forward to say that it appears to me very probable that France will be inclined to treat on this affair with you singly, should the King of Prussia consent that you should be solely trusted with the business on his behalf; and, as I may say, should you be made arbitrator. I feel how important it is to you, to us, and to all, that you should not endanger yourself in the opinion of his Majesty. There are already but too many causes of distance existing between you, and the country is entirely lost if the necessities of the times do not oblige you to take the helm. But, should you find the crisis so alarming as to dread decisive events should be the consequence, it appears to me that then it will no longer be proper to keep beating against the wind. For, if the King of Prussia be fated to commit irreparable faults, it would be as well for all parties that he should begin to-morrow, in order that we might the sooner augur what his reign shall be, and choose our sides in consequence. It is for you, therefore, to know in what degree of favor you are with the King. He cannot love you; for never yet did the weak man love the strong. He cannot desire you should be his Minister, for never yet did a vain and dark man desire to possess one who was himself illustrious and luminous. But it is neither his friendship nor his inclination that are necessary to you; it is power. You ought to acquire that ascend-

ency over him which a grand character and a vast
genius may ever acquire over a confined understanding and an unstable mind. If you have enough of
this ascendency to inspire him with fears for his situation; to convince him that he is already betrayed to
danger; that the sending of Goertz, in your despite
(or, rather, without your knowledge, for you were
not then at Berlin), is a blunder of magnitude, which
has been committed without possessing the least pledge
of docility on the part of the Stadtholder; that the
inconsiderate letters of Hertzberg form another equal
blunder; that this Minister pursues his PERSONAL
INTERESTS, and those only, at the hazard or depriving
his master of PERSONAL RESPECT, even from the commencement of his reign; since it is very evident that,
if he persist in his thoughtless interference (be suppositions as favorable, nay, almost as romantic, as you
please), he will only have played the cards of the English, although they have spoiled their own game—if
you can make him sensible of all this, you will easily
be able to persuade him that he will but be too fortunate in accepting your mediation. And, although
mediation is not exactly the phrase which may be
employed, because it does not exactly square with the
rule of proportion, such is the esteem in which you are
held by the Cabinet of Versailles that, should this
negotiation once be committed to your care, all difficulties will vanish of themselves. Such a measure,
therefore, would have the double advantage of accom-
modating the affair, which you regard as the brand
of discord, and of teaching the King to feel that
he presumes too much if he imagines that, by the sole
magic of the abrupt and *tudescan* French of Count
Hertzberg, he will be able to preserve the same respect for his Court which a succession of great acts,
heroical prosperity, vigilant activity, and perseverance,

even to a miracle, for forty-six years, have procured it; that he has need of a man whose name abroad and whose influence at home should attract confidence and serve as the keystone to an arch which, according to its dimensions, has but little solidity; or, to speak without a metaphor, a kingdom, ill-situated, ill-constituted, ill-governed, and which possesses no real strength, except in opinion, since its military position is wretched and its resources precarious. For, with respect to the treasury, it will vanish if a hand of iron, yet not a hand of avarice, should not guard it; and, as to an army, who can be more convinced than you are, that years scarcely are sufficient for its formation; but that six months of relaxed discipline may degrade it so that it shall no longer be cognizable?"

This discourse, which fixed the attention of the Duke, and which was particularly intended to divine what he himself imagined he might be able to accomplish, and what he might become, appeared to produce a very great effect. Instead of beginning, as he always does, by ambiguous and dilatory phrases, which may serve any purpose he shall please, he immediately entered into the spirit of my discourse, and, after having felt and owned, with an effusion of heart and a penetrating tone, that I presented him a prospect of the greatest honor his imagination could conceive, and which he should prefer to the gaining of six victories, he joined with me in endeavoring to find some means of making the overture to the King.

"I do not imagine," said he, "my situation will authorize the attempt without previous measures. I am more afraid of injuring the cause than of injuring myself, but it is certainly necessary the project should be conveyed to him, and, should he afford the least opportunity, I will explain everything. Cannot you speak to Count Finckenstein, should he recover?"

"No, for he strictly confines himself to his department. Neither is this anything more than an idea of my own, and of small diplomatic value, since I have no credentials."

"You have but few opportunities of speaking in private to Welner?"

"Very few. Besides, how can that man ever be devoted to you? He determines to act the principal part himself. He is industrious for his own interest, being very sensible that, because of his obscurity, he has an immense advantage over you, not to mention that he is the intimate friend of your brother, who does not wish your company at Berlin."

In fact, this brother hates the Duke, by whom he is despised, and hopes for favor and influence under the reign of mysticism.

We had proceeded thus far in our discourse when the whole Court, leaving the opera for supper, and the Duke of York, by entering without any precursor, obliged us to break off. He has appointed to meet me this morning, the day of my departure, at nine o'clock, and to him I am now going.

The Duke, as I expected, was shaken to-day in his resolution of having himself named to the King. I say as I expected, for his brilliant imagination and ambitious energy easily catch fire at his first emotions, although he should betray no exterior symptoms except those of tranquillity. But the rein he has so long put upon his passions, which he has eternally had under command, and in which habit he has been most persevering, reconducts him to the hesitation of experience, and to that superabundant circumspection which his great diffidence of mankind, and his foible, I mean his dread of losing his reputation, incessantly inspire. He made a circumstantial display of the delicacy with which the petty glory, or, to speak plainly, said he, the vainglory of the King must be managed.

Taking up the conversation at the point where we had left it, he assured me that, with respect to Welner, I was deceived; that he was one of the persons in Berlin on whom he depended, and who rather wished to see him in power than any other; that I might easily speak with him at the house of Moulines (his Resident, an artful man, but too ostensibly artful, ready to serve that he may better perform his office of spy, but proffering his services with too much facility; appointed to take part in the education of the Prince of Prussia, but, hitherto, without any title; a deserter from Prince Henry, since it has become pretty evident the Prince will never be in power; inclined to serve France, in general, and, indeed too visibly, for he is styled the Privy Counselor of Comte d'Esterno, but, in his heart, solely attached to himself); that Welner goes there very often; that he certainly would not speak openly, at first, but that he would at length repeat to the King whatever I should say.

The Duke often reiterated that he thought it useless and dangerous for him to be named; and, in fine, although with difficulty, and, as I may say, against his inclination, he gave me the true reason. In a fortnight, he was to be at Berlin, or, perhaps, sooner, for (take particular notice of what follows) IT APPEARS THAT THE HOPE AFFORDED BY SIR JAMES HARRIS (the English Ambassador at The Hague) OF A POWERFUL AND EFFICACIOUS SUCCOR, SHOULD THE KING OF PRUSSIA RESOLVE, WITH AN ARMED FORCE, TO CREATE HIMSELF UMPIRE OF THE AFFAIRS OF HOLLAND, HAS INSPIRED THE KING WITH A WISH TO CONFER WITH HIS SERVANTS. I literally repeat the words the Duke pronounced, who fixed his eyes upon me, but whom I defy not only to have observed the least trait of emotion in my countenance, but still more not to have been struck with a smile, almost imperceptible and very ironical, as if I had known and contemned the fact. My only reply at the end of his sentence was, shrugging up my shoulders:

" There is little need I should remark to you, monseigneur, that the conquest which Louis XIV., Turenne, De Condé, De Luxembourg, De Louvois, and two hundred thousand French, could not make of Holland, will never be effected by Prussia, watched by the Emperor, on that same country, now that it is supported by France."

The Duke therefore is going, or wishes to make us believe he is going, to Berlin; where deliberations are to be held on the propositions of England.

So be it. So much the better. Do not be alarmed. The Duke is rather German than Prussian, and as good a statesman as he is a great warrior. He will prove such a proposition to be so absurd that it is probably no more than the personal conception of the audacious and artful Harris, who wishes, at any expense, to make his fortune, and in a fit of madness to poniard his nation, which is more able than sage.

Still, however, I think my journey to Brunswick is a lucky accident; for I confess, and with great pleasure, I found the principles of the Duke to be moderate, prudent, and, politically speaking, wholly French. I depicted the affair, or rather affairs, as a whole, under new points of view; and if, as I persist in believing, or rather as I have believed more strongly since I have known that he depends upon Welner for strengthening his party, his measures have long been taken (for Welner has been a canon at Halberstadt, where the regiment of the Duke remains), if, I say, the necessity of accident should oblige him to take the helm, I shall have acquired the greatest advantages to treat with and make him a party in our designs.

He has desired I would give Comte d'Esterno the very good advice, should Count Finckenstein die, or even should he not, to demand to treat on the affairs of Holland, and on all that relates to them, immediately with his Majesty. This is the most certain means of battering Hertzberg in breach, who certainly has been controverted with great firmness in these affairs by the King, and to obtain that which we shall seem only to expect from the judgment and personal will of the Monarch. It is a proceeding which is successful with all Kings, even with the greatest. Vanswieten obtained from Frederick II. himself the most important concessions by acting thus; and this is certainly a much more safe, as it is a more noble mode, than all the deceitful efforts which flattery can employ with Prince Henry, whose glaring protection is more injurious to the French Embassy than it ever can be productive of good, under the most favorable contingencies. For I am not very unapt to believe, as the Duke affirms without disguise, that this PARTITION PRINCE, were he master of affairs, would be the most dangerous of the enemies of Germanic freedom. I must conclude, for I have not time to cipher; the remainder of this inestimable conversation will be sent you hereafter. Inform me, with all possible expedition, how I ought to act under the present circumstances, and be persuaded that, if you can find any means whatever of giving me secret official credit with the King, or even with the Duke, you will act very wisely.

Additional Note

If you do not imagine I am totally doting, mark me. I conjure you to read, and cause this to be read, with the utmost attention; and not to suffer me to wait a single moment for an answer, even though it should be absolutely necessary, for this purpose, to borrow some few hours from the levity of the country, or to be consistent for a whole day together.

LETTER XXXVIII

BERLIN, *October 21st,* 1786.

I ARRIVED at half-past five in the morning. The King was to exercise his cavalry at six. I immediately mounted my horse, that I might discover the state of his health, observe what aspect he wore, and if possible to find some person to whom I might address myself. His health is good, his brow cloudy; the troops were obliged to wait a considerable time, and after two charges he very abruptly and very ridiculously retired. Nothing sufficiently new or important has come to my knowledge to prevent my employing the few remaining moments before the departure of the courier, and which are greatly abridged by your eight pages of ciphers, in resuming the consequences which I have drawn from the very interesting conversation, an account of which I gave you in my last dispatch. It is impossible I should send you a complete and circumstantial narrative of all that passed, because that the Duke, an hour after I had left him, having sent me his Minister for Foreign Affairs (M. von Ardensberg von Reventlau), I have too much to add.

Four particulars appeared to me evident:

1. That, during the confidential conference with the Duke, a great complication of sensation, emotion, and design was mingled. He wishes we should aid him in becoming Prime Minister of Prussia, but that we should act with caution. He is not convinced that we desire to see him in that post (I did everything in

my power to persuade him of it), yet perfectly satisfied that any interference in the affairs of Holland
would be a stupid error, he is anxious that Prussia
should act with propriety, and that, in this affair at
least, we should acquire influence. He, therefore,
while he informed me, endeavored to discover if I
already had any information, and whether we were
determined in the pursuit of our projects. To the
same purport were the after commentaries of Ardensberg, his deceptive confidences, and Gazette secrets, the recall, not only of M. de Coetloury, but also
of M. de Veyrac, our desertion of the patriotic party,
etc., etc., to all which particulars I replied with a smile.

2. That the great inquietude of the Duke arises
from not knowing whether we are or are not Austrians, or whether we are merely so undecided on the
subject that the errors, or the cold distance, of the Cabinet of Berlin will be sufficient to induce us, at the
hazard of all that can happen, to second the Emperor
in his designs against Germany. In my opinion, were
the Duke freed from his apprehensions on this very
capital article, he would be French, for he is strongly
German, and the English can only set Germany in
flames; we alone have the power of maintaining it in
peace. Should his connections with England appear
to be strengthened, it is but, as I think, because he
distrusts the destiny of Prussia, for he well knows
that his English calculations are rather specious than
solid, and that the Prussian, though perhaps somewhat more subaltern, are much less hazardous.

3. He and his Minister have so often demanded,
and redemanded, on what basis I imagined the pacification of Holland might be established, that I have
supposed the Duke probably thinks, should we exclude
the Prince of Prussia from the Nassau alliance, there
might be a necessity of choosing his daughter, the

Princess Caroline of Brunswick as a consort for the
Prussian heir. The supposition is founded on circumstances so fugitive that it is impossible to give
them written evidence, or perhaps probable, especially
because, not having received any instructions on such
a subject, I have not dared to make any advances. I
therefore only give it for what it is worth. The being but little informed of the affairs of Holland has,
in every respect, been highly injurious to me on this
occasion. Might I have spoken more freely I might
even have drawn the well dry. The only positive proposal which he made on the subject was a kind of
coalition-council of regency, without which the Stadtholder could effect nothing, and in which should be
included Gislaer, Vanberckel, etc., etc., but among
whom also must be seated M. Van Lynden, the governor of the children of the Stadtholder, etc., etc. To
my eternal objection, "How will you support those
measures which shall be taken under the pledge of
your aid?" he continually replied: "Should the Stadtholder counteract these arrangements, we will abandon him." "But how far?" I replied. "And, if but
amicably, how will he be injured, should he be thus
abandoned?" In a word, I continued with a kind
of mysterious obstinacy, to maintain that the Stadtholder would never be brought to reason, unless it
should be declared to him that the King of Prussia
would forsake his party, though his consort might be
secretly informed such was not the real intent.

4. It appeared to me that the Duke was ruminating
on some grand project for the reconstruction of the
Germanic edifice, for this able Prince perceives the
antique, ruinous building must be propped in order to
be preserved, and even in many parts repaired. The
sole wish which he clearly testified was the separation
of the Electorate of Hanover from the English Mon-

archy, and the secularization of certain provinces, which might one day form an equivalent for Saxony. He supposes the first point might be gained, and even without any great difficulty, should our politics become Anglicized, and that the second might be accomplished, though contrary to the confederation of the Princes, because, at the death of the Elector of Mayence, there will be an opportunity of retouching the league, as well as a natural and proper occasion of coming to an explanation with the ecclesiastical Princes, who, more interested than any others in the liberties of Germany, are always the first to tergiversate, etc., etc. Hence, we at least may learn that, however attached he may appear to be to the confederation, means may be found of inducing him to listen to reason concerning modifications.

The instructions which are necessary for me, at present, are:

1. Whether we ought, on this occasion, to bring him on the stage, which would be the real means of driving him from it; and I certainly do not think the latter to be our interest, for he is more prudent, more able, and less susceptible of prejudice and passion, than any other who can be made Minister.

2. Whether his party ought to be encouraged and strengthened, which will be to act directly contrary to the party of Prince Henry; for the plan of the Duke is exclusive; and, to confess the truth, he appears tacitly so convinced that the Prince can effect nothing, that he has greatly fortified my own opinion on this subject.

3. What is the degree of confidence I ought to place in him? For it is impossible to obtain the confidence of, without placing confidence in, such a man; and in my apprehension he had better be told than suffered to divine.

Count Finckenstein is recovering.

The King arrived on the eighteenth, at eight in the morning, after having left Breslau, on the seventeenth, at seven in the morning. This was incredible diligence; no person could keep pace with him. He went on the same day to visit the Queen Dowager, and thus gave occasion to attribute the rapidity and danger of the journey to Mademoiselle Voss. She is said to be pregnant; but, in the first place, this cannot be known, and, in the second, I do not believe the haste would have been so great, had it been truth. According to report, she has demanded two hundred thousand crowns. Should this be so, the circle of her career will not be very ample.

The King made a multitude of nobles in Silesia, as elsewhere. But, without loading my letter, the Gazettes will tell you enough of their names. He is to remain a week at Potsdam, which is to be dedicated to his military labors. Great changes in the army are spoken of, such as will be favorable to the subalterns, and the reverse to the captains.

The Dantzickers, who, according to appearances, supposed Kings were hobgoblins, were so enraptured to meet with one who did not eat their children that, in the excess of their enthusiasm, they were willing to put themselves without restraint under the Prussian Government. The Magistrates eluded the folly of the populace as well as they could, under the pretence that Dantzic was dependent on Poland; but so great and so violent was the tumult, that Prussian and Polish couriers were sent off. This event will no doubt rouse the Emperor and Russia; a favorable circumstance to our affairs in Holland.

Count Hertzberg, who has indulged himself in very headlong acts in Silesia, and particularly in his discourse on the day of homage, in which he really braved

the Emperor in a very indecent manner, as if it was
not in his nature to accommodate himself to a peaceable order of affairs; Hertzberg, I say, has had the
influence to retard the nomination of Alvensleben for
the French Embassy, which had been announced by
the King at supper. How might I have expected to
be thus deceived, since, when I sent you the intelligence, I supposed it to be an affair so public that I
did not even write it in a cipher?

LETTER XXXIX

October 24th, 1786.

I SHALL begin my dispatch with an anecdote, the truth
of which is undoubted, and which appears to me the
most decisive of all I have learned concerning the new
reign. Recollect that, in Number XVIII., August
29th, I wrote:

" The King apparently intends to renounce all his
old habits. This is a proud undertaking. He retires
before ten in the evening, and rises at four. Should
he persevere, he will afford a singular example of
habits of thirty years being vanquished. This will be
an indubitable proof of a grand character, and show
how we have all been mistaken."

When I spoke thus, I, like the rest of the world
judged by appearances. The truth is that at half
after nine the King disappeared, and was supposed to
be gone to rest; whereas, in the most retired apartments of the palace, like another Sardanapalus, he
held his orgies till night was far advanced. Hence it is
easy to understand why hours of business were obliged
to be inverted. Health would not allow him to be
equally active upon the stage and behind the scenes.

Prince Henry regards himself as kept at a distance as well from system as from inclination. He is, or believes himself to be, persuaded that the innumerable follies which will result from his absence, for in his opinion the country without his aid is undone, will occasion recourse to be had to his experience and his abilities, and he then intends to refuse that tardy succor which his genius will be implored to yield. Even granting him the truth of all these vain dreams, he does not recollect that the expression of an undone country is only true relative to a certain lapse of time and that therefore in all probability, he will be dead before the want of his assistance will be perceived. He comes to reside four months at Berlin, there, according to him, to suffer martyrdom, that it may not be supposed he has deserted the public cause. His places of asylum are afterward to be Rheinsberg, the Lake of Geneva, and France; but such he will easily find everywhere. Consolation will not be wanting to him, since consolation can be found at playing at blind man's buff, or hot cockles, with actresses more insipid than the very worst of our provincial companies can afford.

The distribution of influence continues the same. Hertzberg violently seizes on the King, who probably has more esteem for Count Finckenstein; but whom, not being so eternally hunted by him, he leaves in a subaltern degree of credit, which from apparent may become real, the easy temper of the master considered. The remaining Ministers are held to be so many ciphers.

Welner daily increases his jurisdiction, and Bishopswerder his influence, but he does not appear to exercise this influence either as a man of ostentation or a dupe. He neither asks for titles, ribbons, nor places. At most he will but make Ministers; he will never be one. Three hundred thousand livres for each of his daughters, an excellent fief for himself, with military rank (he is said to be a good officer), these are what he wishes, and these he most probably WILL obtain. In the meantime no person HAS anything; neither he nor Welner nor Goertz, who lives by borrowing.

Bowlet?—The influence of a mason engineer, and no other; for of no other is he capable.

Goltz the Tartar?—Artful, sly, dexterous; perhaps ambitious, but very selfish and covetous. Money is his ruling passion, and money he will have. He will probably have the greatest influence over military affairs, unless the Duke of Brunswick should take them to himself. The memorials relative to fortification are transmitted to him.

Colonel Wartensleben is evidently kept at a distance, and probably because of his family connections with Prince Henry; who, to all his other disadvantages, adds that of having every person who is about the King for his enemy.

Subalterns?—Their kingdom is not come. It should seem that having long, while Prince of Prussia, been deceived by them, the King knows and recollects this; although from compassion he wishes not to notice it, at least for a time.

The master?—What is he? I persist in believing it would be rash, at present, to pronounce, though one might be strongly tempted to reply KING LOG. No understanding, no fortitude, no consistency, no industry; in his pleasures the Hog of Epicurus and the hero only of pride; which, perhaps, we should rather denominate confined and vulgar vanity. Such hitherto have the symptoms been. And under what circumstances, in what an age, and at what a post? I am obliged to summon all my reason to divine, and to forget it all again to hope. The thing which is really to be feared is lest the universal contempt he must soon incur should irritate him, and deprive him of that species of benevolence of which he shows signs. That weakness is very formidable which unites an ardent thirst after pleasures, destitute of choice or delicacy, with the desire of keeping them secret in a situation where nothing can be kept secret.

Not that I here am writing a second part to Madame de Sévigné; I do not speak ill of Frederick William because he overlooks me, as she spoke well of Louis XIV., because he had lately danced a minuet with her.

Yesterday, at the Court of the Queen, he three times addressed himself to me, which he never before did in public. "You have been at Magdeburg and Brunswick." "Yes, Sire." "Were you pleased with the manœuvres?" "Sire, I was in admiration." "I ask to be informed of the truth, and not to be complimented." "In my opinion, Sire, there was nothing wanting to complete the splendor of this exhibition, except the presence of your Majesty." "Is the Duke in good health?" "Exceedingly good, Sire." "Will he be here soon?" "Your Majesty, I imagine, is the only person who knows." He smiled.

This is a specimen. You will well imagine it was, personally, very indifferent to me what he should say to me before the whole Court, but it was not so to the audience; and I note this as having appeared to make a part of the arranged reparation to France, which reparation was as follows. (From this, imagine the wit of the Court of Berlin; for I am convinced there was a real desire of giving satisfaction to Comte d'Esterno.)

First, it was determined the Queen should have a Lotto, and not a private party, in order that the company at her table might be the more numerous. After all the Princesses, Prince Henry, Prince Frederick of Brunswick, and the Prince of Holsteinbeck, had been

invited, and taken their places, Mademoiselle Bishopswerder, the maid of honor, who regulated the party,
named Comte d'Esterno. The Queen then, perceiving
Lord Dalrymple, beckoned him, and at the same moment desired him to sit down. The Ambassadors of
France and England were the only foreign ministers
that were of the party, so that Princes Reuss and Romanzow were now excluded, as they before had appeared to have been favored. It would be difficult to
imagine anything more awkward, or more inconsistent; and this increases my regret at remembering
that Comte d'Esterno thought himself obliged to take
offense on the first Court day of the Queen; for, after
the absurdity of yesterday, I can see no possible hope
of reparation which would not be slovenly daubing.

I am certain, however, that, far from wishing to
wound, they were desirous to heal; and, to treat the
subject less petitely, I am persuaded it is wrong to affirm the King hates the French. He hates nothing;
he scarcely LOVES anything. He has been told that he
must become wholly German, in order to pursue a new
and glorious track, and he descends to the level of his
nation, instead of desiring to elevate his nation
superior to himself. His conduct is the result of the
narrowness of his views. If he have a cordial dislike
to anything, it is to men of wit; because he imagines
that, in their company, it is absolutely requisite he
should hear wit, and be himself a wit. He despairs of
the one, and therefore hates the other. He has not
yet learned that men of wit only are the people who can
appear not to possess wit. He seems to have made a
determination to treat all persons in an amicable manner, without haughtiness or threat. The Stadtholder
always receives two very different accounts from Berlin, and does not fail to believe that which flatters his
ruling passion.

A mile from this place some very secret experiments are making on the artillery, which are confided to Major Tempelhoff. A small number of superior officers are admitted; captains are excluded. The ground is covered by tents, and guarded by sentinels, night and day. I shall endeavor to learn the particulars.

I forgot to write you word from Brunswick, that the Duchess informed me the Prince of Wales was consulting the most able civilians in Europe, to learn whether, by marrying a Catholic, the positive laws of England, the laws of any other nation, or the maxims of the civil laws of Europe, would disinherit an heir, and particularly an heir apparent. There appears to be much imprudence in this appeal of an heir apparent from the opinions of Great Britain to those of the civilians.

An anecdote less important, but perhaps more poignant, is that the Margrave of Baden-Baden has sent M. von Edelsheim here as his complimentary envoy, the brother of one of his ministers who is called the Choiseul of Carlsruhe. The following is the history of this complimentor, who has arrived long after all the others.

At a time when the prolific virtues of the father of the five royal children were held in doubt, there was a wish to bestow a lover on a lady (the afterward divorced Queen, banished to Stettin), who, had they not done so, would have made bold to have bestowed one on herself. The care of choosing was committed to the brothers of the Duke of Brunswick. They descended a little too low, and in consequence an eye was cast on Edelsheim, who was publicly enough charged with this great work. He was afterward sent to Paris to execute another commission, of which he acquitted himself ill. I have been assured he was thrown into the Bastille. On his return he was disgraced, but afterward employed, and sent to various courts of Germany in 1778. And this is the man whom, in his high wisdom, the Margrave selected for his envoy to the King of Prussia. The Monarch himself, when he saw him, could not forbear laughing.

POSTSCRIPT.—Yesterday, at eleven in the morning, the King, hidden in a gray coach, went alone to Mon-Bijou, where he remained an hour, whence he returned in a great glow. What does this mean? Is this the triumph of the Lady Voss? It is impossible at present to know. Neither has anything transpired concerning the letters which M. von Calenberg has brought from the Stadtholder.

Muller and Landsberg, private secretaries of the Cabinet, demanded their dismission with considerable chagrin, their services not being apparently necessary, said they, since they were not thought worthy of being instructed concerning the answers they had to return, and since the letters were sent ready composed to the King. They remain in their places, and the accommodation was effected by Bishopswerder. It appears that he is in league with Welner against Hertzberg, which he does not take any great precautions to conceal. The King will not go to Potsdam to make the military arrangements before Friday, in order, as it is supposed, to give the Duke time to arrive. The attempting to account for all the caprices of kings is a strange kind of frenzy.

LETTER XL

October 28th, 1786.

I PASSED yesterday evening with Prince Henry. The King had dedicated almost the whole afternoon of the day before to this palace, for, after having been

with the Prince, he visited the Princess, where he
played, and drank tea with Mademoiselle Voss, among
other ladies of honor. This kind of reconciliation with
the Prince (which, however, is nothing more than a
simple act of courtesy, as is evident from the succeeding visit to the Princess, whom the Prince regards as
his most cruel enemy), this reconciliation (which is
nearly an accurate phrase, for the coolness between
them was very great) appears to be the political work
of Welner, who wishes, in his struggle against Hertzberg, if not the support, at least the neutrality of the
Prince; and the hatred of this feeble mortal is so blind
in effect that, united with the hopes of his ambition,
of which he is not easy to be cured, it was sufficient to
induce him once more meanly to offer his services to
the King, consequently to cast himself, if possible, to
a greater distance. Not that he himself places any
great dependence on this type of peace, which is the
more suspicious because it happened on the eve of a
succeeding fortnight's absence, after which it will not
be difficult to find pretenses not to meet again for some
time longer, should the King think proper. But the
Prince imagines his enemy dead, and he enjoys himself, and chuckles like a child, without recollecting that
this is the very way to promote his resurrection.

In reality, Count Hertzberg appears to have cast his
own die. He had a tolerable run of ill luck in Silesia,
—abrupt disputes, contradictions, the chagrin of seeing the name of the brother of his former mistress
struck off from the list of Counts; he ought, even while
in Prussia, to have perceived that his sounding
speeches gave no pleasure. On the day of receiving
homage, he read over the names of the Counts, and
when he came to his own stopped, that the King,
seated on his throne, might pronounce it himself, and
the Monarch was malicious enough to remain silent,

so that the inauguration of Count Hertzberg did not take place till the day after, and in the antechamber.

But what probably has occasioned his downfall, if fallen he has, was his haughty behavior to Welner, the least forgetful of men, and who, amid his ambitious projects, needed no such cause of rancor to occasion him to hate and injure the Minister. Hertzberg has made him wait for hours in his antechamber, has received and kept him standing, spoken to him a very short time, and dismissed him with airs which are only proper to give offense. Welner vowed his destruction, and he is seconded by Bishopswerder.

Such at least are probabilities, according to every acceptation of the word influence; and I should have divined them to-day from the very politeness of Hertzberg. He gave a grand dinner to foreigners, among whom, for once, Comte d'Esterno and myself were invited. His attention seemed all directed to us. Such proceedings are awkward and mean. This mixture of stiffness and twining is a strange singularity by which half-formed characters ruin themselves. Machiavel rightly affirms that "all the evil in the world originates in not being sufficiently good, or sufficiently wicked." Whether my conjectures are or are not true, still it is certain Count Hertzberg has been very dryly and positively forbidden all interference, direct or indirect, in the affairs of Holland, from which country Callenberg does not appear to have brought any remarkable intelligence. He is really come to obtain admission into the Prussian service, and his letters were only recommendatory.

It is not the influence of Hertzberg that prevents the recall of Thulemeyer, but that of Count Finckenstein. The mother of the envoy has had a lasting and tender friendship for the Count; and indeed it was her husband who procured the Count a place in the Ministry. In fact it appears to me to be a matter of little moment, for the present, whether Thulemeyer should or should not be recalled. His embassy ended on the arrival of Goertz, nor do I believe he sends any dispatches.

The destiny of Launay was decided the day before yesterday by a very severe letter. He is no longer allowed to act, and they offer him a pension of only two thousand crowns to retire on, with the proviso that he shall remain in the Prussian States. It must be owned his estimate is a *chef-d'œuvre* of egotism and folly, and that he might be completely refuted; although the memorial of the commissioners who have undertaken his refutation is a pitiable performance. He has proved two facts, the one of which is curious, and the other decisive against his own administration. First, that, in the space of nineteen years, he has brought into the King's coffers a surplus of 42,689,000 crowns of the empire, exclusive of the fixed revenue, which annually amounted to five millions of crowns. What dreadful oppression! The second, that the collecting of the customs is an annual expense of more than 1,400,000 crowns, which, on a first view of the business to be transacted, and of local circumstances, might at least be reduced two-thirds. But not one man is at this moment employed who appears to understand the elements of his profession. It is a fact that they have not yet been able to make any general statement of debtor and creditor, nor to class any single branch of the revenue; so that there is not one object, not even the King's dinner, which is yet regulated.

This is a chaos, but it is a chaos at rest. Finance, military and civil, are each alike in a state of stagnation; and such a state in general would indeed be better

than the rage of governing too much, in a country
with a fixed constitution, in which individual prudence
might preponderate over public folly.   But men are
here so accustomed to see their King active or rather
exclusively active; they are so little in the habit of
doing what he leaves undone, though, having once
issued his orders, they very well understand the art of
deceiving him; they even think so little of laying any
proposals before him, that the stagnation is a real clog
on the machine.   But how injurious may this clog
become in a kingdom which rests on so brittle a basis,
though inhabited, indeed, by a people so tardy, so
heavy, so unimpassioned, that it is scarcely possible a
sudden shock should happen?   The vessel, however,
must continue to sink, more or less sensibly, if some
pilot does not come on board, although she will not
suddenly founder.

Wait we must; it would be an act of temerity to
attempt to look into this darkness visible.   I repeat,
we must wait before we can know whether the King
will, or will not, have the courage to take a Prime
Minister.   Such an appointment would be equal to a
revolution; and, well or ill, would change the whole
face of affairs.

The Duke of Brunswick is the person who ought to
be narrowly watched, if we wish to foretell the fate of
this Government; although he should not be the person appointed, and should there be any appearance of
a shipwreck.   This Prince is only fifty, and is indis-
putably ambitious.   Should he ever resolve on hazardous and daring designs, and should he no longer depend on Prussia, he would shake all the German
combinations as the north wind shakes the reed.   His
manners and his prudence are incompatible with the
English party.   Neither can England act on the Continent, except accidentally.   But I can imagine circum-

stances under which I think him capable of going over to the Emperor, who would receive him with open arms. And what might not the Duke of Brunswick perform at the head of the Austrian army? How great would be the danger of Germany! How vast a prospect for him whose passions might be unbridled, should he be obliged to act a desperate part; for he almost hates his sons, unless it be his youngest, who promises not to be so stupid as the others.

The best manner of securing him has been missed, which would have been to place him unconditionally at the head of the Germanic Confederation. Should he desert it, I greatly fear he will be its destroyer.

Baron H—— is arrived, and has not been received by the King in a manner equal to his expectations. A certain musical demoniac, named Baron Bagge, is also at Berlin. I imagine they are all in too much haste. The King is in the high fervor of the German system, and anxious to have it known that the ship is to be differently trimmed. Since his accession, the banker of La Valmour has received orders to send in his account, that it may be discharged, and to stop all future payments to that girl who had formerly so much power over him. It is said he is to return from Potsdam on the third, and I imagine it will be found that he goes there to the chase. The Prince of Dessau is to arrive there to-morrow evening, and I have no doubt there is to be a calling of the faithful.

LETTER XLI

October 30th, 1786.

AT the request of Struensee, I have sent him the following information: First, on the possibility of public loans to France, and, secondly, on the treaty of commerce, and on the manner of placing money in the French funds.

There are two species of public funds in France: those the interest of which is fixed and certain, and which does not vary with circumstances; and those which produce dividends, or a participation of gain, subject to vicissitudes and to rise or fall.

The public and favored companies principally appertain to this last class,—such as the Caisse d'Escompte, the Paris waterworks, and French East India Company; the prices of stock in which have successively, or all together, been agitated by every frenzy of stockjobbing. All true estimate of their real value and their effective gains has been, as it were, lost, that men might yield to the rage of gambling in funds which never could be reduced to any exact valuation. These jobbers have been less occupied by endeavors to reduce the price of shares to their true value than artfully to affect their price, by disputes and pretended reasonings on the impossibility of delivering all the shares that had been sold. Monopoly has succeeded to monopoly, association to association; some to raise, others to lower the price; to effect which every imaginary species of deceit, cabal, and cunning has been practiced; and, though this gambling mania has not continued more than two years, many people have already been ruined, and many others dishonored, by taking shelter under the laws to elude their engagements.

The other species of public funds, and the only one perhaps which merits the name, consists in contracts, and royal effects, properly so called. The contracts yield an interest of from five and a half to six per cent at the utmost. One only fund, the stock of which is paid at sight, is more productive. This is the loan of one hundred and twenty-five millions. Shares are sold, at present, at an advance of but two per cent, although there are nine months' interest due, and the real interest amounts to nearly seven per cent. The stock cannot remain long at this price, and, whether the purchasers wish to be permanent stockholders, or only to speculate for some months, this loan merits a preference to any other. Its advantages annually increase, since, while receiving uniform interest of five per cent, a part of the capital is to be periodically repaid. In January, 1787 and 1788, these reimbursements are to be made at the rate of fifteen per cent on the capital advanced. They are afterward to proceed to pay off twenty per cent, and at intervals of three years to twenty-five, thirty-five, forty, forty-five, fifty per cent, till, in the last year, the whole will be repaid, independent of the interest of five per cent to, and including, the years of reimbursement, the last year of payment only excepted. The stockholders may either have bills payable at sight, according to the original plan, or, if they please, may receive contracts in their stead, without any change taking place in the order of reimbursement.

Those who buy in with the design of remaining stockholders, must prefer contracts, because these are liable neither to be stolen, burned, nor destroyed. Those who purchase stock on speculation, intending to sell out, should rather receive bills, because the transfer would then be subject to none of the delays of office.

We ought to regard the public loans of France as at an end, all the debts of the war being paid, so that if any loans henceforth should take place, they can probably be only for small sums to pay off the annual reimbursements with which the finances will, for five or six years to come, be burdened. But these loans can only offer trifling advantages to the moneyed men. The rate of interest must have a natural tendency to fall, because of the general prosperity of the kingdom, and, consequently, the loan of one hundred and twenty-five millions presents the probability of rising in price, which rise is each day liable to take place, and which variation cannot be profited by, unless stock is immediately purchased. This probability might even be called a certainty, when, on the one part, we recollect the nature of the loan, which is the most wise, solid, and advantageous to the moneyed men, and in every respect the best that has ever been imagined; and, on the other, the concurrence of circumstances, which, all uniting, lead us to presume that the credit of France, and the public confidence in its royal effects, must daily increase.

ON THE COMMERCIAL TREATY

It appears that the Treaty of Commerce is highly acceptable to both parties. The English perceive in it a vast market for their woolen cloths, wrought cottons, and hardware; we depend on the great exportation of our wines, linens, and cambrics, and probably both nations are right, but under certain modifications, the value of which can only be taught by time.

The Treaty, in general, seems to have held a principle as sacred which has too often been misunderstood, which is, that moderate duties are the sole means of preserving the revenue, and preventing illicit trade. Thus the English merchandise is rated at from ten to twelve per cent. Should the advantage for some years appear to be wholly on the side of the English, still it is evident the French trade will gain ground, since nothing can prevent our manufacturers gradually imitating the products of English industry, whereas, Nature having refused soil and climate to England, our wines cannot be made there, and, in this respect, the English must always depend on us.

True it is that the wines of Portugal will continue to be drunk in England in great quantities, but the rising generation will prefer the wines of France. Of this, Ireland affords a proof, in which ten times the quantitiès of French wines are drunk in comparison with the wines of Portugal. The French wines, henceforth, are only to pay duties equivalent to those which the wines of Portugal at present pay in England, that is to say, forty pounds sterling per ton, or about one shilling per bottle. Our wines of Medoc may there be sold cheap, and will be preferred to the wines of Portugal. The English, it is true, are allowed to lower the present duties on the wines of Portugal, but they will fear to diminish them too sensibly, lest they should injure the revenue arising from their beer, which is the most essential of their excise duties, and annually produces more than 1,800,-000 pounds sterling.

The Treaty, in fact, will incontestably be advantageous to both countries. It will procure an increase of enjoyment to the people, and of revenue to their respective monarchs. Its tendency is to render the English and French more friendly, and in general it is founded on those liberal principles which are worthy two such great nations, and of which France ought to be first to give an example since, of all countries on earth, it would, from its natural advantages, be the greatest gainer, should such principles be universally established in the commercial world.

LETTER XLII

October 31st, 1786.

.   .   .   .

They have also affirmed (that is, Prince Ferdinand has) that it was I who refuted the estimate of Launay. From that moment I have daily left my card at the house of Launay, and have declared that to torment people seemed to me to be a thing so unnecessary that, exclusive of the cowardice of wantonly striking a man under misfortunes, none but a fool could have invented so silly and malicious a tale.

On the reply of the refutation of his estimate, Launay received so severe a letter that he immediately demanded permission to retire. The King answered this should be granted him, when the commission should have no more need of his assistance.

It is loudly rumored here, after having been long whispered, that a treaty is concerting between Russia, Austria, and Prussia; the pretext for which is the pacification of Holland. I own that at present I do not see the least probability of truth in the report. Neither the King, nor any one of his Ministers, appears to me to have an understanding sufficiently enlarged for such a project. Not but we most assuredly ought to pay very serious attention to the rumor.

As I was finishing my phrase, I received information that Dr. Roggerson, the favorite physician of the Czarina, the same whom she sent to Vienna, and of whom I spoke to you in my former dispatches, is just arrived. Now or never is the time for an EYE WAR; but this kind of tilting can be performed only by ambassadors; they alone possess the means, were we to exclude every other except the all-puissance of supper parties, which are the very sieves of secrets.

Roggerson returns from England by way of Amsterdam, and Berlin is directly in his road. Still, I repeat, we ought, watchfully to observe Vienna and Petersburg,—convinced as I am at present that the Emperor is only spreading nets for this country. I must further add that I imagine I very clearly perceive the Gallomania of Prince Henry is on the decline. But this to him will be of no advantage, for it is to oppose the Prince that they are Anti-Gallican here. It is not to oppose the French that he is opposed. Prince Henry is turbulent, false, and perfidious. He formerly was successful at Petersburg. He may flatter himself that, should there be any need of that Court, he may be employed; and never will there be a better resemblance of the morality of the late Erostratus.

The Duke of Brunswick arrived on Saturday at Potsdam. That is a kind of secret at Berlin. Nothing had been done on Sunday, except listening to music and looking at reviews; but two couriers were certainly sent off, from the Sunday to the Tuesday. I know nothing more. I am in want of pecuniary and other aid. The domestic disorder is a thing so inconvenient, some of the favorites are so interested to put an end to it, or to certain parts of it, since they have not a sixpence, and it is carried to such excess in the palace, that I cannot help supposing there is some grand object which employs the whole attention of the King, and the few moments he can prevail on himself to dedicate to business.

There has been a quarrel in the household, in which the master has committed some violence on himself. One of his favorite ushers, Rumpel, a man naturally very insolent, insomuch that at a review he once struck a gentleman without any serious notice being taken of the affair, has had a very passionate brawl with Lindenau, the new first usher, who is a Saxon, and the friend of Bishopswerder, who procured him the place. Lindenau put the insolent favorite under arrest, and gave an account of his proceeding to the King. The Monarch started with astonishment; but, after a momentary silence, he not only approved of the act of Lindenau, but confirmed the arrest in a very cool manner, and for an indefinite term. By this he has given some energy to the head servants, and somewhat tempered the insolence of the subalterns.

Discord, on the other hand, reigns among the favorites. Goltz and Bishopswerder had a very serious dispute in Silesia. The King, having made some new appointments, in favor of I know not whom, Goltz kept so cool a silence that the King insisted on knowing the reason of this tacit disapprobation. Goltz replied: "Your Majesty is overflowing the land with Saxons, as if you had not a subject of your own." Bishopswerder came in, a few moments afterward, and proposed another Saxon, on which the King very abruptly exclaimed, "Zounds! you never propose anybody but Saxons." Probably, in the explanation which succeeded this pettishness, the King told what Goltz had said. Certain it is that Bishopswerder and Goltz have been very warm. The wall is whitewashed over, but we may with good reason conclude that Goltz, the Tartar, and Bishopswerder, the debonair, neither do, nor ever will, cordially esteem each other. It was the latter who brought the insignificant Duke of Holstein-beck hither, and who is endeavoring to advance him to the command of the guards, that he may deprive the former favorite, Wartensleben, of the place.

To descend a step lower, it appears that Chauvier is regaining credit. He imagined, at the beginning of the reign, that the surliness of the secretary would promote his interest. It did the reverse. Apparently he has altered his route, and is in the pandar department, submits to subaltern complaisance, and even to act the spy, in which he finds his account.

The King returns on Wednesday, as it is said, to depart again on Thursday. I cannot understand what this means, unless it should be to keep Prince Henry at a distance, without openly quarreling. The Prince will remain ignorant of affairs by not knowing where to find the King. The Minister, Blumenthal, has rather resolutely demanded his dismission, complaining that his Majesty, having bedizened some of his servants, who were not of so long standing as himself, with ribbons, had not bestowed on him that mark of honor. His retreat, which is not granted, is a matter of little moment; though it is affirmed the King could not be better pleased, for he would then have a place to bestow. I have heard, and from a good quarter, that this place, or rather a place of principal trust, will very soon be given to a remarkable man to the dissatisfaction of everybody. I can neither divine who this man is, nor believe the King has the fortitude to dissatisfy everybody. The credit of Hertzberg, if not ruined, is still on the decline. It is certain that he has not dined with the King since the return from Silesia.

Welner is at Potsdam.

Do not suffer your Ambassador to persuade you that there is nothing to apprehend from Austria; I am convinced the King is undetermined, that the Emperor is sounding him, and that there is something in agitation with which we are unacquainted. For my own part, nothing would appear less extraordinary to me. I own I am surprised at all the intelligence I obtain, however little that may be. But nothing can here be kept secret from a French Ambassador, who is in want of neither money nor industry.

I have just been told that General Rodig has sent a challenge to Count Boertz. I have not learned what was the cause of quarrel, and the truth of the news scarcely appears to be probable; yet it comes from a person who should know, though he is a young man.

LETTER XLIII

November 4th, 1786.

A NEW letter, excessively rigorous, and tolerably incoherent, has suspended Launay in the exercise of all his functions. Yet I scarcely can believe it is intended to sully the beginning of a reign by useless cruelty. The victim is immolated to the nation the moment the man is no longer in place. The remainder would only be the explosion of gratuitous hatred, since the unfortunate Launay no longer can give umbrage to anyone. Verder is placed at the head of the customs. We shall see what the new established order will produce; or rather, whether they will know how to establish any new order. In the meantime the discharge of forty Frenchmen is determined on, *in petto.* But I cannot perceive that these kind of Sicilian vespers are likely even to gain the public favor. The theater here is not sufficiently vast to conceal from the pit what is passing behind the scenes. There is scarcely any illusion possible, except that of actually doing good. I shall endeavor to save Launay, by causing Prince Henry to say, who has at least preserved the privilege of uttering all he pleases, that hitherto the King has really acted in this business as the man of the nation; but that, should he go further, he will become the man of the persecutors of Launay; that there are public murmurs which affirm he has espoused their hatred, etc. Certain it is that the repetition of the self-important *I,* in Launay's estimate, has put the King out of humor, and even in a passion.

His Majesty arrived yesterday, and returned this morning. This seems to be an episode in the romance of Voss which approaches the *dénouement,* and which is suspended to obtain the three following articles: (1) two hundred thousand crowns for her portion. The King refuses (or will only count out a thousand crowns per month, so that the payment will not be completed in less than sixteen years and eight months, which will render the sum a little problematic); (2) a left-handed marriage (to this he consents, but the lady finds that a very equivocal kind of circumstance), or (3) to marry her to a man who shall depart on the bridal day as Ambassador to Sweden (there is no certainty of finding a man sufficiently base, in that class which should rank him among ambassadors). Mademoiselle avows that, without being amorous, she is rendered exceedingly sensible by a three years' siege. But what shall become of her, of her uncle, her family? What place shall she hold in the public opinion, in city, and Court? Such is the purport of the negotiation conducted by Bishopswerder. I do not suppose him young enough to be the King's substitute; so that the speculation does not appear to be very certain.

As to the King, there is, indeed, some little curiosity, a degree of obstinacy, and somewhat of vanity, but still greater want of a companion with whom he may be as much of a gossip, may loll, and dress as slovenly as he pleases. The circumstance that shackles the negotiation is that Rietz and her tribe must evacuate the country, and the King is exceedingly attached to her son. It is necessary, however, to add to all this that Mademoiselle Voss relates herself all the tales repeated in public, and even of the most secret courtiers, which concern herself; and this may render the probability of these conjectures suspicious.

The King, it is said, returns to Potsdam till the 8th. He is not there so entirely occupied by business or secret pleasure as to exclude all company. M. Arnim is one of his society; a kind of unfinished man of the world, who has acquired many friends by the affability and amenity of his manners and his great fortune, and whose understanding, sufficiently upright and little brilliant, being timid and wavering, neither gives umbrage to the King nor inspires him with fears. In all despotic countries, one grand means of good fortune is mediocrity of talents. If it be generally true that no positive assertions ought to be made in the presence of princes, and that hesitation and deliberation always please them, I think it peculiarly so applied to Frederick William II.

It is affirmed the assignments are made out, and that this has been the labor of Welner alone. For this reason all the ministers, Schulemburg excepted (perhaps because of his connections with Count Finckenstein, whom the inauguration of Mademoiselle Voss must render powerful), are restless and terrified. Some of them have not yet given in the least account to the King. Estimate by this the state of a country in which everything depends on the industry of the King. Be not astonished that so little mention is made of business, for no business is transacted; the affair of Launay is the only one which is pursued with activity and hatred; everything else slumbers.

A person who comes from Russia assures me that the Empress has long omitted going any more to the Senate, and that she habitually intoxicates herself with Champagne and Hungary wine (this is contradictory to every account I have hitherto received); that Potemkin elevates his ambition to the grandest projects, and that it is openly affirmed he will either be made Emperor or be beheaded, at the accession of the Grand Duke. This artful and decisive man, possessed of uncommon fortitude, has not a single friend; and yet the number of his creatures and creditors who with him would lose their all, is so great in every class of the people, that his party is extremely formidable. He amasses immense treasures, in a country where everything is venal. Accustomed never to pay his debts, and disposing of everything in Russia, he does not find any difficulty in accumulating enormous sums. He has an apartment, the key of which he keeps himself, partitioned out from top to bottom, and divided into a great number of boxes, filled with bank bills of Russia, Denmark, and particularly of Holland and England. A person in his employment proposed to him the purchase of a library, appertaining to a great lord that had lately died. Potemkin took him into his bank-bill apartment, where the only answer he made was asking whether he imagined this library was of equal value with the one proposed. Possessed of such pecuniary aid, he has no need of any other to perform whatever he shall dare to undertake at Petersburg.

I must here mention that Doctor Roggerson, who yesterday departed on his return to Petersburg, affirms that no person in Europe leads a more sober or regular life than Catherine II. He, however, has been eight months absent.

I have collected some particulars that are rather curious, relative to the usurpation made on the ducal rights of postage in Courland, of which I have spoken to you in my former dispatches. This is an object of some importance, in so small a State, independent of the inquisition that thence results, and of the infraction of the rights of nations. This branch of revenue does not annually amount to less than a hundred and sixty thousand livres. But the following is a singular circumstance, which characterizes Russian politics.

Not to commit an act of violence too openly, and to avoid marching troops, which always draws the attention of neighboring Powers, the Court of Russia proposed, or rather demanded, an amicable conference between the deputies of Courland and commissaries, named to that effect; and appointed their sittings to be at Riga, a Russian fortress on the frontiers of Courland, under the presidency of the Governor of that town. Four deputies from Courland repaired thither at the time appointed; and the Governor signified to them that he had received orders from his Sovereign to arrest them if they did not sign an act, which he produced ready drawn up, by which the ducal rights of the postage of Courland were transferred to Russia. The deputies, should they refuse, having no other prospect before their eyes but Siberia, purely and simply affixed their signatures: after this, several stipulations, which alienated lesser rights and even portions of the borders of Courland, were in like manner presented and sanctioned. One of the most artful, and the most important, of these stipulations is that which relates to reclaiming the subjects of Russia, who may be found in Courland, and in which the Cabinet of Petersburg have included the very descendants of those who may have been naturalized for ages. It is very evident that this concession leads to unlimited abuse, and innumerable disputes, which will be more injurious to Courland than the most burdensome tax could be; for nothing can prevent the Russian superintendents from feigning, whenever they please, the existence of one or of several of such or such Russian subjects, in such or such a part of Courland, or from taking the refusal of restitution for granted, in order to lay the country under the contribution of an equal number of hundreds of ducats (the sum fixed by the stipulation for each Muscovite whom the Courlanders shall refuse to deliver up), whenever the Russian treasury, or the Russian delegate, shall stand in need of, or whenever the country shall be enabled to pay, such sums of money. I again repeat that similar practices, openly in Courland, in other parts more secretly, similar projects I say, are carried on in all the countries that border upon Russia. Let us return to Berlin.

Trumpel, the groom whom I mentioned to you in my last, is discharged. This exertion has excited much astonishment. The King certainly rouses himself as much as he can, that he may not be governed, and this is the most distinct act of self-will which has hitherto been discernible in the Monarch.

On Thursday evening he supped at the confidential table, at which there are no servants, but the guests are supplied by *tours*. The supper was more than gay. Ten persons were present. When it was over, the ladies of honor were visited, one after the other.

Prince Henry, who has this week given grand dinners to the civil and military officers of the Court, a thing he never did before, supped on Monday with the reigning Queen and her whole Court. This proves nothing, except a desire to keep up the appearance of politeness. I forgot to say that he is to give a dinner to-morrow to all the subalterns of the regiment of Braun. This is gratuitous and ridiculous affectation, and will never make his peace with the army, by which he is truly despised.

Baron Bagge, after refusing to pay any visits here, even those that common decorum required, saying that, according to the manner in which he had lived with the Heir Apparent, it was for the King to send him an invitation, yesterday received this invitation to Potsdam. The incident proves that music still is a passion.

That infamous C—— has written to Chauvier, affirming that he knew, past all dispute, it was to him he was indebted for the obligation of not being permitted to see the King! that he was going into a country in which he should find it easy to injure; and that he would use every exertion to effect his ruin; exclusive of the means with which he has been furnished by Chauvier himself. Chauvier has acted with propriety, and laid the letter before the King.

The nocturnal jaunts continue. I still remain ignorant of the object of the grand motions toward Austria, and reciprocally.

LETTER XLIV

November 7th, 1786.

THE King himself has interfered to produce a reconciliation between Bishopswerder and Goltz, the Tartar. Peace for the present, therefore, is concluded; and the more firmly, because that war, open and avowed, is hotly carried on between the first favorite and Count Goertz. There has been great difficulty in preventing them coming to blows. What may be argued of a King for whom they thus openly contend? Probably a regiment will be given to Goertz to send him out of the way; but the payment of his debts is the difficulty, for it appears that the last thing the King will part with is money. The treatment of the aides-de-camp is at length determined on. Bishopswerder has two thousand crowns; Goltz, the Tartar, and Bowlet each seventeen hundred. The head groom, Lindenau, also has two thousand crowns, with eight places of forage, which may be estimated at six hundred crowns, and fire and candle. Behold how the sandy plains of Brandenburg, with the aid of Silesia, be it understood, are capable of maintaining an army of two hundred thousand men

The thermometer of business remains still at the same fixed point. There is no riddance of letters; one chamber is full of packets that remain unopened. The State Minister, Zedlis, has not been able to obtain an answer to his reports for more than three weeks. Everything is in arrear. Yet the mode of living at Potsdam appears to have been tolerably well regulated, though Madame Rietz has been there. The latest hour at which the King has risen has been six o'clock. The Prince of Dessau has never seen him before half-past twelve, and perhaps not half an hour each day, dinner time excepted. It is at supper that the women make their appearance and that wrinkled cares are discarded.

Welner has not quitted Potsdam, and two men are continually writing in his apartment. Hitherto he may be regarded as the monarch of domestic affairs. That he is neither deficient in talents nor information is a point undisputed; and the eternal disorder of the accounts, added to suspicion of the financiers in power, must have impelled the King to have abandoned himself wholly to Welner, whose obscurity is his recommendation.

I say the ETERNAL DISORDER; because in effect Frederick William I., with whom all domestic regulations originated, in which no alterations were made by his son, kept no general and exact accounts,—and acted thus, systematically: being acquainted himself with the whole of his affairs, as he would not suffer any one of his Ministers to divine what the state of them was, he made out imperfect, over-charged, and false accounts. Frederick II., who never understood anything of finance, but who very well knew that money is the basis of all power, confined his views to the amassing of large sums; and he was so certain that his savings were enormous that he was satisfied with partial accounts. Such an interpretation is certainly more probable, in my opinion, than the imputation of having burned the general state of debtor and creditor, with the malicious intention of embarrassing his successor. The present King wishes for order, and he has reason so to do; but it is an Augean stable, and I see no Hercules,—at least among those by whom he intends to be served.

Count Finckenstein has written in very warm terms to the King, to inform him that the provocations of Count Hertzberg are so frequent that they are become insupportable; and that his great age and his last illness made him sincerely desirous of retreat. The King returned a very mild answer, very obliging, and what may be called apologetic; in which he earnestly requested him to remain in office, and promised that the cause of his complaints should cease. He promised, perhaps, more than he can perform. Men of the most opposite tempers served together under Frederick II., and this is one of the characteristic traits of his reign. But it is no small presumption to imitate his manner; it cannot be expected that such imitation should succeed; for, in spite of the servility of the country, liberties are taken that were not permitted under the late King, of whom the world spoke very freely, but with whom no person was familiar. The very Academicians now make encroachments. Three new members have been proposed—one Boden, an astronomer; one Meierotto, the rector of a college; and one Ancillon, a minister of the Holy Gospel. Admirable choice! The King testified his surprise with asperity at this unusual proposition, made without its being even known whether he did or did not intend to increase the number of Academicians. The indiscretion will probably occasion some regulation. He has, however, signed a large YES to the proposal for I know not what Druid of the name of Erman, author of a multitude of vile sermons, and a refugee history, of which four volumes are already written, that might be reduced to thirty pages; and who has been proposed by the curator only, Count Hertzberg, without the question having been put to the vote.

The Boden of Paris seems to be forgotten, or worse. The King was told that he had written three letters to his Majesty without having received any answer. " I have no answer to give; the fellow came here without orders." Such was the royal decision! The King returns to-morrow for a few days. He has been so accustomed to run from place to place, and to make only a momentary stay, that the habit seems to have become one of his wants. M. de H—— wrote to him, three days ago, to know when he might take his leave, but has received no answer.

The grand dinner of Prince Henry to the regiment of Braun was given yesterday, as I before wrote, All the officers and forty subalterns, who had served under him at the battle of Prague, sat at the Prince's table. He gave a medal worth fifteen ducats to each officer, a ducat to each subaltern, and a crown to each private. It would be difficult to be more awkwardly ostentatious. Had there been any need to have further injured himself in the King's opinion, he could not have found a better method; but this was completely done before, and it must be well known too, for Roggerson, who had often visited Prince Henry during his two journeys into Russia, has not been to pay him his respects. The King gave him an audience, it is said, but only for a few moments.

I do not at this instant recollect the name of the person who is arrived from Vienna, and who at the King's table was very pleasant at the Emperor's expense, which occasioned a coolness in the King and some gloominess, so as to denote marks of disapprobation—silent but strong.

The new ribbons are preparing. Moral coin seems to cost the King least. Never was the remark of Frederick II. to Pritwitz more true than at present. The latter complained that the ribbon had been bestowed on Braun before himself. "My ribbon," said the King, "is like saving grace; it may be given, cannot be merited."

Count Arnim has been appointed master of the hounds and a Minister of State, with a vote and a seat in the grand directory. In one of my former dispatches I have spoken of him circumstantially. This is a pure choice of favor (and is the more marked because that the place of master of the hounds, taken from Schulemburg, had continually been solicited by Colonel Stein, who was rather in the King's good graces), but of favor founded, as I imagine, merely on the pleasure taken in the company of Arnim who is irreproachable in mind and manners. It is only another person of incapacity added to the Ministry.

ROTTEN BEFORE RIPE. Such I greatly fear will be the motto of the Prussian power. But their millions are good. It will, therefore, be of use to remit new propositions for a loan, if it be really intended to erect a bank, as all packets, gazettes, and private letters affirm, so that, myself excepted, everybody is informed of the project; for in my opinion these would be of more importance than the loan of a hundred and twenty-five millions, which the bank apparently will be able to borrow on its own credit. Struensee, who doubtless will be glad of this occasion of rendering himself useful to the King, has in plain terms asked what he is to think of the disorder of the Caisse d'Escompte; of the letter of the Comptroller General to his administrators; of the project of a bank; of its approaching realization; of the principles on which it is to be established; and especially what kind of directors shall have the management. He thinks the plan good, but is convinced that everything depends on those who shall have the direction. To all these questions, as you must be sensible, I know not what to reply; yet it is requisite I should soon know, because not to mention that any negotiation of this kind cannot succeed here except by his aid,—for not one of the others understands anything of such affairs,—he has a right to interrogate me, since I made the first advances.

LETTER XLV

November 20th, 1786.

UNFORTUNATELY, I cannot be blind to what is here daily confirmed by traits which are each more pitiable than the others, concerning the opinion that I have so long forborne to take of the man and of affairs.

The King has just bestowed the ribbon of the Black Eagle on Anhalt. This gentleman is the son of a cookmaid, and of a multitude of fathers. He was originally a groom; he next sold smuggled coffee to the officers. I know not by what means he became what he is, but I know that his principal function was that of a spy. He was afterward placed in the service of the present King while Prince of Prussia; and, as he mingled poisonous advice and odious tales, THEY destined him, as it is said (and the word THEY is in this

case the most bitter of the enemies of the late King),
to execute a crime which THEY neither had the address
to color nor the courage to consummate. Anhalt possesses more military talents than his native folly
could promise. His warlike vocation seems to be
remarkable by this singular characteristic, that he
never possesses coolness except when heading his
men. He has arrived, whether by these or other
means, at the rank of Lieutenant General. As he
is without understanding (the little he had he was
deprived of by a dreadful fall, for which he was
obliged to be trepanned), he continued in favor.

He was detested at Königsberg, where he commanded, and this was a kind of recommendation to
him at Potsdam, where the kingdom endured forty-
six years of disgrace.

Some days before the King's death, General Anhalt
was sent for to Sans Souci. "You have lately married one of your daughters," said the King. "Yes
Sire, I feel I have." "How much did you give with
her?" "Ten thousand crowns." "That is a large
sum for you, who have nothing." On the morrow
they were sent him by the King. Anhalt returned into
Prussia. His benefactor died; he beheaded his portrait, and substituted the head of his successor. The
new King repairs to Königsberg to receive homage,
and bestows a superb box on Anhalt; but, indeed, gives
him notice he must quit the government of Prussia
in two months' time, that is to say, at present. Anhalt, being at an auction some days since and seeing
the portrait of the late King sold at a low price, very
coolly said, "Right, I'll give you the other into the
bargain." He retires with a pension of five thousand
crowns, a ribbon, and a promise of being employed
in war. This prostitution of reward, apparently extorted from weakness, is endeavored to be excused by

alleging the fear that Anhalt should pass into the service of the Emperor, as he threatened in the following speech, which does not want dignity: "If you refuse me this favor, I must then go elsewhere, and prove that it is not because of my want of merit." I do not think this a sufficient reason, for the estates he had purchased near Magdeburg were a sufficient pledge for his person.

Be this as it may, and, however singular the choice may appear, which has made a strong impression upon the public, it must be allowed that Anhalt is a great commander, an officer worth preserving, and that some recompense was due to him for the loss of his government of Prussia, with which, mad as he was, and often furious, he could not be intrusted.

But none of these reasons can be alleged in behalf of Manstein, a simple captain, a common and even ignorant officer, but a devout mystic; who, without any pretext, has been sent for and is destined, as it is said, to be governor of the young Princes, with the title of Lieutenant Colonel. To those who look into futurity, this is fearful. The whole army is offended. Indeed, it is probably not true; but the very suspicion speaks the public opinion.

A singularity which has not excited less murmuring is that Heynitz, Minister of State for the department of the mines, is placed at the head of the commission against Wertenberg, a kind of disagreeable man who has long had the clothing of the troops; a subaltern knave, and perhaps nothing more; or perhaps less so than his predecessors. This species of inquisition, which appears to be the adopted method, and which will not easily be made familiar to the people, whom it will be difficult to persuade that the late King was negligent and a bad economist,—this species of inquisition, I say, seems to indicate suspicions of the commanding officers, since the direction of such trials is taken from these officers, to whom they entirely appertained. There are great complaints, and still greater contempt. This must be an ill symptom, especially after a reign of only two months.

Indolence and stagnations, its necessary result, continue to be felt. In consequence of not having the letters sent after him, as was the custom of Frederick II., the King is prodigiously in arrear. He found thousands on his return from Silesia, his journey through which is a striking contrast to the incredible activity of the late King; who, however, did not devote more time, or rather who devoted less, than another to his trade of King. He only set apart an hour and a half each day on ordinary occassions for this purpose; but he never put off the business of the present day to the morrow. He knew, so well was he acquainted with man, that a bad reply was better than none. A heap of memorials and projects are on the table of the present King, most of which relate to military changes, on which he has never cast his eyes, and which have been productive of nothing, except for his vehement aversion for memorials. He regards them as a tax on his sovereign authority; and supposes advice of any kind to be an avowal of an opinion of his incapacity. Among the useless writings which have been remitted to him, there is said to be a memorial from Baron Knyphausen, on foreign politics. There are indications which lead me to believe it is favorable to our system, and this has given him particular displeasure; its fate, therefore, was to be thrown aside, without hesitation, as the reveries of dotage. The Baron, however, has disowned to me that he is the author of this memorial.

To the same sensation, apparently, which makes him so much detest advice, we must attribute the following singularity: Welner has only had a stipend of three thousand crowns, deducted from the pensions formerly paid to the head officers of the commercial departments; the smallest of which pensions only is granted him, so that he is but the equal of those who have least influence, and have not the same industry. As the few preparations which are made are all made by him his labor must be very great. A single statement of the money accounts is said to have given him much trouble. At present, the exceedings of the receipts over the expenditure, at least the civil, are known. The sum is greater than was supposed by near one-quarter, which is much. It is imagined that the chief part of this surplus will be applied to increase the pay of subalterns. Private soldiers undoubtedly deserve no greater honor than that of dying with hunger. But I scarcely can believe they will dare to offend the corps of the captains.

If the King give but little to those who seem to be his greatest favorites, yet there are indications that he bestows secret largessess; or that he has secret reasons for conferring such on some persons. The chamberlain Doernberg, an insignificant person in my opinion, who quitted the service of the Princess Amelia with ingratitude, she having paid his debts, to enter into that of the Queen, has twice within five days had his salary considerably augumented. At present he has two thousand crowns as chamberlain, a sum hitherto unheard of. What does this denote? Have they at length determined on the scheme of marrying Mademoiselle Voss? Have they cast their eyes on this fortunate mortal, who resembles a baboon? Do they intend insensibility to make his fortune? A captain in the Gendarmes said to me yesterday, " Since royal munificence is so amply showered on Doernberg, I for my part expect an annual gratification of fifty thou-

sand crowns. This must be either an affair of mysticism, pimping, or marriage. But, if the last, why
make so ridiculous a choice? What courtier is there
who would refuse Mademoiselle Voss, with plenty of
money? I did them too much honor in supposing such
were to be found in this Vandalian Court. Not in
places where men are accustomed to walk double will
any be found who shall stand erect when such temp-
tations are thrown in their way. Besides, what cannot
money effect in a nation so poor! I not long since saw
Brederic, late lackey to Prince Henry, become a kind
of favorite, because of his art as a CHAMBER COUN-
SELOR, and ostentatiously display the cross and ribbon
of a canonry of Magdeburg (Prince Henry is provost
of this chapter). Seven thousand crowns, lent by the
Prince, have purchased the stall; and the Prince's well-
beloved groom bears the sacred insignia, in a country
where there is so much delicacy pretended on the article of birth.

Apropos of his patron. For a week past I have not
heard this musical Prince mentioned, the height and
depth of whose thermometer are the greatest that ever
fell under my observation. The Count of Brandenburg requested permission of him to be present at
the banquet he gave to that part of the regiment of
Braun who fought under him at Prague. The Prince
granted the child permission; and, after highly caress-
ing him, said, " It is difficult, my little friend, to converse with you here, but ask your father leave to come
to my palace, and I shall be very glad to see you."
Thus artful are his politics. He must employ a quantity of such stratagems to reimburse himself for his
grand dinners. One of his table-confidants and admirers said to me the other day, " Is it not very singular that the Prince is so little esteemed, after all he has
done for the army? "—and he meant by this to crim-

inate the army! It appeared to me a notable speech.

The anecdote respecting the Academy is still more curious than according to the manner in which I related it in my last. The Academician Schultz has written a very violent letter to the King, against Count Hertzberg, and concerning the arbitrary manner in which he governs the Academy. The King sent the letter to Hertzberg, a marked token of disapprobation in this country. Busching, the geographer, on the same day, refused a seat in the Academy, unless a pension should be granted him of a thousand crowns. The only answer given to the complaints of Schultz was the nomination of Erman, by Hertzberg, without consulting any person; and the King signed his YES, without objecting to this nomination. Schultz wrote another letter, still more violent; what the consequences were I do not know.

The disgrace of Launay is not so mild as it appears. It is openly avowed that Government only waits till he has furnished Silesia with coffee, and that then he is to be displaced. He very rashly undertook this contract, which he has bargained with traders to fulfill, who are emboldened by his downfall to disown or break their engagements at the moment when, all the navigable canals being frozen, there are such few means of repairing so great a deficiency. But the truth is the commission is suspended, because that they are secretly sending, through different parts of the kingdom, in search of proofs; a truly cruel and tryannical inquisition, which shows that they are rather desirous of the guilt of Launay than of the public benefit.

A man named Dubosc, formerly an eminent merchant at Leipsic, where, if I do not mistake, he failed, and well known for his visionary adherence to mysticism, has been sent for, and is at present employed, as is supposed, to give in a plan of commercial regulations as a substitute for exclusive privileges. It should seem they meditate a sally against the Splittgerbers, and that means are seeking to deprive them of the monopoly of sugar; a very just and salutary, but a very difficult and delicate act.

An article of intelligence still more important is that Baron Knyphausen has had a secret conversation with the King; but, though it comes from a good quarter, I will not warrant it to be true. Not that this would much astonish me. I know past doubt that the King, enraged at being obliged to send Count Goertz to Holland, at the very moment when the House of Orange itself complains of this Ambassador, wished after venting a torrent of passion and abuse, to recall both Goertz and Thulemeyer; but that he was stopped short, because of the impossibility of finding a MAN in a country where there are none; and particularly none fit for Ambassadors, a part of administration that was highly neglected by the late King. His successor, perhaps, will be taught that fools are not good for any one purpose.

POSTSCRIPT.—Nothing new since I wrote this long letter. Various particulars assure me that the Princess Frederica, the daughter of the King, gains great influence, and never meets with any refusal. This doubtless appertains to the history of Voss.

LETTER XLVI

TO THE DUC DE L——

November 12th, 1786.

I FLATTERED myself that M. de H—— would bring me a packet from Your Grace. He informed me you

had intended to intrust him with one, and I am exceedingly grateful for the intention, although I have
not profited by it; this I attribute to unforeseen circumstances, which, while I pray for you, have my hearty
maledictions.

I hope that the Abbé de P—— has sent you the
news of the country, concerning which I have not
neglected occasionally to remit anecdotes tolerably
characteristic of the moment. I feel the poverty of
my own harvest more forcibly than any person; but it
ought not to be forgotten that I am neither provided
with the pecuniary nor the ministerial means. It is
impossible anything should escape the man of France
if he be adroit, active, liberal, and has the art to invite
proper guests to his DAILY dinners and suppers; for
these are the efficacious means, and not PUBLIC dinners. He is, besides, a kind of register office, to which
all the discontented, the babblers, and the covetous
resort. Besides that, his intercourse with subalterns
is natural to him and permitted; I, on the contrary,
have need of great art and circumspection, in order to
speak without offense or intrusion on public affairs. I
rarely can address my discourse to persons in power.
My very aspect terrifies them too much. The King
never deigns to look at me but their countenances
lengthen and grow pale. I have acted however, to the
best of my abilities, and, as I believe, done all I could
with means that are very mutilated, very ungracious,
and very sterile; nor can I tell whether the person on
whom the King bestows a salary of sixty thousand
livres, and a post of honor here, sends much more information than I do. But I well know that I, under
the same circumstances, would have penetrated many
clouds through which, stationed as I am, I have very
dark views; and that I would not discredit my nation,
as he is accused of doing, by his haughty behavior, his

bittersweet aspect and idleness that greatly resembles
ignorance.

M. de H——will more fully relate, as I suppose, the
particulars I have sent. He will tell you our cause is a
lost one here, unless a change should take place among
the Judges; that the way to re-establish our affairs is
not to be over hasty; since this would but prolong resistance among men naturally phlegmatic, and whose
phlegm we may safely conclude will not suffer them to
continue long impassioned; that he himself was too
hasty to come to a country which at the beginning of
the present reign, when each is looking for advancement, is too restless and jealous to suppose that a general officer and an inspector in the service of France
could really wish to be in the service of Prussia; that
the chaos (for so affairs at present may well be called)
must be suffered to subside, and from the nature of
things acquire consistency (if on the contrary it should
not suffer destruction), though it be but the consistency of apathy, before attempts should be made to
interfere; that no person is at present firmly placed;
that the grand question—" Will the King, or will he
not, have the courage to take a first Minister?"—is
far from being resolved, even by the calculation of
probabilities; that on this determination, however, the
fate of the country depends, and even the ultimate
capacity of the King, whose inability will be of little
import if this remedy should be found to be a substitute
for his indecision; that the symptoms are vexatious,
and indeed disagreeable, but that we must not pronounce too hastily, because our information is the reverse of complete.

It appears to me indubitable that Prince Henry is
ruined past resource; and I fear (in his behalf) that,
on this occasion as on many others, chance has arranged affairs better than our precaution. But

whether or no, his cunning, his boasting, his inconsistency, the intemperance of his tongue, and the vileness of his creatures, seconded by the most universal discredit, have added to personal antipathy, and the general and habitual fear of appearing to be governed.

The destiny of the Duke of Brunswick is far otherwise uncertain; nor do I believe it will be decided before there is an open rupture. But it is peculiar to him, and to him alone, that, should he once grasp power, it will not afterward escape him; for a better courtier, a man of deeper views, more subtle, and at the same time more firm and more pertinacious, does not exist.

You may well imagine, Monseigneur, that, if I suppose facts are too partial, and hitherto not sufficiently numerous to be reduced to system, on which conjectures may be formed respecting the King and politics, I am still much farther from thinking I can, with any appearance of probability satisfactory for a wise man, divine what will be the grand foreign connections, and political influence of Prussia, under the present reign. I have sketched my ideas on the subject in a memorial, which is a work of labor; but which (except the proofs the country affords, and which here, as I imagine, will be found united and compared more accurately than anywhere else) is only a succession of conjectures. It contains many things which may, and perhaps not one of which will, happen. I am fortunate if, in this calculation of the arithmetic of chances, I have so far succeeded as to describe things as they are, and as they may be. From this memorial, accompanied by three or four others, on parts of Germany which lucky chance has given me opportunities of perfectly knowing, a plan may be formed according to which the Germanic edifice may be reconstructed, a work that ought to be begun, if its ruin is not desired. And here, I confess, the indecision of man, the complication of incidents, and the obscurity of future contingencies arrest me at each step; and I have no other guide than what is offered by your grand and noble project of coalition, between France and England, the end of which is to give happiness to the world, and not afford amusement to orators and news-writers.

M. de H—— has informed me that Your Grace intends coming hither in the spring. This certainly would be the only means of rendering my stay here supportable. But I hope you will not so long be left in inactivity so unworthy of your talents. As to myself, after having paid a tribute for six months, during which I have the satisfaction conviction gives of having employed uncommon assiduity and research, in compensation for the want of natural talents, I think I have a right to shake off an equivocal and doubtful existence, every way embarrassing, requiring dexterity and fortitude seldom found to preserve personal respect, and in which I consume my time and my strength in a species of labor that has no charms for me, or in the languor of etiquette and company still worse than this labor. Of this I have informed the Abbé de P—— in express terms.

LETTER XLVII

November 24th, 1786.

THE most distressing incident possible has just happened to me. It is a very extraordinary story. Madame de F—— the famous *Tribade,* coming from the waters of Schwalback, has dropped here as if from the clouds, under a borrowed name, with an immense train, and not a single letter of recommendation except to bankers. Can you imagine what project this profoundly audacious and indeed capable woman has entertained? The conquest of the King! And as, in punishment for my sins, I have known her long and well, the damnable siren has addressed herself to me, to lay down a chart of the country for her; and, in return, receive, as a deposit, that high confidence which I should most willingly have bequeathed to Beelzebub. However, as she is a demon of seduction, as she does not ask for money, at least not at present, and as her qualities of body and mind in many respects correspond with those of the Monarch, if this be not an opportunity to be sought after neither is it one to reject. Besides, as the design is begun, and as it will be better to undertake the direction than be exposed to ridiculous broils, I am at present in search of means to afford her a decent pretense of remaining here a fortnight; taking care to draw my stake, or rather taking care not to put it down.

If the Comte d'Esterno were not in every respect one and the same, the affair might presently be managed. She might be going to Petersburg, through Warsaw, —waiting here till she could travel in a sledge, which from the setting in of the frost cannot be long delayed; might give a few select suppers; excite curiosity, etc., etc. But this mode is not to be depended on; it is too subtle for his understanding.

Were not Prince Henry indiscretion itself, nothing could be more easy than by his aid to introduce her to the Court. She might have brought him letters. But in an hour's time the aide-de-camp, Tauensien, would be informed of everything; as would his aunt, Madame Knibbeck, in five minutes afterward; and her I suspect to be the go-between of Mademoiselle Voss. We must depend on our resources. I shall take care not to entangle myself; though, indeed, her very first step has entangled me. It is a kind of a fatality; and how might I escape?

I have made many reflections on this odd adventure. Our plan must be not to abandon our purpose, and not to be too scrupulous concerning the means. The few we have are, in truth, impracticable.

If she remain in her present situation, there will be no means of seeing the King. The mystics, the Voss party, and the anti-French in general, will all be her enemies. If she conceal her intentions, she will be opposed by the party of the Rietz, and the subalterns. Either I must often visit her, which will render her suspected; or I must not, and she will conduct herself improperly.

If this partake of the adventurer, I voluntarily engross the blame.

Nothing can be done in haste, with a German prince. Should her stay be long, that stay will of itself divulge the secret.

It is not possible but that, in a week, her true name must be known. The reputation she has acquired will then spoil everything, in a country where seductive qualities will not excuse vice, and where a trip is not the less a trip because made by a woman.

The follies most inexcusable are those which expose to ridicule without compensation, of the number of which this is one. D'Esterno will relate his trifling tales; Boden his trifling scandal; Tauensien propagate his trifling intrigues; before appearance, it will be necessary to let the crowd go by, who will come and endeavor——I will, therefore, send her to Warsaw, and procure her letters. She may return with other letters, if you do not inform me by what means she may be prevented, should such be your wish; for, though I can delay, how may I forbid her return? Such I have thought the least hazardous proceeding in this fantastic farce, which I, with good reason, think of greater importance than you may be tempted to do, because at Paris Madame de F—— is, like many others, little more than a courtesan; while here, the niece of an Ambassador and the widow of a P—— G——, etc., will never be supposed not to have been sent by Government, or, at least, not to have come hither under its protection. She, therefore, must not be suffered to commit any great folly.

The King has lately terminated a suit which had been in contest for three-and-twenty years. The Duke of Mecklenburg-Schwerin formerly borrowed a hundred thousand crowns of Frederick II., and gave some *bailliages* (or districts) as a security. Hither Frederick immediately sent a regiment of hussars into quarters. The regiment, as you may well suppose, raised recruits. The people of Mecklenburg were shocked by this act of despotism, and offered to repay the late King; who, during twenty-three years, always found pretenses to avoid receiving the money. His successor has withdrawn the troops. It is true he loses an opportunity of enlisting some of the country people, but he will annually save thirty thousand crowns; and there is likewise a new member gained for the Germanic confederation, and what that might be valued at, this is worth.

On Sunday (the 12th), at the principal inn in Berlin, the marriage of the Countess Matuska and a Prussian officer named Stutheren, was celebrated. The Countess is a sister of Mademoiselle Hencke (Madame Rietz). She thought to have married a Polish gentleman, who some months since withdrew. Once deceived, she next made choice of a young officer. The King has given money, and money enough. It is supposed that Mademoiselle Hencke, who now is said not to be married to Rietz, will retire and live with her sister, that she may not impede the projects formed to enjoy the maid of honor in peace.

There are whisperings of a very remarkable and very secret supper, at which the shade of Cæsar was taken. The number of mystics increases. They affirm that the credit of Bishopswerder declines. I do not believe a word of it.

No new act of finance. Depositions against poor Launay are poured in, and in all probability his fortune must purchase his freedom.

Nothing new, or at least nothing certain, from Holland, except that Count Goertz has found the way to displease the States, the House of Orange, and the principal persons who are enumerated among the French faction. I well know what a philosopher would deduce from this: the politician will perceive there are commissions, the discharge of which he never ought to undertake.

LETTER XLVIII

November 18th, 1786.

IT IS every day more apparent that the King does not forget those who were attached to him before his accession to the throne; and this propensity, which is successively developed, proves him, at least, an honest man. Count Alexander Wartensleben, an officer in the guards, whom I have several times mentioned, had been educated with him. Hence that intimacy which will not admit of secrets. The late King sent for Wartensleben, and said to him, " I am pleased to see you so very intimate with my nephew; continue your friendship. But it is also necessary you should serve the State. I ought to be informed of the proceedings of my successor. *Mein liebes Kind,* you will come and let me know what passes at your parties of pleasure. I shall not forbid them. I shall only warn you when there is any danger; and of this you yourself will inform the Prince of Prussia. Depend upon me, *mein Schatz.*" Wartensleben, who knew the old fox, replied " that he was the friend of the Prince, the friend of his heart, and that he would never become his spy." The King then assumed his furious countenance. " HERR LIEUTENANT, since you will not serve me, I will at least take care that you shall obey." On the morrow he was sent to Spandau, where he was imprisoned three months, and after that ordered to a garrison regiment in the very farther part of Prussia. On the new King's accession he was recalled. After a momentary displeasure, which Wartensleben's refusal to go to Sweden occasioned, and which perhaps was the contrivance of the other favorites, the King has bestowed a prebendary on him, the income of which is valued at twelve thousand crowns; and, according to all appearance, intends to give him the command of the guards.

The following is a second example of a like kind. When the suit was carried on against the Minister Goern, who was superintendent of the College of Commerce, among his papers was a bill on the Heir Apparent for thirty thousand crowns. The money must be procured within twenty-four hours. Arnim went in search of the Prince, and offered him the sum, which was most joyfully accepted. This probably is the origin of the favor which the new Minister enjoys; I cannot conjecture any other, except what may be deduced from the King's easiness of character, his indecision and mediocrity of mind; which, however, is just and clear, as I have said in my former dispatches.

The King has done a third humane and generous act. His first wife, the Princess Elizabeth of Bruns-

The supper was more than gay. —p. 204

From the painting by J. Lomax

wick, has received an increase of allowance, consisting of the revenues of the *bailliage* of Ziganitz, which amount to twelve thousand crowns, with liberty to retire whenever she pleases. Certain of not being received by her family, she will remain at Stettin. But the news has transported her with joy. She has publicly declared that the lady of General Schwerin, her *gouvernante,* has no more right to give her any orders; and, for the first time these eighteen years, she took an airing on horseback with Mademoiselle Plates, that she might immediately enjoy that liberty to which she was restored.

A trait which we ought to add, in proof of the King's morals, is his having given up the letters to Prince Henry, which passed in his correspondence with Frederick. Their number amounts to five hundred and eighty-seven, on State affairs, from the year 1759 to the year 1786. It had been unseasonably reported that the Prince was privately of his brother's opinion concerning their nephew. These letters, however, have proved that he did not wish it should be known. He even rendered him services; and, for example, when Count Wartensleben of whom I have just spoken, was imprisoned, he sent him a grant of a pension of a hundred a year, which he still enjoys.

The famous chamber hussar, Schoening, the confidential man of the deceased King, has lately been appointed assistant to the cashier of the military chest, with a salary of three thousand crowns. This certainly is not a rancorous act. Schoening, indeed, is not a man without intelligence; and he is the depositary of numerous secrets, which ought not at present to be made public, perhaps never.

In opposition to all these good actions, we must place the apathy of the King, on the subject of his personal debts. He is in no haste to pay those that are not of the household, and there is a very considerable sum appertaining to the latter which remains unsettled.

It is determined that the King is to discharge all the persons employed as tax gatherers on the French finance system, which in itself is a laudable act; for were there a necessity for some years to prolong the farming of the customs, yet, either the French collectors already have, or never will have, taught the Germans the mode of transacting the business. And is not the Prussian Monarch the King of Germans? But innovation is a very delicate thing; and I see no preparations made to lessen the shocks that must be received. The farmers of tobacco and snuff have been informed that their administration must cease on the 1st of June, 1787. All persons thenceforward will be allowed to cultivate tobacco, and to make and sell snuff. This is a very important object; for the tobacco that grows on these barren sands is some of the best in Germany, and formerly was a very considerable branch of trade. On the 1st of July grants are to be delivered, gratis, to whoever shall make the requisition. (Nay, freedom is promised for coffee, too.) From 1783 to 1786, the duties on snuff and tobacco had yielded about sixteen hundred thousand livres more than the sum they had been estimated at by the King; so that these formed a revenue of something more than a million of crowns, and sometimes a million four hundred thousand. Yet the collectors had not the right of buying the leaf tobacco; they were obliged to purchase it from the warehouses of the Maritime Company, by whom it was sold at a profit of cent per cent. These collectors committed infinite vexations on the subject, to obtain a surplus, with which it was necessary to come before the King when they delivered in their accounts; otherwise, he could neither find wisdom in their proceedings nor talents in themselves. The King leaves the collectors their salaries till they can be provided for, and this is humane; for the change will affect not less than twelve hundred families. But how will they find a substitute for this revenue? A capitation tax is spoken of, and is certainly under deliberation. The subjects are to be comprised in twelve classes; the rich merchants are to pay twenty-four crowns; the rich inhabitants twelve crowns; two crowns for obscure citizens; and the peasants something less than two francs. What a manner of beginning a reign it is, to tax persons before property! In the collection of this odious tax, which sets a price on the right of existence, the tobacco excisemen are to be employed. The capitation, however, is somewhat softened by being paid by the family and not by the head. But the proselytes to, and even the apostles of, this project do not estimate the tax at more than two millions of crowns annually; which sum is the product of tobacco and coffee united, but which scarcely will supply the deficiency; and those who understand calculation in finance will be careful not to estimate a tax equally productive in figures and reality. I am surprised that he does not first gain a better knowledge of substitutes; and that he should begin by operations which I have pointed out as things to prepare, and should defer those with which I thought he ought to commence.

Heinitz, Minister for the department of the mines, and president of the commission commanded to examine the administration of General Wartenberg, warned no doubt by universal clamor, has remonstrated to the King that it is requisite to add some military men to the commissioners. His Majesty has in consequence appointed General Moellendorf.

To give a specimen of the malversations attributed

to the Jew Wartenberg, which it is said were highly
surpassed by his predecessors, the following trait is
cited. He made up clothing for a regiment of foot,
without having shrunk the cloth. The coats were so
tight that they scarcely would button on the men.
The first day they were worn by the regiment there
happened a heavy shower. The quartermaster said
that, if the soldiers pulled off their regimentals, they
never could put them on again; accordingly they were
commanded to lie all night in their clothes, and dry
them upon their backs.

The next is an example of another kind, and characteristic of Frederick II. One of the cash keepers of
Wartenberg stole eighty thousand crowns. The General informed the King, and waited his commands.
Frederick replied he had nothing to say to the matter,
for he was for his own part determined not to lose
the money. Wartenberg understood this jargon, assembled all the army clothiers, and requested they
would divide the loss, under pain of being no more
employed. The clothiers cried, cursed, lamented their
wretched destiny, and subscribed. Wartenberg wrote
to the King that the money was again in the military
chest. Frederick sent a very severe answer, and concluded his letter by telling him " this was the last time
he should be pardoned."

Private anecdotes continue much the same. The
general report is that the King is to espouse Mademoiselle Voss with the left hand,—a German mode of
ennobling courtesans, invented by pliant courtiers and
complaisant priests to save appearances, say they.
This lady still continues a mixture of prudery and
cynisme, affectation and ingenuousness. She can find
understanding only in the English, whose language
she speaks tolerably well.

Manstein is suspected to be the author of some of

the intended changes in the army, the purport of which is to better the condition of the soldier and the subaltern, at the expense of the captain. I repeat, this last is a formidable cohort; and that innovations of such a kind require great foresight and inflexible fortitude. Prince Henry, who is profoundly silent, in public, concerning all operations, will very warmly take part with the army, should it find cause of complaint; and hopes thus to regain what, by his excessive haughtiness, he has lost. But the army aristocracy know him too well to confide in him; they know that the *Gitons* have been, and will always continue, with him, the sovereign arbiters; that, when circumstances have obliged him to seek the aid of men of merit, he has always found their presence a burden, which his crazy frame has shaken off as soon as possible,—that, in fine, his day is ended, with respect to war, and that he is odious to the Ministry.

It seems one Count Brühl is chosen governor of the Prince Royal; and nothing better proves the influence of Bishopswerder than this eternal preference of Saxons. Count Brühl, son of the ostentatious satrap of the same name, brother of the Grand Master of the Saxon Artillery, amiable, well informed, really or pretensedly believing in the reveries of the mystics, with little of the soldier, yet willing to profit by circumstances and to enter the military career with gigantic strides—this Count, I say, demands to enter the service as a lieutenant general; a thing unheard of in the Prussian army, and which will cause infinite discontent.

An interdict has lately been issued, prohibiting the discount of bills at the bank; which is very wise in theory, but here accompanied by great inconveniences in practice; for either the bank or the King must pay the interest of two and a half per cent for about seventeen millions of crowns, which is the amount of the capital of, and the money brought into, the bank, in a country where moneyed men find no means of employing their capitals. The bank cannot pay this two and a half per cent without becoming burdensome to the King, except by discounting bills of exchange; and it will hereafter be the less able, if the Maritime Company, founded as I have before said, on so frail a basis, and obliged to give at least ten per cent to the proprietors, should lose any one of its most beneficial exclusive privileges,—that of wood, for example,—and should not be able to afford the bank, to which the Maritime Society pays five per cent for all the money it there borrows, the same sources of profit which have hitherto been open.

FIRST POSTSCRIPT.—The Minister Schulemburg has resigned; his resignation is not yet accepted.

The King yesterday supped with his daughter, Mademoiselle Vierey—the intimate friend of Mademoiselle Voss, and placed by her in his daughter's service since his accession to the throne—and the well-beloved. Hence it should seem that the romance draws toward a conclusion.

It is more than ever certain that the King transacts no business, and that he is mad after pleasure. The secrets of the palace on this subject are very ill-kept indeed; and nothing, as I think, can better prove the feebleness of the master, the little awe in which he is held, and the worthlessness of his creatures.

SECOND POSTSCRIPT.—The King is so terrified by the universal clamor which the capitation tax has excited, that it is renounced. Some of his intimates to-day spoke to me of substitutes; but what can be expected from an avaricious and weak Prince, whom two days' murmurings have caused to retreat, and to whom we can only say, " Tax the estates of the nobility, and lend out some of your millions; that you may procure the interest which nations in debt are obliged to pay."

LETTER XLIX

November 21st, 1786.

THERE are suspicions—which are daily strengthened —of a secret negotiation between the Emperor and Prussia; or at least that propositions have been made, either by the first or reciprocally, on which deliberations are held. I neither have the money nor the requisite means to discover what they are. An Ambassador can effect anything of this kind, and with impunity. But, though I even possessed the great engine of corruption, what danger should I not be in, should I set it in motion? I have no credentials, direct or indirect. An act of authority might dispose of me and my papers in an instant; and I should be ruined, here and elsewhere, for my too inconsiderate zeal. Spur on your Ambassador, therefore, or hasten to oppose to this puissant coalition, which nothing could resist on this side of the Rhine, the system of union with England, the basis of which you have traced out, and which shall be the salvation of the world. Think on Poland, I conjure you. What they have done (if they did not extend their acquisitions it was in fact because they would not) they will again do, and that even without the intervention of Russia; of that sleeping giant, who, waking, may change the face of the globe.

In truth, it is the coolness between the two Imperial Courts which most confirms the suspicions of a new system. All that I can imagine, concerning its foundation, is that its pretext is the election of a King of the Romans, and its purport a strict alliance, which shall destroy the Germanic confederation. As this confederation was the work of the King while Prince of Prussia, or as he wishes to believe it his, and as he regards it as a masterpiece, it may be doubted whether the Emperor will succeed. But, if the news of yesterday be true, there is a great point gained. Advice is received that the Electress Palatine is beyond hope. Should she die, the Elector would marry again on the morrow, and affairs may and must assume a different face. If I am not mistaken, it is difficult to reflect too seriously on this subject. For my own part, unless my instructions and my means are amplified, I only can observe, according to the best of my power, the internal acts of government and the Court.

The reason that Count Schulemburg, one of the Ministers of State, has demanded to retire is, in part, that he was charged to carry the capitation tax into execution, which he neither conceived nor approved, and which he truly regarded as a very unpopular, if not a very odious, office. This Minister, a man of understanding, and who would have again been at the head of affairs if, at his first cause of disgust, he had determined to resign his place, is infinitely disagreeable to the domestic agents. The long favor he has enjoyed, his rapid fortune, and his watchful perspicacity, have angered or disturbed all his rivals. Neither is he one of those pliant instruments that will bend into any form. The incapacity of most of the other Ministers afforded him the pretense of being obstinate in opinion. The absurdities of the courtiers, not to say their extravagant follies, emboldened him to return that contempt which the reputation of his abilities incites with usury. For what will not such a reputation eradicate, especially in a country where men are so scarce? But if, as it is said (I have not yet had time to verify the fact), there be a coalition between Struensee and Welner, Schulemburg is undone, for they will no longer stand in need of him. As he made illness his pretense, the King, in a very friendly letter, only accepted his resignation *per interim* and on condition that his signature should sanction whatever related to his department.

Meantime the Aulic systems, that of mysticism, and the favor of the mystics, are continued, or, rather, increased and adorned. The Duke of Weimar arrived here last night. He has the apartments of the Duke of Brunswick at the palace. This Prince, the great apostle of the fashionable sect, and of whom I spoke in my dispatches from Brunswick and Magdeburg, had long had the character of being only an *arbiter elegantiarum;* a zealous promoter of letters and arts; an economist by system; and a spendthrift by temperament. I some months since suspected him of military enthusiasm. It is now avowed. He comes to enter into the Prussian service. Such generals will never renew the War of Seven Years.

In other respects affairs continue the same. The King invited himself to sup with Prince Henry today. The Prince, who continues his awkward plans, stifling his pent-up rage, has informed the foreign ambassadors that the doors of his palace would be opened every Monday, and that, if they thought proper to form card parties there, he should receive them with pleasure. He wishes to change the custom which hitherto has prohibited all who appertain to the *corps diplomatique* from eating with princes of the blood, and insensibly to invite them to suppers. His credit is at the lowest ebb; yet I still believe, would he persevere in silence, abstain from all pretensions, impatience, and avidity of power, he would highly embarrass the opposite party, and would at length be triumphant.

Murmurs become general against the obscure agents of the Cabinet; and the nobility, now neglected to make room for the Saxons, would be better pleased to behold a prince at the head of administration than obscure clerks, who never can acquire great and acknowledged fortunes, except by great changes. Yet the aristocracy is little dependent on such subalterns, and holds them in little dread.

The Duke of Courland is soon to arrive. As he is to be reimbursed considerable sums, it is to be presumed that the whole of the debts of the Heir Apparent, which it is not decent to have left unpaid for several months after his accession, will then be discharged. This fact, combined with the suppers of the procuresses, the number of which suppers increases at the Princess Frederica's, and for which purpose her establishment has evidently been granted, seriously attaint the moral character of the King.

Madame de F——, who would not depart for Warsaw without making some attempt, yesterday had a very gay audience of the King; an audience of anecdote, at which he complained of his tiresome trade, and was earnest in his desires that she should remain at Berlin; reproached her with having stolen the portrait of Suck from him; and complained to her of the impoliteness and blunders of the Prince de P——, who thought his very daughter, the Princess Frederica, ugly and slatternly. This continued an hour, and probably if Madame de F—— had come hither with greater precaution and for a longer time, she might have had some success. But it is a being so perverse, so avaricious, and so dangerous, that it is perhaps best she should travel with her talents elsewhere; to Paris, for example, where she is known, where she would not increase licentiousness, and never could obtain any important influence; whereas, if admitted to the privy council of Kings, she might set Europe in flames to obtain money, or even for her own private diversion. I took advantage of the moment that she thought proper to depart from the route I had traced out, to reiterate my information that her proceedings might have consequences much more serious than result from wounded vanity, and to declare I no longer should be a party concerned.

1. Because it did not become me to risk my character, in an affair where my advice was not followed.

2. And because the ambition of ladies has not, cannot have, the same motives, principles, proceedings, and conclusions, as that of a man who has a respect for himself.

Should she succeed, which appears to me impossible, she is too much in my power to escape my influence.

POSTSCRIPT.—Lord Dalrymple, it is reported, is recalled, and Ewart remains at the head of the embassy without a superior. Dalrymple is a man of honor and sense; sometimes wearisome, because he is continually wearied, but endowed with more understanding than will be believed by those who have not carefully observed him; and also with generous, liberal, and fixed principles. If pacific coalition be sincerely intended, it is necessary to bring Dalrymple Ambassador to Paris. With respect to Ewart, I believe the Cabinet at St. James's finds it convenient to maintain a spy here, who is the intimate friend of one Minister and the son-in-law of another. But what can be alleged in excuse of the Cabinet of Berlin, that shall tolerate such an encumbrance? This is but public report, which I suspect.

Commissions of inquiry begin to be fashionable;

one has lately been appointed to examine the monopoly of sugars. The people of Hamburg offered to supply the same articles at less than half price.

Another to examine the cloth manufactory.

Another the wood monopoly, which is to be reduced to half its present price (independent of the suppression of the company, by which it is furnished). But how? By what means? The change is assuredly one of the most urgent, and the most profitable that could be made for the country; but the abolition of all these monopolies, sugar excepted, which is granted to an individual, supposes the destruction of the Maritime Company, that strange firm, which has promised the proprietors a dividend of ten per cent, be circumstances what they may. This fantastic superstructure cannot be pulled down, unless by a very able hand, without risk of danger from its ruins. Therefore, in his letter to the Minister Schulemburg, the King renounces this project, and commands that it should be contradicted in all the public papers. What a fluctuation of plans, orders, and intentions! What poverty of power and of means!

LETTER L

November 24th, 1786.

COUNT HERTZBERG has made a new attempt to interfere in the affairs of Holland, which had been interdicted him by the King, and has presented a memorial on the subject, in which he pretends to prove that crowned heads have several times stood forth as mediators between the States and the Stadtholder; and that the insidious reply of France stated that as fact which was in dispute. Prince Henry believes this memorial has produced some effect. I have my reasons for being of a different opinion; however, I informed him that, if he could procure me a copy, its futility should soon be demonstrated. I doubt whether he has even thus much power.

Here let me remark, we are reconciled. I refused two invitations, and he has made every kind of advance to me, which decorum requires I should receive with politeness.

The journey of the Duke of Weimar certainly had no other end but that of his admission into the Prussian service, which is to strengthen the rising fame of the Germanic confederation. This prince in reality warmly protects the system of those who find, in the depth of their mystical abilities, rules for governing a kingdom. The favor in which these systems are held continually increases in fervor; or rather, is become visible, for it never was cool. The brother of the Margrave of Baden, a fashionable enthusiast, has a natural son, for whom he wishes to provide. This is the great affair of which he is come hither personally to treat, and he has met a miraculously kind welcome.

Business is not quite so well. There is so much confusion in domestic affairs that the King only issues money on account to the various officers of the household. It is determined that all his debts, while Prince of Prussia, are to be paid; that the Prince Royal shall have an establishment, and a table of ten covers; that the Princess Frederica shall have another, equal to the establishment of the Queen; and that the period when these arrangements are to take place is to be after the statements of expense have been formed.

The army is discontented.

1. Because the King appears on the parade only once a week.

2. Because commissions of major and lieutenant

colonel are multiplied to satiety (for example, all the captains who have been in actual service have obtained them; this is the second chapter of titles, and patents of nobility, by scores) ; a favor which never was formerly granted, not even at the solicitation of the greatest princes.

3. Because much is talked of, little done; because few are punished, and little is required; and, in a word, because the army does not now, as formerly, absorb the whole attention of the Sovereign.

It does not appear that Manstein diminishes the credit of the aide-de-camp Goltz, who has become a count, and who, in what relates to military affairs, has evidently more influence than his rivals. He has great abilities, without having such as are necessary to that place, which, in fact, is equivalent to that of minister for the war department.

It is the subject of astonishment to the few men of observation who are attentive to whatever may lead to a knowledge of the moral character of the new King, that he should behave so coldly to one of his aides-de-camp named Boulet, whom I have before several times mentioned. Boulet is a French refugee of no superior understanding; an honest man, with little ambition; a very ordinary engineer, though here a distinguished one, because here there are none. He has been twenty years attached to the Monarch, but never was admitted a party in his secret pleasures, which were formerly almost necessary to support the solitude of Potsdam and the hatred of the late King. He neither increases nor diminishes in favor, and his influence is almost a nullity. Such a repugnance for a man of some consequence in his profession, and who neither can offend nor disgust, is enigmatical.

It is nearly certain that the capitation plan will be rejected. This hasty expedient would not have been

a substitute equal to their wants. But you must feel
how much so many variations will diminish all confidence in the subaltern and concealed administrators,
who act instead of the ministers; and how every circumstance occurs to render a prime minister necessary.
Nothing seems determined on except a desire to
change. There is no system; for I cannot call the
vague desire of easing the people by that term; nor
any regular plans, formed from knowledge, examina-
tion, and reflection.

None of the difficulties, for example, had been foreseen that arise from the suppression of the monopoly
and administration of tobacco, which afforded an
asylum to twelve hundred invalids, army subalterns,
and even lieutenants. These invalids must live, and be
maintained by the King. Nor is this all. Shares in
the tobacco company originally cost a thousand
crowns, and brought in eleven per cent; the price afterward rose to fourteen hundred crowns. The contract
granted by the late King was to be in force to the
year 1793. Should the King buy in these shares, at a
thousand crowns each, this would be unjust; since
they have been purchased at fourteen hundred, on the
faith of a contract of which seven years are unexpired.
If he should pay interest for them, at the rate of eight
per cent till the year 1793, he must then himself become a loser. Would it not have been better not to
have made any change till the contract should expire
of itself, or till he had found a proper substitute?
The effects which are the representatives of the capital, consist in utensils, warehouses, houses, carriages,
etc., etc. These cannot all be sold without a loss,
which must likewise fall on the King. The monopoly
was burdened with pensions, bestowed on persons by
whom they had been merited; or, if you please, obtained for that very affair which paid those pensions.

They must hereafter be discharged by some other fund, etc.

Heaven forbid I should pretend such difficulties ought not to be surmounted! Improvement would then be accomplished. But they ought to have been foreseen, which they have not; so that the public only perceives, in this suppression, a real evil in return for an unasked good. This mania to undersell the smugglers, or to destroy illicit trade, if great care be not taken, will be more injurious to the people than the trade itself was to the State. Opposition to contraband trade ought to be the consequence of one comprehensive system; and those are short-sighted views which endeavor to correct partial abuses, that appertain to the general vices of administration. The refining of sugar, the fabricating of arms, silk, gauze, stuffs, cloths, in a word, whatever relates to industry, all are directed by regulations destructive to commerce. But may all this vanish by a single act of volition? Impossible; without producing convulsions in the State. And thus the truth and benevolence discredited, and kings discouraged. Woe to him who pulls down without precaution!

The principles of the two Kings, concerning their personal dignity, appear to be so different as to give room for reflection, relative to this country. When Frederick II. established the coffee monopoly, the citizens of Potsdam were daring enough to load a cart with coffeepots and coffeemills, to drive it through the town and overturn it into the river. Frederick, who was a spectator of this burlesque procession, opened his window and laughed heartily. Here we have an anecdote of him whom they call the Tiberius of Prussia. The following is another of the Prussian Titus:

The day before yesterday, the clerk of a merchant,

named Olier, was imprisoned; and he was not informed, till the morning after, that the cause of his imprisonment was some trifling speech relative to the King; and that, should he commit a similar offense, the dungeon would give a good account of him! Such are the first fruits of a gloomy internal administration, of which the vanity and poverty of mind of the King have been productive. What a foreboding of tyranny, —whether it be royal, or, which is worse, subaltern! Under what circumstances, and in what a country! There, where the master, whose vanity is so irascible, wishes to appear good; and where there is no counterpoise to his power, in the public opinion; for the public has no opinion!

The commission of inquiry, sitting on Launay, remains silent, retards its proceedings, forces or seeks for facts, and decides on nothing. Du Bosc is very industrious. Two merchants are arrived from each province, who are to give their advice, relative to the best manner of rendering trade flourishing. It is not yet known here that, though merchants only should be trusted with the execution of a commercial plan, they never should be consulted concerning a general system; because their views and their interests are always partial. One of them, however, has given advice which is very sage, in the present state of affairs; and that is to forbid the silk manufactories, which are all on the royal establishment, to make any but plain silks. Should they determine so to do, the King of Prussia may supply Sweden, Poland, and a part of Russia.

The Princess Elizabeth, the divorced consort of the King, has requested to have a place five miles from Berlin, and that his Majesty would appoint the ladies and gentlemen who shall be her attendants. It is supposed that the attempts this Princess makes have been

suggested to her by an adroit and intriguing officer;
but it is not she who will become formidable to the
Queen, though I really dare not say so much for Mademoiselle Voss. What must be the destiny of a
country which soon is to be divided among priests,
mystics, and prostitutes?

In despite of all my diligence to divine what is in
treaty with the Court of Vienna, I can only form conjectures. However, when I reflect that the Prussian
Ambassador to Austria is an incapable person, Count
Podewils; and that the Emperor's Ambassador, Prince
Reuss has not altered his conduct; that Prince Henry,
though generally ill-informed, would have some positive intelligence, if anything positive had been done,
and that he has only vague suspicion,—I scarcely can
believe any important or probable revolution is on the
tapis. Did the Prince (Henry) possess but one of the
twenty wills of which he is composed, and which do
not all form the equivalent of a whole, so that he could
expend his money properly, and act with consistency,
his superior information must give him a great ascendency in the Cabinet.

But why do we not rid ourselves of this complication of political affairs, by at once changing our
foreign system, and breaking down the only opposing
barrier? I mean to say, by respectable arrangements
and sincere advances. Why do we not stifle commercial jealousy, that mother of national animosity, which
has silenced good sense, and pompously predicted,
supported by the sophisms of mercantile cupidity, that
total ruin, whether it be for France or England, must
be the result of the unfavorable balance to which a
freedom of trade could not fail to give birth? Is it,
then, so difficult to demonstrate that the trade of
France might be much more advantageous to Great
Britain than that of any other country, and *vice versa?*

Who that will but open his eyes will not see the reason? It is in the will of Nature, by which those monarchies are nearer each other than they are to other countries. The returns of the trade which might be carried on between the southern coast of England and northwest of France might take place five or six times a year, as in the more internal commerce. The capital employed in this trade might therefore, in both countries, be productive of five or six times its present quantity of industry, and might afford employment and subsistence to six times as many inhabitants as the same capital could effect in most other branches of foreign trade. Between those parts of France and Great Britain which are most distant from each other, the returns might at least be made once a year; and would consequently be thrice as profitable as the trade, formerly so much vaunted, with North America; in which the returns usually took place only once in three, and very frequently only once in four or five years. The sage Smith asks, "If we consider its population, wants, and wealth, is not France at least a market eight times more extensive (for England), and, by reason of its quick returns, twenty-four times more advantageous than ever was that of the English colonies of North America?" It is not less, or rather, it is more evident that the trade with Great Britain would be in an equal degree useful to France, in proportion to the wealth, population, and proximity of the two countries. It would eventually have the same superiority over that which France has made with her colonies. Oh, human folly! What labors do we undertake to deprive ourselves of the benefits of Nature! How prodigious a difference between that trade which the politics of the two nations have thought it right to discourage, and that which has been the most favored! It appears to me that a work which should develop these ideas, and which begin no longer to be thought monstrous by the English, would be very useful, and could not be intrusted to a man of too great abilities.

POSTSCRIPT.—I have circumstantial evidence that the King is more than ever indolent. Letters are answered in eight or ten days, and in a more long and careful manner than under the late King; which sufficiently proves that secretaries have great interference. Yet what must we say of a Cabinet in which the King never acts, although it is impossible to cite any minister whose influence has effected such or such a thing? Even into the assembly of the general directory, which sits twice a week, the King never comes. And this is the King who wishes to change the fiscal system! None but a Hercules can cleanse the Augean stables.

LETTER LI

November 28th, 1786.

PEOPLE are not agreed concerning the kind of services which the committee of merchants, convoked from the different provinces, may render Government. These good folks are highly astonished to hear themselves consulted on affairs of State; for there is as great a distance between them and Mont-Audouin and Prémores, as there is between the Prussian Ministers and our Sully and Colbert. The question should be to reverse the general and fundamental system, and they seek only palliatives. The blood is infected, and instead of purifying it, they endeavor but to heal this or that ulcer. They will inflame the gangrene, and render the virus more envenomed.

There are great disputes concerning the manufac-

tures. But, good God! ought they to begin with these?
And, should they well and clearly have determined
which were necessary to preserve, and which to
neglect, ought they not, before they prescribe rules, to
assume as a *datum*—that Berlin is not a place for
manufacturers; because that the dearness of the labor,
local, and national inconveniences, etc., etc., are there
united; and because that the establishment of manufactures must there become a disastrous extravagance?
for which reason the manufacturers themselves carry
on a contraband trade, and sell French for Prussian
stuffs. As they have no competitors, they affix what
price they please on their merchandise; and, as nothing
is easier than to smuggle, they take a part of their
goods to the fairs of Frankfort, which they sell or do
not sell, as it shall happen, and purchase Lyons silks,
to which they affix Berlin stamps, and enter them
without any other precaution, or the least risk: since
the customhouse officers of the barriers, who are invalids either of the Court or army, cannot distinguish
whether what is shown them is taffeta or satin; still
less, whether it be woven at Lyons or Berlin. This
city neither possesses industry, emulation, taste,
genius, nor money, to effect such changes. Another
age, and I know not how many transitions among the
Germans, are necessary for them to imitate that luxury
of embellishment for which they have the folly to
wish. Incapable of choosing between that which is
possible and proper, and that which is chimerical and
injurious, without means, principles, or system, the
present attempts of these men, to which they owe their
ephemeral existence, will have no other effect than
that of leading, the King first, and afterward the
vulgar and the foolish, to believe that the evil is irreparable.

The inheritance of the margraviate of Schwedt is

an affair at this moment, which, in other hands, might have important consequences. The Margrave approaches his end. After the partition of Poland, the late King wrote to his brother, Prince Henry, that he was desirous of bestowing on him a peculiar mark of his friendship and gratitude, for the service he had rendered the State. Frederick thought he should have rid himself of his promise by a statue; but he was privately given to understand that fame was left to the care of posterity, and that the present question was an increase of possession. A few months afterward, the Margrave of Schwedt, brother of the present Margrave died; the King seized the occasion to release himself from his word. In a very authentic patent, and at a long term, he conferred on Prince Henry the reversion of the margraviate, on condition that he should discharge all the burdens with which this great fief is loaded. Frederick dies, and his successor declares that all survivances, and donations *in futuro,* etc., are null, and that he will not confirm them. Prince Henry finds himself among the number of those on whom reversions were bestowed. There is little probability these lands will be given him. The question is, will he or will he not have any compensation?

Prince Henry certainly has pretenses to exclaim against ingratitude, and exclaim he will. There it will end. Melancholy mad at one moment, he will rave the next; and thus, giving vent to his griefs, will save his life; for mute affliction only is dangerous.

Those, however, who are not among his partisans, will observe this proceeding with the greatest inquietude, because it begins to appear that even the personal promises of the King are susceptible of wavering. I spoke to you in one of my dispatches of the restitution of some *bailliages* to the Duke of

Mecklenburg, which had been promised to the envoy
of the Duke by the King himself. He has since withdrawn, or at least suspended, his promise. So much
facility in departing from recent engagements, combined with the clamors of the people, and the exclusive
contracts that are trodden under foot without pity,
appear to be but ill omens. It has been inserted, for
example, BY COMMAND, in the public papers, "that the
King declares to all the army clothiers that, from
paternal motives,"—all of which have been announced
with emphasis, as you will see in every gazette,—"the
King annuls their contracts; even those that have been
recently confirmed." Which clause is the more
gratuitously odious and absurd, as he had not confirmed anyone; he therefore, need not have taken the
trouble SOLEMNLY to inform his subjects that he knew
very well how, when occasion should serve, SOLEMNLY
to break his word.

The King spoke to me yesterday concerning the
woolen manufactory. I endeavored to make him
understand that, before we pulled down our house,
we should know where to find a lodging, or how we
might dispose of the ruins. He answered me, laughing, "Oh! Schmits is your banker." (He is the con-
tractor for this manufactory.) "Very true, Sire,"
replied I; "but he has not hitherto made me a present
of the money which has been remitted ıe through his
hands." This may show you what engines are set at
work to keep me at a distance. The following is a
more circumstantial proof:

I was six days very ill, and did not make my appearance at Court, which I the less regretted because that
nothing is learned in such grand company. The day
before yesterday, the King said at his Lotto, "Where
is the Comte de Mirabeau? It is an age since I saw
him." "That is not astonishing, Sire," said one of the

household. "He passes his time at the house of Struensee, with Messrs. Biester and Nicolai." You must understand that Biester and Nicolai are two learned Germans, who have written much against Lavater and the mystics; that they never enter the house of, nor are they, as I believe, personally acquainted with, Struensee. The intention was to lead the King to suppose I was an anti-mystic.

The appointment of Count Charles Brühl to the place of Governor of the Prince Royal has made the party more than ever triumphant. To the merit of appertaining to that honorable sect, Count Leppel, the most incapable and ridiculous of men, is indebted for his Swedish Embassy; as are Baron Doernberg for favors of every kind, Prince Frederick for his intimacy, the Duke of Weimar, the brother of the Margrave of Baden, and the Prince of Dessau for their success, and the courtiers that surround the King for their influence and favor. It looks like a tacit confederacy, and that there is a determination to admit none but proved and fervent sectaries into administration. No one dares combat them; everybody bows before them. The slaves of the Court and the city, who were not the first to yield, mutter disapprobation, and, by degrees, will range themselves on the side of the prevailing party.

There is no parasite, however great, that attempts to excuse the prostitution of titles, patents of nobility, ribbons, academical places, and military promotions, which daily is aggravated. Seventeen majors, for example, have been made, merely in acquittal of vague and inconsiderate promises; and that there may be the semblance of recollecting, at LITTLE expense, hopes that he had been given when every LITTLE aid was acceptable.

The King makes himself too public not to talk very

idly. It would be better that, at the commencement of a reign, the Prussian Monarch should not find time daily to have a tiresome concert, or a more languid Lotto; especially when the world knows the nothings, or the worse, that employ his mornings. He more and more every day, constitutes himself the redresser of the wrongs committed by his uncle. Those colonels or generals that were dismissed return to the army with the promotions or appointments that recompense their sufferings. The counselors that formerly were degraded, concerning the affair of the miller Arnold, have been reinstated in their functions. To say the truth, their punishment was one of the most iniquitous of the acts of Frederick II. But his principal victim, the Chancellor Fürst, has hitherto been forgotten. His great age, indeed, will not permit him to occupy any post. But some solemn mark of good will, some flattering recompense of strict justice, while so many other recompenses are granted, which are favors that are often more than suspicious—would this be impossible?

Under the late reign, the mines solely depended on the minister of that department. An arrangement has just been made, according to which four tribunals, erected in the provinces, greatly moderate his authority; and this was very necessary in a country where the public right of the mines was the most revolting tyranny. But the arrangement does not announce the disgrace of Heinitz. He has, on the contrary, had several new departments committed to his charge within this fortnight; and particularly some that belonged to Schulemburg. It is a part of the plan to restore all things to the state in which they were left by Frederick William in 1740. This criticism on the last reign may be vengeance dearly purchased. At least it is necessary to be consistent; and, since the grand directory has been restored according to its first institution, it ought not to be left in indolence, and in a state of humiliating insufficiency. The dismission of the Minister Gaudi is reported, who is the man by whom Government might best profit, if he were employed. This conspiracy against capacity and knowledge, with good reason, alarms those who know the persons that inspire predilection.

If I am not mistaken, there is here, at this moment, an acquisition to be made, worthy of the King of France, and M. de Calonne is the very man who ought to lay the proposal before his Majesty. The illustrious La Grange, the greatest mathematician that has appeared since Newton, and who, by his understanding and genius, is the man in all Europe who has most astonished me; La Grange, the most sage, and perhaps the only true practical philosopher that has ever existed; worthy to be commended for the pertinacious calmness of his mind, his manners, and his conduct; in a word, a man affectionately respected by the small number of men whom he would admit to be of his acquaintance; this La Grange has lived twenty years at Berlin, whither he was invited, in his youth by the late King, to succeed Euler, who had himself pointed him out as the only man proper to be his successor. He is much disgusted, silently but irremediably disgusted, because that his disgust originates in contempt. The passions, brutalities, and lunatic boastings of Hertzberg; the addition of so many as Academicians with whom La Grange cannot, without blushing, associate; the very prudent dread of seeing himself held in painful suspense, between the philosophic repose which he regards as the first good, and that respect which he owes himself, and which he will not suffer to be insulted; all induce him to retire from a country where the crime of being a foreigner is not to be forgiven, and where he will not support an existence which will only be tolerated. It cannot be doubted but that he would willingly exchange the sun and the coin of Prussia for the sun and the coin of France, the only country on earth where men pay homage to the genius of science, and confer lasting fame; the only country where La Grange, the grandson of a Frenchman, and who gratefully recollects that we have made him known to Europe, would delight to live, if he must renounce his old friends and the abode of his youth. Prince Cardito di Laffredo, Ambassador from Naples to Copenhagen, has made him the handsomest offers, in the name of his Sovereign. He has received pressing invitations from the Grand Duke and the King of Sardinia. But all these proposals would easily be forgotten, if put in competition with ours. And will not the King of France likewise, aided by a worthy comptroller general, at the time when he would extend that empire of benevolence which appertains to him alone—would not the King of France endeavor to acquire a man whose merit is known to all Europe? La Grange here receives a pension of six thousand livres. And cannot the King of France dedicate that sum to the first mathematician of the age? Is it beneath Louis XVI. to invite a great man, from a miserable academy, who is there misunderstood, misallied, and thus, by the most noble warfare, to extirpate the only literary corps that has wrestled against his proper academies? Would not this act of generosity be superior to those that are usually performed? France, with pernicious policy, has been the asylum of Princes, with whose necessities she was burdened. Why will she not welcome a great man who would but add to her worth? Has she so long enriched others with her losses, and will she not enrich herself by others' errors? In fine, to speak of the Minister I love, one De Boynes has given eighteen thousand livres a year, for a useless place, to one Boscovich,—a man despised by all the learned of Europe, as a literary quack of poor abilities; and why will not M. de Calonne grant a pension of two thousand crowns to the first man in Europe of his class, and probably to the last genius the mathematical sciences shall possess; the passion for which diminishes, because of the excessive difficulties that are to be surmounted, and the infinitely few means of acquiring fame by discovery?

I have the hope exceedingly at heart, because I think it a noble one, and because I tenderly love the man. I entreat I may have an immediate answer; for I own I have induced M. de la Grange to suspend his declarations on the propositions that have been made him, till he has heard what ours may be. I need not repeat that—he whose hands are tied must call for help.

LETTER LII

December 2d, 1786.

ON THE 29th, between one and two o'clock, a person from Courland came to me and asked for the Baron de Noldé. He said he was charged with some secret commission, and delivered him a letter from M. Rummel, his brother-in-law, a Syndic of the nobility, and fifty Prussian gold Fredericks. The letter desired Noldé would give faith to what the bearer should relate, and informed him that the regency of the Republic intended to confer on him the place of assessor, if he would repair to Courland that he might be put in nomination; and that the appointment was to be made at the beginning of the year. The bearer of the letter said he had known the Baron Noldé when a boy. The Baron supposed him to be an advocate, or a notary, of whom he had some confused idea. He neither told his name, where he lodged, how he traveled, when he came to Berlin, nor where he was going. Hamburg, Lübeck, Vienna, Munich, etc., are places through which he has passed, or means to pass. His journey has been very secret, very enigmatical, very mysterious. He only gave it to be understood that great changes would soon be seen in Courland, and that Woronzow was there to enact a grand part, of which he spoke so as to make it suspected he might become Duke. Such are the chief points of this odd interview.

We must combine this with the return of the Duke, who arrived three days ago, and with innumerable indications which demonstrate that a revolution is either in agitation or preparing in Courland. Consternation has seized on the Duke. It is only whispered, but it appears evident that the States have stopped the payment of his revenues, because he does not expand the money in the country; and this is the least of the griefs, entertained at Petersburg, against this detested man. Certain it is that he has sent his wife, who is far advanced in her pregnancy, to Mittau, whither he dares not return himself; hoping she shall be delivered of a male child, and that this presumptive heir will reconcile him to his country.

Add, further, that Baron Noldé is of one of the first houses of Courland; that his uncle, the Chamberlain Howen, a capable and enterprising man, is at present first Minister or Land Marshal; that all affairs pass through his hands, and that he is in the greatest credit; which, to say truth, may be reduced to this : that he has the power of selling, with more or less meanness, this fine but unfortunate province; which, however, should it be abandoned by all its neighbors, cannot act otherwise than to bestow, rather than suffer itself to be seized upon. It is very possible that the family of

Noldé, which knows how much this studious young Baron has continually preferred a civil to a military life, has only thought of placing him advantageously. (The post of assessor, which is worth from four to five thousand livres of Courland, per annum, is the post of preferment.)   But it is equally possible, and, all circumstances considered, very probable, that his assistance is wished for in effecting a revolution.

This young Baron is possessed of honor, information, and understanding; has a great respect for the rights of mankind, an utter hatred for the Russians, and an ardent desire his country should rather appertain to any other Power. From his infancy the sport of chance, ruined by misfortunes of every kind, which all had a worthy origin; disgusted with the gloomy rank of subaltern officer, which impedes the progress of his studies, and moderate in his desires, he would accept a place which should bestow on him the *otium cum dignitate;* but he would not be the slave of Russia. He loves France, and is attached to me, to whom he thinks himself obliged. He is desirous of serving his country, the Cabinet of Versailles, and his friend. The indecision of his mind must have been afflicting, especially under circumstances when, laboring for these six months like a galley slave, and certainly in a manner more useful than had he been mounting guard, you have even neglected to prolong his furlough. This, at least, was perplexing. I have decided for him.

Making myself responsible for this prolongation, which it would be so iniquitous to refuse, and which surely will be granted if it be only out of respect to me, who find his coadjutorship necessary; imagining he still has the right of returning into Courland by throwing up his commission, or even without throwing it up, by suffering another nomination to take place; convinced that no one can inform us more exactly of the situation of the country in which he has so many relations; persuaded that this is an important step for several reasons, the principal of which I shall presently demonstrate, and not believing (independent of the expense of a journey of more than four hundred leagues) that I should be justified in absenting myself without having received express orders; confiding in the honor of this affectionate young gentleman, as well because of the recommendations of those to whom he is intimately known, as from having myself proved his principles and his conduct; and still farther convinced that confidence is the most powerful of motives with men of honor,—I have thought it the most prudent mode to suffer him immediately to depart on his promise of sending me information of whatever passes, and of returning to Berlin within two months. It has seemed to me that this will conciliate his interest and ours,—the latter because we shall be perfectly informed of whatever we wish to know concerning Courland, of which many things are to be learned, and by which step, at all events, we shall make a party in the country, where the simple title of consul, or the permission only of wearing our uniform, with a small pension, will secure to us a man of merit, should he determine to accept the offers of the regency; first, because Baron Noldé will inform himself, by this journey, what is the degree of stability and profit of the place they propose for him, and because, if he be not satisfied with this, he may again return to the service of France, with the recommendation of additional labors and strong zeal in her behalf; and, should he be satisfied with the offers of Courland, he may accept them, while we may better his situation and augment his respect and safety, by suffering him to wear our uniform, etc., etc.

Summarily, this young gentleman, who has served at the sieges of Port-Mahon and Gibraltar; who is esteemed and beloved by his commanders; who for six months has labored, under my direction, with uncommon zeal, and assiduity not less uncommon; I repeat, this gentleman would certainly merit such a mark of favor, though it had been on his own business solely that he had made a journey into Courland. But the truth is I send him thither because I am strongly invited by circumstances, and am convinced of two things. First, that were it only perfectly to understand this part of the politics of Russia, it is of importance to us at once to know at what to estimate the worth and destiny, as well as the changes of which this country is susceptible; which, independent of all interior circumstances, stands by situation the sentinel of Poland and of the Baltic, now that Sweden, our arm of the north, is so seriously menaced. My second conviction is that Baron Noldé is the most proper of men faithfully to send us this information. Wherefore not afford him aid? Wherefore not preserve such persons?

You must have seen, but perhaps you have not remarked, in the thirty-second abstract from the gazettes, that Springporten, formerly a colonel in the service of Sweden, has lately entered into the service of Russia, with the rank of major general; that he is the man who best knows Finland; that the Empress has granted him three thousand roubles for his equipment, an estate of six hundred peasants, in White Russia, and the key of chamberlain; that he is incessantly to make a journey into the Crimea, etc., etc. Though by acquiring such men, with the knowledge and connections which they bring with them, preparations are made for the execution of the greatest projects, still, by the same methods, such projects are rendered abortive.

There was not time, last post, to write the postscript in cipher, which contains a curious fact, of which Panchand will probably make use and application.

I informed you in No. VI. that " they have lately interdicted discounting bills of exchange at the bank, etc." This fact has not been verified. The merchants indeed required it might be done, but their request has not been granted, and it was opposed by Struensee. But to the news of the day.

There are two versions concerning Mademoiselle Voss. Both are derived from excellent sources, and probably the real one will be that which may be composed from the two.

1. There will be no marriage. Mademoiselle will depart in a month, for I know not where; and afterward will return to Potsdam. " I know," said she, " that I dishonor myself. All the compensation I ask is not to see any person; leave me in profound solitude; I neither wish for riches nor splendor." It is certain that, if she can keep him thus, she will lead him much the farther.

2. Wednesday, the 22d of last month, was the remarkable day on which Mademoiselle Voss accepted the King's hand, and promised him her own. It was determined the Queen should be brought to approve the plan of the left-handed marriage as a thing of necessity, should she obstinately display too much repugnance. It is singular that, for the consummation of this rare business, the arrival of the Duke of Saxe-Weimar was waited for, who is the brother-in-law of the Queen. The King thus will be father to four sorts of children. The priests, who have been consulted on the manner of reconciling the claims of heaven with the pleasures of earth, have decided that it will be better to concentrate his enjoyments by an extraordinary marriage than incessantly to wander from er-

ror to error. Nothing has transpired concerning the manner in which this arrangement is to be made known to the uncles; of the name the new Princess is to bear; or of her future establishment, etc., etc. In all probability she soon will interfere in public affairs; and, should she do so, the credit of Bishopswerder will diminish. She loves neither him nor his daughters. Her party is, besides, very opposite to that of the mystics, which gains ground in a very fearful manner. I am going to relate a recent anecdote on that subject which happened in the last months of Frederick II., and which it is infinitely important, at least for my security while I remain here, to keep secret; of the irrevocable authenticity of which you yourself will judge; and which will show you whither tends this imaginary theory of the mystics connected with the Rosicrucian-Freemasons, whom among us some look upon with pity, and others treat as objects of amusement.

There is a rumor whispered about which terrifies worthy people, and which, true or false, is a faithful indication of the public opinion. It is affirmed that Prince Henry, the Duke of Brunswick, and General Moellendorf, mean to quit the army. The two first probably do not yet think of such a step; but the latter is indubitably the most discontented of the three. Rich, loyal, simple, firm, he possesses virtues which would do honor to a soil on which virtue is more fruitful. He certainly has not been treated either as he himself expected, or as good citizens have wished. They were desirous, indeed, to create him a count; but among so many counts, what need had he of such a title? For which reason this respectable man replied, "WHAT HAVE I DONE?" This artless, noble question was too severe—on the herd of nobles and the multitude of titles that have sprung up, warmed by the breath of royal munificence—to be agreeable. His modest and antique manners are become reproachful to the Court; yet is the only reform truly beneficial and universally approved, under the new reign, the work of this general. I mean the abolition of that iniquitous contribution called GRASS FORAGE, which subjected the open country to pillage, during three months of the year, under the pretense of accustoming the cavalry to forage. He has not since been consulted on any subject, or he has had no influence. I should not be surprised should he retire to his country seat; and it is impossible to exaggerate the unamiable light in which such a tacit profession of faith would place the King and his Government.

Three months more of similar proceedings, and he will have no respect to lose,—at least, in his own country. Every corrupt symptom is manifest. Rietz, a rascal, avaricious, chief pimp, and an avowed *Giton,* insomuch that *ipse confitetur, sibi cum Rege, dum princeps Borussiæ esset, apud eius amicam stupri commercium fuisse.* In a word, Rietz, the vilest and the most debased of men, manages the royal household, and enjoys a great part of the Court favor. Here it ought to be noted that he is very susceptible of being bought; but he must be dearly bribed, for he is covetous and prodigal, and his fortune is to make, should ever France have occasion to direct the Cabinet of Berlin. So long as the King shall have any power, Rietz and Prince Frederick of Brunswick are the two men most liable to temptation.

The following is an anecdote of a very low species, but very characteristic for those who know the country. The Italian and French dancers have received orders to dance twice a week, at the German theater. The purport of such a capricious injunction was to give disgust to this species of people, who are expensive enough, and to find a pretense for dismissing them. They have been well advised, and will dance; but such is the low spirit of cunning which presides over the administration. Politics are treated as wisely as theatrical matters.

I this moment learned that Heinitz, one of the Ministers of State, a man of mediocrity, but laborious, has written a letter to the King, of which the following is nearly the sense: " Being a foreigner, not possessed of any lands in your States, my zeal cannot be suspected by your Majesty. It is consequently my duty to inform you that the projected capitation tax will alienate the hearts of Your Majesty's subjects; and proves that the new regulators of the finances are, at present, little versed in public business." The King said to him two days after, " I thank you," and made no further inquiries. Irresolution does not exclude obstinacy, although obstinacy is far from being resolution. I should not be astonished were the tobacco and snuff company to remain on its former footing. As for the respect which government should preserve, that must take care of itself.

It was an attempt similar to that of Heinitz which produced the last military promotion, to the disadvantage of General Moellendorf. The General wrote, with respectful but firm dignity, against the nomination of Count Brühl, and entreated the King would show less indifference for the army. Thanks were returned, accompanied with these words: " The place has been promised a year and a half"; and two days after seventeen majors were created. Since this time, coldness toward the General has increased, and civility has been substituted for confidence. The letter is not thought well of. It is said that he ought to have reserved this vigorous blow for some occasion on which he should not appear to be personally interested; and it is he himself who seemed most proper to fill the place of governor.

The Duke of Weimar is preparing to make a very pompous wolf hunt, on the frontiers of Poland. The orders and adjustments for this party of pleasure do not very well agree with the projects and ceremonials of economy. Twelve hundred peasants are commanded to be in readiness; sixty horses have been sent, and eight baggage wagons, with the masters of the forests, gentlemen, huntsmen, and cooks for this hunt, which is to continue six days.

At present, I am nearly certain that my second version, relative to Mademoiselle Voss, is the true one; and that the Queen is coaxed into the measure. The King never lived on better terms with her. He has often visited her within this week, pays her debts, and has given her a concert. Probably she has made a virtue of necessity. It appears evident that this connection of the King highly deranges the plan of the mystic administrators. The family of Mademoiselle Voss wishes to profit by her elevation; and their advice no way agrees with that of the present favorites. Bishopswerder, far from gaining upon the King, declines in his esteem. In a word, revolution may come from that side. Will public affairs be the gainer? This question it is impossible to answer. We can only turn the telescope toward the spot; or rather the microscope; for, in truth, we are in the reign and the country of the infinitely minute.

[Postscript, mentioned in the body of the letter.]

The current coins in Poland were formerly as follows: The mark of fine silver of the Cologne weight was coined at 13-3 r. or 80 fl. of Poland.

As to gold coins, there were none but Dutch ducats that had any nominal value; that is to say——

At the royal treasuries, they were taken for 16¼ k.

By the public, for 18 k.; both of which rates were fixed by decrees of the Diet.

In the Diet of 1786, the ducats were universally raised to 18 k. each.

The assay of the silver consequently cannot any longer be maintained; and it is affirmed there is a determination, hereafter, to coin the fine mark at 14 r. or 84 fl.

But neither can this coinage support itself; for, should Berlin coin at 14 r., Poland will be obliged to keep up an equal value at a greater expense, because of carriage.

Under the present circumstances, it might be advantageous to draw on Poland for ducats at 3 r. if the assay of silver is at 14 r.

But, if the relative value of gold should fall, comparatively to that of silver, silver may be there bought with profit.

Generally speaking, it appears to me that the recent operations on gold should lead us to reflect on the state of the silver, especially in Spain, should that power persist in the folly which, with the greatest part of Europe, it has given into, of keeping two species of coin, and hoarding the gold.

SECOND POSTSCRIPT.—The King, attended by a single lackey and much disguised, has been to the corn and straw warehouses, where he inquired of the soldiers who worked there what their wages were. "Five groschen." A moment after he put the same question to the superintendents. " Six groschen." Three soldiers being called to confront the superintendents, and the fraud being proved, a subaltern and three soldiers

were ordered to conduct the two superintendents to
Spandau, a civil prison; and there they are to be tried.
The fact is very praiseworthy. He makes evening
peregrinations almost unattended, and addicts himself
to the minute inquiries of a justice of the peace. At
least this is the third time he has acted thus. Some of
his attendants imagine he means to imitate the Emperor. After what has passed between them, this
perhaps would be the most severe symptom of absolute
incapacity.

LETTER LIII

December 5th, 1786.

THE news of the cabals, which the Emperor again
wishes to excite at Deux-Ponts, and which our
Cabinet has published here, seem to have produced a
very good effect upon the King, in despite of those
who exclaim, *Ne crede Teucris*—an adage which is
become the signal of rallying among the English,
Dutch, anti-French, etc., etc. May we conduct ourselves so as never to admit of any other reproach.
This discovery will probably, both at Berlin and Deux-
Ponts, counteract the Emperor. It was very ill-judged
of him not to suffer that torpor to increase, which is
the infallible consequence of the languor of labor, or
of the confusion which doing nothing produces.

But I resign these foreign politics to your ambassadors, to whom they are known, because I gained this
intelligence by that means only by which I gain all
other; because Comte d'Esterno did not say a word
on the subject to me; because it would have been weak
and little decent to have put many questions on a
matter which I ought to have known; and because I,

therefore, satisfied myself with vague annotations on our fidelity. I am not, and probably shall not be, circumstantially informed of the affair. You, perhaps, may feel on this occasion how important it is that better intelligence should be sent me from Versailles; but you will doubtless acknowledge I perform all I can, all I ought, when I trace the outlines of internal —since I have not the key to external—politics; though assuredly I shall not neglect the latter whenever lucky chance shall afford opportunities.

The libellist Crantz, who was expelled the country by Frederick II. for theft, and for having sold the same horse three times, is recalled, with a pension of eight hundred crowns. The King wrote to Count Hertzberg to give him some post. The Minister replied that the abilities of the gentleman were great, and that he was very estimable, but that he had too little discretion to be employed in foreign affairs. The King proposed him to the Minister Werder, who answered, the gentleman was exceedingly intelligent, exceedingly capable, but that there was money in his office, which, therefore, M. Crantz must not be suffered to enter. At last, the King has thrown the illustrious Crantz, praised by all and by all rejected, upon the States; and he receives a pension of eight hundred crowns for doing nothing.

The Minister Schulemburg, after having twice demanded his dismissal, has finally obtained it, without a pension. This is severe; but the ex-Minister is adroit. He has cast all the burden upon the first branch of his department, which has been retrenched. If there are any means of being restored, this was well done. You are acquainted with the qualities of this man. He had understanding, facility, and sagacity in the choice of his coadjutors; was indifferent concerning the means he employed; vain in prosperity; despairing in misfortune, of which his feelings are the sport; ready to serve others; susceptible of affection, and believing in friendship after having been fifteen years Minister of Frederick II. He thought himself immovable because he was necessary, and hopes that this necessity will surmount the cabals by which he has been driven from his post. Perhaps he deceives himself; for, while we are not difficult in our choice, and when the business is not of itself beyond vulgar capacities, agents may at any time be found. If monarchs wish for a Newton, they certainly must employ a Newton, or the place must remain vacant. But who is there who does not think himself capable of being a minister, and of whom may it be demonstrated he is not capable?

I am assured, from a good quarter, that Count Hertzberg regains confidence. He has bowed to the new agents, who have had the weakness to bring him again into favor because Mademoiselle Voss is the niece of Count Finckenstein, and because, her family being unable to obtain any advantage by her promotion except by the overthrow of those who surround the King, who are not ignorant that the lady detests them, it is requisite some one should be opposed to her. But, if she be a dame of mettle, change must be looked for on that side, which more or less address will hasten or retard. Whether or no, Hertzberg has advised Count Goertz to take part with Renneval, of whose prudence he has spoken in the highest terms to the King.

A new blunder has been committed in the military. All the first lieutenants have been made captains; and the captains, whether on whole or half pay, of the regiment of guards, are advanced to the rank of major. Except the war chancery, I do not see who will be the gainer by this arrangement. It is said the King intends to pay his personal debts, the payment of which, by the way of parenthesis, is more than ever eluded, with the produce of the commissions of officers, and the diplomas of counts, barons, chamberlains, etc.

The plan for the capitation tax was represented to the King as a kind of voluntary act, and which the people themselves would meet half way; but informed of the public disgust this project had occasioned, alarmed by the rumor, and heated by the letter of Heinitz, he told Werder, " People ought not to meddle with matters they do not understand." (Take good note that this be said to his Minister of Finance). " Launay should have been consulted " (now under the fetters of the commission of inquiry). Werder excused himself in the best manner he could, by saying the plan did not originate with him (in fact, the project was Beyer's), as if he had not appropriated by approving it.

The general directory, that species of Council of State at which the King is never present, has projected remonstrances concerning the humiliating inactivity in which it is held; but Welner opposed them, giving the invincible repugnance of his Majesty for every species of advice to be understood. This arises from the strange supposition that those who give him advice have adopted the sentiments of his uncle, relative to his capacity. He is yet to learn that no one ventures to advise among the great, except such persons as they esteem.

In the meantime the mystics continue in the same degree of favor. Their conspiracy was denounced by the great person whom I spoke of to you in my last, to General Moellendorf, the intimate friend of the brother of Mademoiselle Voss (a man esteemed for his moral character; in other respects obscure, at

least hitherto, yet who probably will soon appear upon
the stage), in order that he might terrify his sister,
and by her intervention the Sovereign, concerning the
crimes of a sect who would sacrifice all whom they
cannot rule. Biester—the same, to say the least, to
whom it has been insinuated that he should spare the
mystics—has a lawsuit in which they are interested,
which it is said he will lose. He has accused M. Starck
of being a Catholic. Starck is a Professor of Jena,
a man celebrated for the gift of persuasion, as well
as for his understanding and knowledge, a Lutheran
born, and a Lutheran minister, but a known professor
of the Catholic religion. He has, notwithstanding,
instituted a criminal action against Biester, for having
said this, and has summoned him to prove his calum-
nious assertion. Never would such a suit have been
heard of under Frederick II. Starck has recently
published a book entitled " Nicaise," in which he attacks Freemasonry. The Freemasons have replied by
another, entitled " Anti-Nicaise," in which are inserted authentic letters from several princes, and,
among others, from Prince Charles of Hesse Cassel,
and Prince Ferdinand of Brunswick; which well prove,
what all know who have conversed with him, should
they not likewise know his creatures, Bauer and Wet-
sall, that a great general, or rather a FAMOUS general,
may be a very little man.

The statement of the expense is at length made out,
and the result is that the King may increase his treasury by two millions of crowns, and still reserve a considerable sum for his pleasures or his affections. But,
in this calculation, it is supposed that following receipts will equal the preceding, which certainly is
doubtful. One paternal act has been performed; the
country people have been freed from the obligation of
lodging the cavalry gratis, and supplying forage at

a very low price. This reform will cost the King two hundred and seventy thousand crowns per annum. But it was extremely necessary. It is the result of the plan of Moellendorf for the abolition of the GREEN FORAGE.

One M. Moulines is the editor of the manuscripts of the late King. I have before given you his political character; and, as a literary man, he is destitute of taste and discernment, and without any profound knowledge of the language. But he is the friend of Welner; of that Welner to whom the King, at seven o'clock in the morning, sends the letters and requests of the day before, and who at four o'clock goes to give his account, or rather to instruct the King. As for the Ministers, they receive orders, and do not give advice. Welner has had the wit to refuse the title of Minister, and to satisfy himself with that of superintendent of the buildings; but he is already fawned upon by the whole Court. These manuscripts are to be printed in eighteen volumes octavo. The two parts most curious are the "History of the Seven Years' War," and the "Memoirs of My Own Times." In the former, Frederick has rather recounted what he ought to have done than what he did; and this is itself a trait of genius. He praises or excuses almost everybody; and blames only himself.

The Marquis of Lucchesini, who had been, not the friend, not the favorite of Frederick, but his LISTENER, is, though he does not own it, highly piqued at the choice made of Moulines. He has demanded leave of absence for six months, to make a journey into his own country, from which, no doubt, he will no more return. How did it happen that he did not feel that the personal respect in which he would have been held would have been immense had he quitted Prussia a week after the death of the King, with this only reply

to all the offers which would have been made him?—
"I was ambitious only of a place which all the Kings on
earth could not take from me, cannot restore; that of
being the friend of Frederick II."

Two successors have been appointed to Count Schulemburg; for, as the King of France has four Ministers, twenty are necessary to the King of Prussia.
One of these successors is M. Moschwitz, a magistrate;
of whom neither good nor harm is spoken. The other
is a Count Schulemburg von Blumbert, the son-in-law
of Count Finckenstein. The latter possesses knowledge, an ardent and gloomy ambition, and a moral
character that is suspected. He is studious, intelligent,
assiduous, and is certainly a capable man. But he is
supposed to want order; to possess rather a heated
brain than an active mind; and to have more opinions
of his own than dexterity to blend them with the
opinions of others and render them successful.
Neither is he at all accustomed to business; and is an
absolute stranger to banking and commercial speculations, that is to say, to the principal branches of his
department.

FIRST POSTSCRIPT.—The King, who is paying off
the debts of his father, has granted twenty thousand
crowns for the maintenance and privy purse of his two
eldest sons. Their household is a separate expense.

SECOND POSTSCRIPT.—I did not believe I was so
good a prophet. The brother of Mademoiselle Voss
has the place of the President Moschwitz. This is
the foot in the stirrup.

The course of exchange on Amsterdam is so exceedingly high that, there being no operation of finance or
of commerce by which it may be accounted for, I have
no doubt but remittances are made to pay off the

personal debts of the King. Struensee is of the same opinion; but he has no positive intelligence on the subject.

LETTER LIV

December 8th, 1786.

YOU may take it for granted that there are three principal shades in the character of the King—deceit, which he believes to be art; irascible vanity, whenever the least remonstrance is made to him; and the accumulation of money, which is not so much avarice in him as the passion of possessing. The first of these vices has rendered him suspicious; for he who deceives by system continually imagines he is deceived. The second induces him to prefer people of middling, or inferior abilities; and the latter contributes to make him lead an obscure and solitary life, by which the two former are strengthened. Violent in private, impenetrable in public, little animated by the love of fame in reality, and making this love to consist chiefly in leading the world to suppose he is not governed; rarely troubling himself with foreign politics; a soldier from necessity, and not from inclination; disposed to favor the mystics, not from conviction, but because he believes he shall, by their aid, examine the consciences and penetrate the hearts of men—such is the outline of the man.

His debts will be paid by the surplus money. Under the late King there was annually a considerable sum which was not brought to the Treasury, but was kept apart to raise new regiments, to increase the artillery, or to repair the fortresses. Now, as the artillery was not increased, as new regiments were not raised, and as the fortresses were not repaired, the money consequently accumulated. It is now employed in liquidation.

The revenues are upward of twenty-seven millions of crowns, including the customs; or about a hundred and eight millions of French livres. The expense of the army is twelve millions and a half of crowns; of the civil administration, two millions three hundred thousand crowns; of the King's, the Queen's, and the Princes' household, one million two hundred thousand crowns; and a hundred and thirty thousand for the payment of pensions. I am not acquainted with all the inferior expenses; but when, for example, we know that the legation chest does not absorb more than seventy-five thousand crowns, and that the supplements amount on an average to twenty-five thousand crowns (on which I have to remark that the same object in Denmark costs three millions of crowns; and in Russia, a country almost unknown to the greatest part of Europe, three hundred thousand rubles), it is easy to understand that the sum total of the annual surplus, the expense being deducted from the receipt, is about three millions and a half of crowns.

The manufacturers have presented a petition, in which they supplicate to be informed whether any alterations are intended to be made in the privileges granted them by the late King, or his predecessors, that they may not be exposed to the buying of materials, or contracting agreements which they shall be unable to fulfill. Frederick William has given his word of honor not to make any change, at present, of this kind.

I have already said that the King intended to have made Welner a Minister, which dignity it is affirmed he refused. This for many reasons was a master stroke, by which he will be no loser; for he has lately been granted an augmentation of three thousand crowns, that he may enjoy the same pension as the Ministers of State. The King not only places no confidence in the latter, but he affects never to mention them, unless it be to Count Finckenstein, the uncle of the well-beloved; or to Count Arnim, who interferes in the negotiations of the so much desired marriage, and who is at present too much a stranger to business to be suspected of any system. The supposition that he has one will, at least for some time, be the rock on which the new Schulemburg is liable to be wrecked. He is supported by strength of character and ardor of ambition. As to the new President, to whom already is attributed a depth of design which probably he never possessed, I believe him little capable of enacting any great part.

The Sieur du Bosc, who is become a counselor of finance and of commerce, is also desirous of making his entrance. He has petitioned to be employed in the customs, and his request has been granted, but without an increase of respect. Speculators, joining this symptom to some others, have drawn a conclusion that this is some diminution in the credit of Bishopswerder, his protector. The party of the mystics, however, does but augment and flourish. To own the truth, the crowd of candidates may injure individuals. One of the most zealous members, Drenthal, is lately arrived. No office was found for him under the King; but he has in his interim been placed with the Princess Amelia, in quality of Marshal of the Court, with a promise of not being forgotten at the death of this Princess, whose end approaches.

Our knowledge of the new Sovereign may be increased by a sketch of the most distinguished people at his Court. Among these are an old count (Lendorf), gentle as Philinta, obliging as Bonneau, a shameless flatterer, an unfaithful talebearer, and, when need is, a calumniator. A prince in his pupilage (Holsteinbeck), smoking his pipe, drinking brandy, never knowing what he says, ever talking on what he does not understand, ready at any time to fly to the parade, to hunt, to go to church, to go to brothels, or to go to supper with a lieutenant, a lackey, or Madame Rietz. Another prince (Frederick of Brunswick), famous for the pains he took to dishonor his sister, and particularly his brother-in-law, the present King; a libertine under the Monarch who was called an atheist; at present a mystic, when the Monarch is supposed a devotee; a pensioner of the Freemason lodges, from which he annually receives six thousand crowns; talking nonsense from system; and, for the secrets which he wrests, returning a multitude of half secrets, which are partly invented, and partly useless. A kind of mad captain (Grothaus), who has seen all, had all, done all, known all; the intimate friend of the Prince of Wales; the favorite of the King of England, invited by Congress to be their president, on condition of conquering Canada; master at pleasure of the Cape of Good Hope; the only man capable of settling the affairs of Holland; an author, a dancer, a runner, a jumper, a farmer, botanist, physician, chemist, and lieutenant colonel in the Prussian service, with an income of seven hundred crowns per annum. A minister (Count Arnim), who dreams instead of thinking, smiles instead of replying, reasons instead of determining, regrets at night the liberty he sacrificed in the morning, and wishes at once to remain indolent on his estate, and to acquire the reputation of a minister. A reigning prince (the Duke of Weimar), who imagines he has wit because he can interpret a rebus; is cunning, because he pretends to swallow his own sarcasms; a philosopher, because he has three poets at his Court; and a species of hero, because he rides full speed in search of wolves and boars. Such being his favorites, judge of the man.

Do you wish to estimate his taste by his diversions? Tuesday was the great day on which he went to enjoy the pleasures of the imagination at the German theater. Here, in grand pomp, he was accosted by a dramatic compliment, which concluded with these words: "May that kind Providence that rewards all, all great and good actions, bless and preserve our most gracious King, that august father of his people; bless and preserve all the royal house, and bless and preserve us all! AMEN!" The King was so highly enchanted with this dramatic homily that he has added another thousand crowns to the five thousand which he had granted the manager, and has made him a present of four chandeliers, and twelve glasses to decorate the boxes. Sarcasms innumerable, on the French theater, accompanied this act of generosity.

Would you judge him by military favors? A pension of three hundred crowns has been granted to Captain Colas, who had been eight-and-twenty years imprisoned in the citadel of Magdeburg; and the rank of lieutenant general bestowed on Borck, his Majesty's Governor, who is eighty-two years of age.

Or by his Court favors? The chamberlain's key sent to that extravagant Baron Bagge; who indeed presented a hundred louis to Rietz, and forty to the person who brought him this gift of royal munificence.

It has been insinuated to his Majesty that he had displeased the citizens, on his return from Prussia; the army, from the first day of his reign; the general directory, by rendering it null; his family, by being polite instead of friendly; the priests, by his project of a third marriage; the pensioners, by the suppression of the tobacco monopoly; the Court, by the confusion or the delay in the statement of the accounts; and that, therefore, it might perhaps be imprudent, for the present, in the moment of effervescence, to accept the statue that has been proposed by the city of Königsberg.

And are you desirous of an index to the respect in which he may be held by foreign nations? The Poles have refused a passage to the horses, for remounting the cavalry, coming from the Ukraine. I need not tell you such a refusal would never have been made to Frederick II.

Count Hertzberg pretends he has received letters written against himself, to persons in France, by Prince Henry. He showed them to the King, who made him no reply. I scarcely can believe there is not some fraud in this affair. I know the persons to whom the Prince writes in France; and, treachery out of the question, they certainly are not interested in favor of Count Hertzberg. But whether or no, there are rumors that Hertzberg and Blumenthal are soon to resign; that the latter will be replaced by M. Voss; and the first, who has imagined himself too necessary to be taken at his word, "by a man who will astonish the whole world." (This, it is affirmed, is the phrase of the King himself.) Hertzberg has the knowledge of a civilian, and is well read in archives, because his memory is prodigious. He also knows something of practical agriculture. But, on the reverse, he is violent, passionate, abundantly vain, and explains himself as he conceives, that is to say, with difficulty and confusion; is desirous but incapable of doing that good by which reputation is acquired; rather vindictive than malignant; subject to prejudices; disposed to injure those against whom he is prejudiced; and devoid of dignity, address, and resource.

Blumenthal is a faithful accountant, an ignorant Minister; ambitious, when he recollects ambition, and to please his family; and full of respect for the Treasury, which he places far above the State; and of indifference for the King, whom he more than neglected while he was Prince of Prussia.

The duty has been taken off beer, which yielded five hundred and fifty thousand crowns per annum, and a substitute, it is said, will be found by an additional tax on wines; but wines are already too much taxed, and cannot bear any such increase. The expenses of this part of the customs amount to twenty thousand crowns; sixty-nine persons employed have been dismissed; but their salaries are continued till they shall be replaced.

FIRST POSTSCRIPT.—Count Totleben (a Saxon), who has been appointed major in the regiment of Elben, was preceded by a letter the import of which was that he was sent to the regiment TO LEARN THE SERVICE. The equivoque of the expression is stronger in the German. The regiment wrote in a body to the King: "If Count Totleben be sent to instruct us, we have not merited, nor will we endure, such humiliation. If he come for instruction, he cannot serve as major." Some pretend that the dispute is already settled, and others that it will have consequences.

The King about a month since was reminded of Captain Forcade, who was formerly a favorite of the Prince of Prussia. His Majesty replied: "Let him write what his wishes are." Forcade requested the happiness of being one of his attendants. The King answered: "I have no need of useless officers; they only serve to make a dust."

SECOND POSTSCRIPT.—By the last courier I sent you some calculations on the coins of Poland. Here follow others more absurd, relative to those of Denmark.

Denmark has adopted, according to law, the nominal value of its currency at $11\frac{1}{3}$ crowns for the fine mark of Cologne; yet it has for several years paid from thirteen to fourteen crowns the fine mark. Hence there are no silver coins in Denmark, and business is all transacted in bank bills, the value of which is never to be realized.

When the evil began to be evident, Schimmelmann wished it might be remedied. He coined crowns in specie $9\frac{1}{4}$ of which contained the fine mark, and calculated that the crown in specie was equal to one crown $9\frac{37}{100}$ sols currency *lubs*. The fact would have been true, if the silver currency had existed at $11\frac{1}{3}$ per mark; but as none such were to be found, each person willingly accepted the crowns in specie at one crown nine sols currency; but no one was willing to give a crown in specie for one crown nine sols currency. The result was that all these fine crowns in specie were melted down.

At present, now the evil is excessive, there is a wish to repeat a similar operation, after the following manner.

1. Crowns in specie are to be coined of $9\frac{1}{4}$ to a fine mark.

2. Bank bills are to be issued, which are to represent crowns in specie, and are to be realized or paid in specie.

3. It is wished to fix the value of these current crowns, in specie, by an edict; and, as they could not coin the crown at the assay of a crown nine sols without loss, it is intended to raise their value.

If, therefore, the present currency of Denmark, that is to say, the bank bills, have no real value, but their value consists in the balance of payment of this kingdom (or the rate of exchange) as it shall be for or against Denmark, this operation will be equally absurd with the former; for, if the bank shall pay crowns in specie, in lieu of the ideal value of the currency, it will rid itself of its crowns in specie, which will pass through the crucible, and the former confusion will continue to exist or perhaps be increased to greater extravagance, by a new creation of bank bills representing the specie, which in like manner will, in a few months, be incapable of being realized.

THIRD POSTSCRIPT.—The new establishment of the bank of specie still appears to be obscure. It is intended to coin one million four hundred thousand crowns in specie, the silver for which should be at Altona.

There have been great debates, in the Council of State, between the Prince of Augustenborg, and the Minister of State, Rosencranz. The first requires the money should be coined at Altona, and the latter at Copenhagen. It is said that the Minister intends on this occasion to give in his resignation.

Bank bills equal to the value of one million four hundred thousand crowns are to be fabricated. This bank is to exchange the old bills of the Danish bank for the new bank bills, at a given rate.

Should this rate, as is very probable, be lower than the course of exchange, it would be an excellent manœuvre to buy up bank bills, at present, and afterward convert them into specie.

LETTER LV

December 12th, 1786.

THE true reason why the Duke of Weimar is so feasted is because he has undertaken to bring the Queen to

consent to the marriage of Mademoiselle Voss. The
Queen laughed at the proposal, and said: "Yes, they
shall have my consent; but they shall not have it for
nothing; on the contrary, it shall cost them dear."
And they are now paying her debts, which amount to
more than a hundred thousand crowns; nor do I believe this will satisfy her. While the King of Prussia
is absorbed by meditations on this marriage, to me it
appears evident that, if the Emperor be capable of a
reasonable plan he is now wooing two wives, Bavaria
and Silesia. Yes, Silesia; for I do not think that so
many manœuvres on the Danube can be any other
than the domino of the masquerade. But this is not
the place in which he will make his first attempt.
Everything demonstrates (and give me credit for beginning to know this part of Germany) that he will
keep on the defensive, on the side of Prussia, which
he will suffer to exhaust itself in efforts that he may
freely advance on Bavaria; nor is it probable that he
will trouble himself concerning the means of recovering Silesia, till he has first made that immense acquisition.

I say that he may freely advance; for, to speak
openly, what impediment can we lay in his way? Omit-
ing the million and one reasons of indolence or
impotence which I could allege, let it be supposed that
we should act—we should take the Low Countries,
and he Bavaria; we the Milanese, and he the republic
of Venice. What of all this would save Silesia? And
what must soon after become of the Prussian power?
It will be saved by the faults of its neighbors. It will
fall! This grand fairy palace will come to the earth
with a sudden crush, or its Government will undergo
some revolution.

The King appears very tranquil concerning future
contingencies. He is building near New Sans Souci, or

rather repairing and furnishing a charming house, which formerly belonged to the Lord Marshal, and which is destined for Mademoiselle Voss. The Princess of Brunswick has requested to have a house at Potsdam; and the King has bestowed that on her which he inhabited as Prince Royal, which he is furnishing at his own expense. It is evident that this expiring Princess, crippled by David's disease, and consumed by inanity, is to be lady of honor to Mademoiselle Voss.

The debts of the Queen Dowager, the reigning Queen, the Prince Royal, now become King, and of some other complaisant people, male and female, are paid; and if we add to these sums the pensions that have been bestowed, the houses that have been furnished, and the officers that have been created, we shall find the amount to be tolerably large. This is the true way to be prodigal without being generous. To this article it may be added that the King has given to Messieurs Blumenthal, Gaudi, and Heinitz, Ministers of State, each a *bailliage*. This is a new mode of making a present of a thousand louis. Apropos of the last of these Ministers, the King has replied to several persons employed in the Department of the Mines, who had complained of being superseded, that hereafter there shall be no claims of seniority.

He has terminated the affair of the Duke of Mecklenburg with some slight modifications.

He has given a miraculous kind of reception to General Count Kalckreuth; who was aide-de-camp to and principal agent of Prince Henry; who quarreled with him outrageously for the Princess; and whom Frederick II. kept at a distance that he might not too openly embroil himself with his brother. Kalckreuth is a man of great merit, and an officer of the first class; but the affectation with which he has been distinguished by the King appears to me to be directed against his uncle; perhaps, too, there may be a mingled wish of reconciling himself to the army; but should Count Brühl persist in assuming, not only the rank which has been granted him, but that likewise of seniority, which will supersede all the generals, with Moellendorf at their head, I believe the dissatisfaction will be past remedy. All that is of little consequence while peace shall continue; and perhaps would be the same, were war immediately declared, for a year to come; but in process of time, that which has been sown shall be reaped. It is a strange kind of calculation which spreads discontent through an excellent army by favors and military distinctions, bestowed on a race of men who have always been such indifferent warriors.

Not that I pretend to affirm there are not brave and intelligent men in the service of Saxony. There are, for example two at present, very much distinguished— Captain Tielke of the artillery, whom Frederick wished to gain but could not, though he offered him the rank of lieutenant colonel and an appointment of two thousand crowns; and Count Bellegarde, who is said to be one of the most able officers in the world. But these are not the persons whom they have gained for the Prussian service. Hitherto, in all the Saxon promotions, the thing consulted was the noble merit of being devoted to THE SECT, or that of being recommended by Bishopswerder.

POSTSCRIPT.—I forgot to mention to you that Comte d'Esterno had, at my intercession, addressed the Comte de Vergennes on the proposition of inviting M. de la Grange into France. It will be highly worthy of M. de Calonne to remove those money difficulties which M. de Brühl will not fail to raise.

LETTER LVI

December 16th, 1786.

GENERAL COUNT KALCKREUTH continues to be in favor. It is a subject worthy of observation, that, should this favor be durable, should advantage be taken of the very great abilities of this gentleman, and should he be appointed to some place of importance, the King will then show he is not an enemy to understanding; he is not jealous of the merit of others; nor does he mean to keep all men of known talents at a distance. This will prove the mystics do not enjoy the exclusive privilege of royal favor. But all these deductions, I imagine, are premature; for although Kalckreuth is the only officer of the army who has hitherto been thus distinguished; although he himself had conceived hopes he should be; although his merit is of the first order; Moellendorf having placed himself at the head of the malcontents, which the King will never pardon; Pritwitz being only a brave and inconsiderate soldier, the ridiculous echo of Moellendorf; Anhalt a madman; Gaudi almost impotent, because of his size, and lying likewise under the imputation of a defect in personal bravery, which occasioned Frederick II. to say of him, "He is a good professor, but when the boys are to repeat the lessons they have learned, he is never to be found." Although his other rivals are too young, and too inexperienced, to give him any uneasiness; in spite of all this, I say, I scarcely can imagine but that the principal cause of the distinction with which the King has treated him was the desire of humbling Prince Henry. At least I am very intimate with Kalckreuth, of whom I made a tolerably sure conquest at the reviews of Magdeburg, and I have reason to believe that

I know everything which has passed between him and the King; in all which I do not perceive either anything conclusive, or anything of great promise.

The King supports his capitation tax. It is said it will be fixed according to the following rates: A lieutenant general, a Minister of State, or the widow of one of these, at about twelve crowns, or forty-eight French livres; a major general, or a privy councilor, at ten crowns; a chamberlain, or colonel, eight; a gentleman, six; a peasant, who holds lands in good provinces, three; a half-peasant (a peasant who holds lands has thirty acres, a half-peasant, ten), a crown twelve groschen. In the poor provinces, a peasant two crowns, a half-peasant, one.

Coffee hereafter is only to pay one groschen per pound, and tobacco the same. The general directory has received a memorial on the subject so strongly to the purpose that, although anonymous, it has been officially read, after which it was formally copied to be sent to the tobacco administration, in order to have certain facts verified. The step appeared to be so bold that the formal copy, or protocol, was only signed by four ministers—Messieurs Hertzberg, Arnim, Heinitz, and Schulemberg von Blumberg.

The merchants deputized by the city of Königsberg have written that, if salt is to continue to be monopolized by the Maritime Company, it will be useless for them to come to Berlin; for they can only be the bearers of grievances, without knowing what to propose. It is asserted, in consequence, that the Maritime Company will lose the monopoly of salt. This intelligence, to say the least, is very premature. Salt is an exceedingly important article; and Struensee, who has exerted his whole faculties to secure it to himself, has been so perfectly successful that he sells five thousand lasts of salt, twenty-eight muids constituting nine lasts. (The muid is one hundred and forty-four bushels.)

I ask one again, if the Maritime Company is to be deprived of its most lucrative monopolies, how can it afford to pay ten per cent for a capital of twelve hundred thousand crowns? When an edifice, the summit of which is so lofty and the basis so narrow, is once raised, before any part of it should be demolished, it were very necessary to consult concerning the props by which the remainder is to be supported. The King has declared that he will render trade perfectly free, if any means can be found of not lessening the revenue. Is not this declaration pleasantly benevolent? I think I hear Job on his dunghill, exclaiming, " I consent to be cured of all my ulcers, and to be restored to perfect health, provided you will not give me any physic, and will not subject me to any regimen."

The munificence is somewhat similar to that which shall restore freedom to all the merchandise of France, by obliging it to pay excessive heavy duties, the produce of which shall be applied to the encouragement of such manufactures as shall be supposed capable of rivaling the manufactures of foreign nations. I know not whether the King imagines he has conferred a great benefit on trade; but I know that throughout Europe all contraband commerce is become a mere article of insurance, the premium of which is more or less according to local circumstances; and that therefore a heavy duty (with respect to the revenue) is equivalent to a prohibition.

The King has ordered his subjects to be numbered, that he may not only know their number, but their age and sex. Probably, the changes which are projected to be made in the army are to be the result of this enumeration. But we know how difficult all such numberings are in every country upon earth. Another affair is in agitation, of a much more delicate nature, and which supposes a general plan and great fortitude; which is a land tax on the estates of the nobles. The project begins to transpire, and the provincial counselors have received orders to send certain informations, which seem to have this purpose in view. I will believe it is accomplished when I see it.

Single and distinct facts are of less importance to you than an intimate knowledge of him who governs. All the characters of weakness are united to those I have so often described. Spies already are employed; informers are made welcome; those who remonstrate meet anger, and the sincere are repulsed or driven to a distance. Women only preserve the right of saying what they please. There has lately been a private concert, at which Madame Hencke, or Rietz, for you know that this is one and the same person, was present, and stood behind a screen. Some noise was heard at the door. A *valet de chambre* half opened it, and there found the Princess Frederica of Prussia and Mademoiselle Voss. The first made a sign for him to be silent. The *valet de chambre* disobeyed. The King instantly rose, and introduced the two ladies. Some minutes afterwards, a noise was again heard behind the screen. The King appeared to be embarrased. Mademoiselle Voss asked what it was. Her royal lover replied, " Nothing but my people." The two ladies, however, had quitted the Queen's card table to indulge this pretty whim. The King was making a joke of the matter, on the morrow, when one of the ladies of the palace who was present said to him, "The thing is very true, Sire; but it were to be wished that it were not." Another lady asked him, the other day, at table, " But why, Sire, are all the letters opened at the post office? It is a very ridiculous and very odious proceeding."

He was told that the German plays, which he protects very much, are not good. " Granted," replied he; "but better these than a French playhouse, which would fill Berlin with hussies, and corrupt the manners of the people." From which, no doubt, you must conclude that the German actresses are Lucretias. You must also especially admire the morality of this protector of morals, who goes to sup in the house of his former mistress, with three women, and makes a procuress of his daughter.

He troubles himself as little with foreign politics as if he were entirely secure from all possible tempests. He speaks in panegyrics of the Emperor, of the French always with a sneer, of the English with respect. The fact is, the man appears to be nothing, less than nothing; and I fear lest those diversions which may be made in his favor are exaggerated. I shall, on this occasion, notice that the Duc de Deux-Ponts escapes us; but he unites himself the closer to the Germanic league, which has so high an opinion of itself that it really believes it does not stand in need of our aid. Under the standard of what chief it has acquired this presumption Heaven knows!

There is an anecdote which to me is prophetical, but the force of which you will not feel, for want of knowing the country. Prince Ferdinand has received the fifty thousand crowns which were due to him, according to the will of the King, on the simple word of Werder, conceived in these words: "His Majesty has given me his verbal command to lay down the fifty thousand crowns to Your Highness, which will be paid to you or your order, by the Treasury, at sight. —Welner." An order for fifty thousand crowns, to be paid down, signed by any other than the King, is a monstrosity in the political regulations of Prussia.

Erect a bank, and blessings be upon you; for it is the

sole resource for finance which would not be horribly
burdensome; the only money-machine which, instead
of borrowing with dearness and difficulty, will cause
you to receive; the only corner stone on which, under
present circumstances, the basis of the power of the
Minister of Finance can be supported. Struensee, who
is more stiff in the stirrups than ever, since he must
necessarily become the professor of the new Ministry,
has charged me to inform you that the King will
probably purchase shares to the amount of several millions, if you will send him (Struensee) an abstract of
the regulations of the bank, according to which he may
make his report and proposals.

Apropos of Struensee, with whom I am daily more
intimate. He has desired me to inform you that the
change of the *commandite* for the dealing in *piastres*
will very powerfully lower your exchange; and the
following is his reasoning to prove his assertion:

" The remonstrances of the Bank of St. Charles to
preserve the remittances of the Court, on commission,
at the rate of ten per cent, have been entirely rejected;
it has only been able to obtain them on speculation,
and on the conditions proposed by the *Gremios;* that is
to say, at an interest of six per cent for the money
advanced.

" The same bank has lately changed the *commandite*
at Paris for the *piastre* business, and substituted the
house of Le Normand to that of Le Couteulx. As the
former does not at present possess so extensive a
credit as the latter, many people foresee that the
Spanish bank will be under the necessity of keeping
a greater supply of ready money with their *commandite*.

" In the interim, it has found itself extremely dis-
tressed. Desirous of settling its accounts with the
House of Le Counteulx, and other houses in France,
it was in want of the sum of three millions of French

livres. To obtain this, it addressed itself to Government, and endeavored to call in sixty millions of reals which were its due. Government having, under various pretenses, declined payment, the bank declared itself insolvent, and that it must render the state of its affairs public. This means produced its effect; Government came to its aid, and gave it assignments for twenty millions of reals, payable annually."

LETTER LVII

December 19th, 1786.

THE comedy which Prince Henry had promised the world every Monday had its first representation on yesterday evening. The King came, contrary to the expectation of the Prince, and highly amused himself. I was a close observer of royalty, as you may suppose. It is incontrovertibly the cup of Circe which must be presented, in order to seduce him, but filled rather with beer than tokay. One remark sufficiently curious, which I made, was that Prince Henry amused himself for his own personal pleasure, and was not subject to the least absence of mind, neither of politics nor of attention to his guests. All the foreign ministers were present, but I was the only stranger who stayed to supper; and the King, who, when the comedy was over, behaved all the evening with great reserve, except when some burst of laughter was forced from him by the obscene jests of Prince Frederick of Brunswick, contemplated me with an eye more than cold. He is incessantly irritated against me by speeches which are made FOR ME; and the most harmless of my acquaintance are represented as personally offensive to his Majesty. For my own part, I am perfectly the reverse of disconsolate on the subject. I only notice this that I may describe my present situation, exactly as it is, without any hypocrisy.

It is true that Count Hertzberg has been on the point of losing his place, the occasion of which was what follows: He had announced the promised arrangement to the Duke of Mecklenburg, notwithstanding which, the affair was not expedited. Driven beyond his patience, and impatience in him is always brutal, he one day said to the members of the General Directory, " Gentlemen, you must proceed a little faster; business is not done thus; this is a State which can only proceed with activity." An account was given to the King of this vehement apostrophe. The Sovereign warmly reprimanded his Minister, who offered to resign. Blumenthal, it is said, accommodated the affair.

Apropos of the Duke of Mecklenburg, the King, when he received his thanks for the restitution of his *bailliages,* said to him, " I have done nothing more than my duty; read the device of my order " (*Suum cuique*). The Poles, when the Prussian arms were erected to denote the limits of the frontiers, after dismemberment by the late King, added *rapuit* to the motto. I do not imagine Frederick William will ever give occasion to a similar epigram.

A very remarkable incident in the history of the human heart was the following: After various retrenchments had been made upon this Duke, especially in the promises that had been given him, one of the courtiers represented to the King that he would not be satisfied. " Well," said his Majesty, " then we must give him a yellow ribbon; " and, accordingly, yesterday the yellow ribbon was given. The vainglorious Duke at this moment found the arrangement of the *bailliages* perfectly satisfactory, and this was the occasion of his coming to return thanks.

Would you wish to obtain a tolerably just idea of the manner of living, in this noble TENNIS COURT, called the Court of Berlin? If so, pay some attention to the following traits, and recollect that I could collect a hundred of the same species.

The Princess Frederica of Prussia is now nineteen, and her apartment is open at eleven every morning.

The Dukes of Weimar, Holstein, and Mecklenburg, all ill-bred libertines, go in and out of it two or three times in the course of the forenoon.

The Duke of Mecklenburg was recounting I know not what tale to the King. The Prince of Brunswick, awkwardly enough, trod on the toe of a person present, to make him take notice of something which he thought ridiculous. The Duke stopped short in his discourse—" I believe, sir, you are diverting yourself at my expense." He went on with his conversation to the King, and presently stopped again—" I have long, sir, been acquainted with the venom of your tongue; if you have anything to say, speak it to my face, and I shall answer you." More conversation and other interruptions. " When I am gone, Sire, the Prince will paint me in charming colors; I beg Your Majesty will recollect what has just passed."

This same Prince Frederick is, as I have very often told you, the chief of the mystics, against whom he uttered the most horrid things to Baron Knyphausen.

" But how is this, my Lord? " replied the Baron; " I understood you were the Pope of that Church." " It is false." " I have too good an opinion of your honesty to imagine you can be of a sect which you disavow; I, therefore, give you my promise everywhere to declare you despise the mystics too much to be one of them; and thus you will recover your reputation." The Prince beat about the bush, and called off his dogs.

A courtier, a grand marshal of the Court, petitions for a place promised to five candidates. I remarked to him, " But how, monsieur, if the place be engaged?" " Oh, engagements are nothing at present," answered he, gravely; " for this month past we have left off keeping our word."

Welner, the real author of the disgrace of Schulemburg, went to see him, pitied him, and said, " You have too much merit not to have many enemies." " I, many enemies, monsieur!" said the ex-Minister; "I know of but three—Prince Frederick, because I would not give his huntsman a place; Bishopswerder, because I dismissed one of his dependents; and you, because— I know not why." Welner began to weep, and to swear that detraction was everywhere rending his character. " Tears are unworthy of men," said Schulemburg; " and I am unable to thank you for yours."

In a word, all is sunken to the diminutive, as all was exalted to the grand.

It is asserted that the Prussian merchants will be allowed a free trade in salt and wax. I cannot verify the fact to-day; Struensee will be too much occupied, it being post day; but if it be true, the Maritime Company, which at once will be deprived of salt, wax, coffee, tobacco, and probably of wood, cannot longer support the burden of eighteen per cent at the least; a profit which no solid trade can afford, and which, perhaps Schulemburg himself, with all his lucrative exclusive privileges, could not have paid, but by perplexing the treasury accounts, so that the gains of one branch concealed the deficiencies of another.

As to the silk manufactures, which are proposed to be laid aside, I do not perceive than any inconvenience whatever will result from this. An annual bounty of forty thousand rix-dollars divided among the master weavers of Berlin, added to the prohibition of foreign silks, will never enable them to maintain a competition. Nay, as I have before explained to you, the very manufacturers themselves smuggle, and thus supply more than one-third of the silks that are used in the country; for it is easy to conceive that purchasers will prefer the best silks, which have more substance than, and are of superior workmanship to, those which monopoly would oblige them to buy. Not that the raw materials cost the manufacturer of Berlin more than they do the manufacturer of Lyons. They both procure them from the same countries, and the former does not pay the six per cent entrance duty to which the Lyons manufacturer is subject; besides that, the German workman will labor with more diligence than the French; nor is labor much dearer here than at Lyons. The one receives eighty centimes an ell for making, and the other, ninety-five centimes for the same quality, of equal fineness, which scarcely amounts to one and a half per cent on the price of the silk, estimated at five livres the French ell. The Berlin manufacturer has likewise, by a multitude of local calculations of trade, to which I have paid severe attention, an advantage of thirty per cent over the Lyons trader, at the fair of Frankfort on the Oder. And, whether it proceed from a defect in the Government, the poverty of the workmen, or the ignorance of the manufacturer, he still cannot support the competition. Of what use, therefore, are so many ruinous looms, of which there are not less than sixteen hundred and fifty, at Berlin, Potsdam, Frankfort, and Koepnic?—the product of which, however, is far from being equivalent to the same number of looms at Lyons. The Berlin weaver will not, at the utmost, do more than two-thirds of the work turned out of hand by the weaver of Lyons. Of these sixteen hundred and fifty looms, we may reckon about twelve hundred in which are weaved taffetas, brocades, velvets, etc. The remainder are employed in fabricating gauze, about nine hundred and eighty thousand Berlin ells of which are annually produced. (The French ell is equal to an ell three-quarters of Berlin measure.) The twelve hundred silk looms only produce about nine hundred and sixty thousand ells; which in the whole amount to one million nine hundred and forty thousand ells. The sum total of the looms consume about one hundred and fourteen thousand pounds weight of raw silk, at sixteen ounces to the pound. (You know that seventy-six thousand pounds weight of raw silk will require about one hundred and fourteen thousand pounds weight of undressed silk.) There are also twenty-eight thousand pair, per annum, of silk stockings fabricated at Berlin; which consume about five thousand pounds weight of raw silk. It is principally in the stocking manufactory that the silk of the country is employed; which, in reality, is superior in quality to that of the Levant; but they so ill understand the art of spinning it, in the Prussian States, that it is with difficulty worked in the silk loom. The stocking manufacturers use it to a greater advantage, because being cheap, and of a strong quality, stockings are made from it preferable to those of Nismes and Lyons, in which cities the rejected silk alone is set apart for stockings. From eight to twelve thousand pounds weight of silk is annually obtained in the Prussian States, in which there are mulberry trees enough to supply thirty thousand pounds weight. This constitutes no very formidable rivalship with the silk produced in the States of the King of Sardinia.

The commission of inquiry has written to inform Launay that it has no further demand to make from him; and in consequence he has addressed the King for permission to depart. The King replied, "I have told

you to wait here till the commission shall be closed."
There is either cunning or tyranny on one side or the
other.

LETTER LVIII

December 23d, 1786.

MADEMOISELLE HENCKE, or Madame Rietz, as you
think proper to call her, has petitioned the King to be
pleased to let her know what she is to expect, and to
give her an estate on which she may retire. The
Sovereign offered her a country house, at the distance
of some leagues from Potsdam. The lady sent a positive refusal, and the King, in return, will not hear any
mention made of an estate. It is difficult to say what
shall be the product of this conflict between cupidity and
avarice. The pastoral, in the meantime, proceeds without relaxation. *"Inez de Castro"* has several times
been performed at the German theater, imitated from
the English, and not from the French. In the fourth
act, the Prince repeats with ardor every oath of fidelity
to a lady of honor. This has been the moment of each
representation which the Queen has chosen to leave the
house. Was it the effect of chance, or was it in-
tendedly marked? This is a question that cannot be
answered, from any consideration of the turbulent and
versatile, but not very feeble, character of this Princess.

When her brother-in-law, the Duke of Weimar, arrived, the King gave him a very gracious reception;
and, by degrees, his countenance changed to icy coldness. Conjectures are that he has been lukewarm, or
has wanted address in his negotiation with the Queen,
on the subject of the marriage, which is far from being

determined on. Two private houses have been bought at Potsdam, and have been furnished with every degree of magnificence. And to what purpose, if marriage be intended? May not the wife be lodged in the palace? Speaking of arrangements, let me inform you that the King has sent a M. Paris, his *valet de chambre,* into France, to pay his personal debts there, and to purchase such things as are wanting to these newly bought houses which are consecrated to love.

The relations of Mademoiselle Voss, who four months since pressed her to depart for Silesia, there to marry a gentleman who asked her hand, are at present the first to declare that the projected royal marriage would be ridiculous, and even absurd. In fact, its consequences might be very dangerous; for, should disgust succeed enjoyment, a thing which has been seen to happen, Mademoiselle Voss must separate with a pension; instead of which, in her rank of favorite, she might rapidly make her own fortune, that of her family, and procure the advancement of her creatures.

Be this as it may, the time is passed at Potsdam in projecting bowers for love; and, though the Sovereign might not perhaps be exactly addressed in the words of LA HIRE to Charles VII.—" I assure you, Sire, it is impossible to lose a kingdom with greater gayety," it may at least be said, " It is impossible to risk a kingmore tenderly." But whatever tranquillity may be affected, there are proceedings and projects which, without alarming, for he certainly has valor, occupy the Monarch. The journey of the Emperor to Cherson, the very abrupt and very formal declaration of Russia to the city of Dantzic, the intended camp of eighty thousand men in Bohemia, for the amusement of the King of Naples, are at least incidents that may compel attention, if not remark. There are doubts concerning the journey of the Empress into the Crimea,

Potemkin being unwilling to make her a witness of the incredible poverty of the people and the army, in this newly acquired garden.

The discouragement of the Ministry of Berlin still continues to increase. The King, for these two months has not acted in concert with any single Minister. Hence their torpor and pusillanimity are augmented. Count Hertzberg is progressive in his descent, and Werder begins to decline. The King remains totally unconcerned; and never was the mania of reigning in person and of doing nothing carried to greater excess. Instead of the capitation, a tax on houses is talked of as a substitute. I begin to think that neither of these taxes will take place. There is an inclination to retract without disgrace, if that be possible; and the pretext will be furnished by the advice of the provincial presidents. It is the more extraordinary that this capitation tax should be so much persisted in, since, under the reign of Frederick William I., a similar attempt was made, and which on the second year was obliged to be renounced.

The Prussian army has made a new acquisition, of the same kind with those by which it has been enriched for these four months past. I speak of Prince Eugene of Wurtemberg. He began his career by an excess of libertinage. He since has distinguished himself in the trade of *corporal-schlag*, and by stretching the severity of discipline to ferocity. He notwithstanding, has not acquired any great reputation by these means. He has lived at Paris, and plunged into mesmerism. He afterward professed to be a somnambulist, and next continued the farce, by the practice of midwifery. These different masquerades accompanied and concealed the real object of his ambition and his fervor, which is to give credit to the sect of the mystics, of whom he is one of the most enthusiastic chiefs. A regiment has lately been granted him, which brings him to Berlin. His fortune will not permit him to live wholly there; but his situation will allow him to make journeys to that city, where he will be useful to the fathers of the new church. Singular, ardent, and active, he delivers himself like an oracle and enslaves his hearers by his powerful and ecstatic elocution, with his eyes sometimes haggard, always inflamed, and his countenance in excessive emotion. In a word, he is one of those men whom hypocritics and jugglers make their successful precursors.

23d, at Noon.

I have just had a very deep and almost sentimental conversation with Prince Henry.

He is in a state of utter discouragement as well on his own behalf as on behalf of his country. He has confirmed all I have related to you, and all I shall now relate,—torpor in every operation, gloom at Court, stupefaction among Ministers, discontent everywhere. Little is projected, less still is executed. When it is noticed that business is suffered to languish, the King's being in love is very gravely given as the reason, and it is affirmed that the vigor of administration depends on the compliance of Mademoiselle Voss. Remarks at the same time are made how ridiculous it is thus to suspend the affairs of a whole kingdom, etc., etc.

The General Directory, which should be a Council of State, is nothing more than an office to expedite common occurrences. If Ministers make any proposition no answer is returned; if they remonstrate they meet with disgust. What they ought to do is so far from what they actually do that the debasement of their dignity occasions very disagreeable reflections. Never was a public opinion produced more suddenly than it has been by Frederick William II., in a country where the seeds of such opinion did not appear to exist.

Prince Henry can find no remedy for domestic vices, but he has no apprehensions concerning foreign affairs; because the King is at present wholly decided in favor of France, and still more destitute of confidence for the favorers of the English faction. Pray take notice that this is the version of the Prince; not that I am very incapable of believing it, if we do not throw up our own chances.

What the public papers have announced respecting the journey of Prince Henry, is without foundation. Some wish to go to Spa and France, but no plan is yet determined on; a vague hope, which he cannot suffer to expire, notwithstanding the blows he receives, will detain him at Rheinsberg. Year will succeed to year; the moment of rest will arrive, and habit will enchain him in his frosty castle, which he has lately enlarged and rendered more commodious. To these different motives, add a nullity of character, a will unstable as the clouds, frequent indisposition, and a heated imagination, by which he is exhausted. That which we desire without success, gives more torment than that which is executed with difficulty.

A second Minister is to be appointed for Silesia; one singly is a kind of viceroy. It is dangerous, say they, to see with the eyes of an individual only. *Divide et impera.* Thus far have they advanced in their politics.

Prince Frederick of Brunswick is ardently active in his intrigues against Prince Henry, and the Duke his brother. What he wishes is not known; but he wishes, and hence he has acquired a certain importance among the tumultuous crowd, who cannot perceive that a contemptible Prince is still more contemptible than an ordinary man. He neither can be of any durable utility, nor in the least degree agreeable or estimable; but, under certain given circumstances, he may be a very necessary spy.

LETTER LIX

December 26th, 1786.

A GRAND list of promotions is spoken of, in which Prince Henry and the Duke of Brunswick are included, as field marshals. But the first says he will not be a field marshal. He continually opposed that title being bestowed on the Duke, under Frederick II., who refused to confer such a rank on the princes of the blood. This alternative of haughtiness and vanity, even aided by his ridiculous comedy, will not lead him far. He intends to depart in the month of September for Spa; he is afterward to visit our southern provinces, and from thence is to continue his journey to Paris, where he is to pass the winter. Such are his present projects, and the probability is sufficiently great that not anything of all this will happen.

The King has declared that he will not bestow any places on persons who are already in office under the Princes. This may perhaps be the cause that Count Nostitz has forsaken Prince Henry. The Count is a very strange kind of being.

First sent into Sweden, where he erected himself a chief of some envoys of the second order, finding himself dissatisfied with the severe laws of etiquette, he passed a slovenly life in an office, which he exercised without abilities. On his return he procured himself the appointment of one of the gentlemen who accompanied the Prince Royal into Russia, but the consent of the Prince he had forgotten to ask. He was consequently regarded as an inconvenient inspector, and was but sparingly produced on public occasions. Hence arose ill-humor, complaints, and murmurs. The late King sent him into Spain, where he dissipated the remainder of his fortune. The merchants of Embden, and of Königsberg, requested the Spaniards would lower the duties on I know not what species of merchandise. Count Nostitz solicited, negotiated, and presently wrote word " that the new regulations were wholly to the advantage of the Prussian subjects." The King ordered the Court of Spain to be thanked. Fortunately, Count Finckenstein, who had not received the regulations, delayed sending the thanks. The regulations came, and the Prussian merchants were found to be more burdened than formerly. His Majesty was in a rage. Nostitz was suddenly recalled, and arrived at Berlin without the fortune that he had spent, destitute of the respect that he had lost, and deprived of all future hopes. Prince Henry welcomed him to his palace, an asylum open to all malcontents. Here he remained eighteen months, and here displayed himself in the same manner that he had done everywhere else—inconsistent in his imaginations, immoral in mind, ungracious in manners, not capable of writing, not willing to read, as vain as a blockhead, as hot as a turkey cock, and unfit for any kind of office, because he neither possesses principles, seductive manners, nor knowledge. Such as here depicted, this insipid mortal, the true hero of the Dunciad, is in a few days to be appointed to the Electorate of Hanover. In excuse for so capricious a choice, it is alleged that he will have nothing to do in the place. But wherefore send a man to a place where he has nothing to do?

Madame Rietz, who of all the mistresses of the Sovereign has most effectually resisted the inconstancy of men, and the intrigues of the wardrobe, has modestly demanded the margraviate of Schwedt from the King, to serve as a place of retreat; and four gentlemen to travel with her son as with the son of a Monarch. This audacious request has not displeased the King, who had been offended by the demand made of an estate. He, no doubt, has discovered that he is highly respected, now that he receives propositions so honorable.

His former friends no longer can obtain a minute's audience; the gates to them are gates of brass. But a comedian, whose name is Marron, at present an innkeeper at Verviers, lately came to solicit his protection. He chose the moment when the King was stepping into his carriage. The King said to him, " By and by; by and by." Marron waited; the King returned, sent for him into his apartments, spoke with him a quarter of an hour, received his request, and promised everything for which he petitioned. Never, no, never will subaltern influence decline; footmen will be all-puissant. Welner has publicly obtained the surname of VICEROY, or of PETTY KING.

The Monarch has written to the General of the gendarmes (Pritwitz), noticing that several of his officers played at games of chance; that these games were forbidden; that he should renew the prohibitions under pain of being sent to the fortress for the first offense, and of being broken for the second. The information and the threat were meant at the General himself, who has lost much money with the Duke of Mecklenburg.

It is affirmed that the Duke of Brunswick will be here from the eighth to the fifteenth of January. But Archimedes himself demanded a point of support, and I see none of any kind at Berlin. There are numerous wishes, but not one will; and the wishes themselves are incoherent, contradictory, and rash; he does not know, nor will he ever know, how to connect a single link in the chain: he will more especially never know how to lop off the parasitical and avaricious sucker. Agriculture is what is most necessary to be encouraged, particularly as soon as commercial oppression shall be renounced; though this oppression has hitherto been productive of gold, thanks to the situation of the Prussian States. But how may agriculture be encouraged in a country where the half of the peasants are attached to the glebe? For so they are in Pomerania, Prussia, and in other parts.

It would be a grand operation in the royal domains, were they divided into small farms, as has so long since been done by the great landholders in England. It is a subject of much greater importance than regulations of trade; but there are so many interested people to be controverted, and the habit of servitude is so rooted, that strength of understanding, energy, and consistency, not one grain of which I can find here, are necessary to make the attempt. More knowledge likewise is requisite than will here be found, for a long time to come, for it to be supposed that there is no town, no province, which would not most gladly consent to pay the King much more than the neat revenue he at present obtains, if he would suffer the inhabitants to assess themselves; taking care, however, continually to watch over the assessments, that the magistrates and nobles might not oppress the people; or for it to be imagined that the subject would not gain three-fourths of the expenses of collecting, and would be free of all those unworthy restraints which are at present imposed upon them by the fiscal treasury.

It is also necessary to recollect that it is not here as with us, where the body, the mass, of national wealth is so great, because of the excellence of the soil and the climate, the correspondence between the provinces, etc., etc., that we may cut as close as we will, provided we do not erect kilns to burn up the grass; and that in France the expenses of collecting only need be diminished; that no other relief is necessary; nay, that we may still prodigiously increase the load, provided that load be well poised. Here, two or three provinces at the utmost excepted, the basis is so narrow and the soil so little fruitful, so damp, so impoverished, that it is only for tutelary authority to perform the greatest part of all which can reconcile Nature to this her neglected offspring. The division of the domains itself, an operation so productive of every kind of resource, requires very powerful advances; for the farmer's stock and the implements of husbandry are, perhaps, those which, when wanting, the arm can least supply.

Independent of this grand point of view, we must not forget THE MILITARY POWER, which must here be respected, for here there are neither Alps nor Apennines, rivers nor seas, for ramparts; here, therefore, with six millions of inhabitants, Government is desirous, and, to a certain point, is obliged, to maintain two hundred thousand men in arms. In war there are no other means than those of courage or of obedience, and obedience is an innate idea in the SERF peasant; for which reason, perhaps, the grand force of the Prussian army consists in the union of the feudal and military systems. Exclusive of that vast consideration, which I shall elsewhere develop, let me add it will not be sufficient here to act like such or such a Russian or Polish lord, and say, " You are enfranchised," for the serfs here will reply, " We are very much obliged to you for your enfranchisement, but we do not choose to be free "; or even to bestow land gratuitously on them, for they will answer, " What would you have us do with lands?" Proprietors and property can only be erected by making advances, and advances are expensive; and, as there are so few governments which have the wisdom to sow in order that they may reap, this will not be the first to begin. It is little probable that the morning of wholesome politics should first break upon this country.

At present it is almost publicly known that the Comte d'Esterno is to depart in the month of April for France. I shall submit it to your delicacy, and to your justice, to pronounce whether I can remain here the overseer of a *chargé d'affaires*. During his absence, functions might be bestowed on me; here I certainly would not remain under an envoy *per interim;* nor would this require more than the simple precaution of sending me secret credentials. But, as no such thing will be done, you will perceive that this is a new and very strong reason for my departure about that time. Those who would make me nothing more than a gazetteer are ill-acquainted with mankind; and still more so those who hope to oblige me to consent tacitly or perforce.

POSTSCRIPT—The Count de Masanne, a fervent mystic, is the grand master of the Queen's household. Welner supped with her yesterday, and had the place of honor; that is to say, he sat opposite her. If he cede to wishes of such indecent vanity, he will presently be undone.

LETTER LX

December 30th, 1786.

YESTERDAY was a memorable moment for the man of observation. Count Brühl, a Catholic, a foreigner,

assuming his rank in the Prussian army, was installed
in his place as Governor, and the capitation tax was
intimated. This capitation, so openly contemned, supported with so much obstinacy, demonstrated to be
vicious in its principle, impossible of execution, and
barren in product, at once announces the disgraceful
inanity of the General Directory, by which it was
loudly opposed, and the sovereign influence of the
subaltern by whom its chiefs have been resisted. How
can we suppose the King has been deceived respecting
the public opinion of an operation so universally condemned? How may he be excused, since his Ministers themselves have informed him that he was in
danger of, perhaps forever, casting from him, at the
very commencement of his reign, the title of well-
beloved, of which he was so ambitious? Here we at
least behold the ambiguous morning of a cloudy
reign.

The Queen is not satisfied with the choice that has
been made of Count Brühl, neither is she with the
regulations of her household, and therefore she is
again contracting debts. She is allowed, for expenses
of every kind, only fifty-one thousand crowns per
annum. It will be difficult for her to make this sum
supply her real wants, her generous propensities, and
her numerous caprices. Blind to the amours of the
King, she can see the disorder of his domestic affairs.
The day before yesterday there was no wood for the
fires of her apartments. Her house steward entreated
the steward of the royal palace to lend him his assistance. The latter excused himself because of the small-
ness of his remaining stock. How, you will ask, can
disorder so indecent happen? Because the quantity
consumed was regulated by the late King on the supposition that the Queen and her children resided at
Potsdam. Since his death no person has thought of

the necessary addition. Such incidents, trifling as they are in themselves, prove to what excess carelessness and the defects of inconsistency are carried.

Count Brühl was waited for in order to furnish the house of the Princes. As he is overwhelmed by debts, and is a Saxon nobleman ruined, it was requisite the King should cause the sum of twenty thousand crowns to be paid at Dresden, to satisfy the most impatient of his creditors. Opinions concerning him are divided.

The only points on which people are unanimous are, that he is one of the flock of the elect (the mystics), and that he plays exceedingly well on the violin. Those who have been acquainted with him fifteen years ago speak in raptures of his amenity. Those whose knowledge of him is more recent are silent. Those who are totally unacquainted with him say he is the most amiable of men. His pupil smiles when he is praised. It is affirmed that the Grand Duke has sent him here, and that it is his intention to take him to himself whenever he shall have the power.

The Prince Royal will soon be worthy the trouble of observation; not merely because Frederick II. drew his horoscope in the following terms—" I shall reign again in him," for perhaps he only meant by that to testify his contempt for the present King; but because all things in him proclaim greatness, but ungraciousness of character; awkwardness, but a speaking countenance; unpolished, but sincere. He asks the wherefore of everything, nor will he ever be satisfied with a reply that is not reasonable. He is severe and tenacious, even to ferocity, and yet is not incapable of affection and sensibility. He already knows how to esteem and contemn. His disdain of his father approaches hatred, which he is not very careful to conceal. His veneration of the late King partakes of idolatry, and this he proclaims. Perhaps the youth is destined to great actions; and, should he become the engine of some memorable revolution, men who can see to a distance will not be surprised.

Launay at length departs; and, as I believe, solely from the fear which the Ministry, or rather which Welner, has that the King should, in some weary or embarrassed moment, restore him to his place. His dismission has been granted to him only on condition that he would give up twenty-five thousand crowns of arrears, which are his due. This is a shameful piece of knavery. They have exacted an oath from him that he will not carry off any papers that relate to the State. This is pitiable weakness. For of what validity is such an oath? He may afford you some useful, or rather curious, annotations. In other respects, the man is nothing, less than nothing. He does not so much as suspect the elements of his own trade. His speech is perplexed, his ideas are confused; in a word, he could only act a great part in a country where he had neither judges nor rivals. But he is not, as he is accused of being, a malicious person. He is a very weak and a very vain man, and nothing more. He has acted the part of an executioner, no doubt; but where is the financier who has not? Where would be the justice of demanding the hangman to be racked because of the tortures he had inflicted in pursuance of the sentence which the judge had pronounced?

He will predict deficiencies in the revenue, and in this he will not be wrong; but he perhaps will not inform you, although it is exceedingly true, that economical principles, which are the guardians of this country, are already very sensibly on the decline. The service is more expensive, the houses of princes more numerous, the stables are better filled, pensions are multiplied, arrangements more costly, salaries of ambassadors almost doubled, the manners more elegant, etc. The greatest part of these expenses was necessary. The real misfortune is that there is no care taken for the proportionate increase of the revenue by slow, but certainly productive, means; and that they seem not to suppose there will be any deficiency, which will at length make an immense error in the sum total; so that, without war, a long reign may see the end of the Treasury, should the present measures be pursued. It is not the prodigality of pomp which excites murmurs. It is a prodigality in contrast to the personal avarice of the King which is to be dreaded. It is an insensible, but a continual wasting. Hitherto the evil is inconsiderable, and, no doubt, does not strike any person; but I begin to understand the country in the whole, and I perceive these things more distinctly than I can describe.

It was a custom with the late King, every year, on the twenty-fourth of December, to make presents to his brothers and sisters, the whole sum of which amounted to about twenty thousand crowns. This custom the nephew has suppressed. A habitude of forty years had led the uncles to consider these gratuities as a part of their income; nor did they expect that they should have SET the first examples, or rather have BEEN MADE the first examples, of economy. Faithful to his peculiar mode of making presents, the King has gratified the Duke of Courland with a yellow ribbon. It would be difficult more unworthily to prostitute his Order.

To this sordidness of metal, and this debauchery of moral, coin, examples of easy prodigality may be opposed. The house of the Jew Ephraim had paid two hundred thousand crowns, on account, for the late King, at Constantinople, during the Seven Years' War. The money was intended to corrupt some Turks, but the project failed. Frederick II. continually de-

layed the repayment of the sum. His successor yesterday reimbursed the heirs of Ephraim.

A saddler who had thirty years been the creditor of
the late King, who never would pay the debts he had
contracted while Prince Royal, demanded the sum of
three thousand crowns from his present Majesty. The
King wrote at the bottom of the petition: " Pay the
bill at sight, with interest at six per cent."

The Duke of Holsteinbeck is at length to go to
Königsberg, to take command of a battalion of grenadiers. I have elsewhere depicted this insignificant
Prince, who will be a boy at sixty, and who will neither do harm to the enemies of the State nor good
to his private friends.

LETTER LXI

January 1st, 1787.

THE King has lately bestowed his Order on four of
his subjects. The one is the keeper of his treasury
(M. von Blumenthal), a faithful but a dull Minister.
The second is the master of his horse, M. von Schwerin, a silly buffoon under the late King, a cipher during
his whole life, a perplexed blockhead, and on whom
the first experiment that was made, after the accession,
was to deprive him of his place. The third is his
Majesty's Governor, a man of eighty, who has been
kept at a distance for these eighteen years past, and
who is destitute of talents, service, dignity, and esteem
for his pupil, which perhaps is the first mark of good
sense he ever betrayed. The last who is not yet named,
is Count Brühl, who is thus rewarded by titles, after
receiving the most effective gratifications before he
has exercised any office. What a prostitution of honors! I say what a prostitution; for the prodigality

with which they are bestowed is itself prostitution.

Among others who have received favors, a mystic priest is distinguished,—a preacher of effrontery, who reposes on the couch of gratifications, at the expense of two thousand crowns. To him add Baron Boden, driven from Hesse Cassel, a spy of the police at Paris, known at Berlin to be a thief, a pickpocket, a forger, capable of everything except that which is honest, and of whom the King himself said he is a rascal, yet on whom he has bestowed a chamberlain's key. Pensions innumerable have been granted to obscure or infamous courtiers. The Academicians, Welner, and Moulines, are appointed directors of the finances of the Academy.

All these favors announce a Prince without judgment, without delicacy, without esteem either for himself or his favors; reckless of his own fame, or of the opinion of the public; and as proper to discourage those who possess some capacity as to embolden such as are natively nothing, or worse than nothing.

The contempt of the people is the merited salary of so many good works; and this contempt is daily more pointed; the stupor by which it was preceded is now no more. The world was at first astonished to see the King faithful to his comedy, faithful to his concert, faithful to his old mistress, faithful to his new one, finding time to examine engravings, furniture, the shops of tradesmen, to play on the violoncello, to inquire into the tricks of the ladies of the palace, and seeking for moments to attend to ministers, who debate in his hearing on the interests of the State. But at present astonishment is incited if some new folly or some habitual sin has not consumed one of his days.

The new uniforms invented by his Majesty have this day made their appearance. This military bauble, prepared for the day on which men have the ridiculous custom of making a show of themselves, confirms the opinion that the sovereign who attaches so much importance to such a circumstance possesses that kind of understanding which induces him to believe that parading is a thing of consequence.

Is his heart better than his understanding? Of this men begin to doubt.

Count Alexander Wartensleben, a former favorite of the present King, who was imprisoned at Spandau for his fidelity to him, being sent for from the farther part of Prussia to Berlin, to command the guards, has lately been placed at the head of a Brandenburg regiment; and by this arrangement he loses a pension of a hundred guineas, which was granted him by the King while Prince Royal. This frank and honest officer is a stranger to the sect in favor; and, after having languished in a kind of forgetfulness, finally receives a treatment which neither can be called disgrace nor reward. This is generally considered as a deplorable proof that the King, to say the least, neither knows how to love nor hate.

Mademoiselle Voss has been persuaded that it would be more generous in her to prevent her lover committing a folly than to profit by such folly; for thus is the marriage publicly called, which would have become a subject of eternal reproach whenever the intoxication of passion should have slumbered. The beauty, therefore, will be made a countess, become rich, and perhaps the sovereign of the will of the Sovereign, but not his spouse. Her influence may be productive of great changes, and in other countries might render Count Schulemburg, the son-in-law of Count Finckenstein, first Minister. He has acted very wisely in attaching Struensee to himself, who teaches him his trade with so much perspicuity that the Count imagines his trade is learned. He has besides an exercised understanding, and an aptitude to industry, order, consistency, and energy. Aided by his tutor, he will find no difficulties too great; and he is the man necessary for this King, whose will is feeble and cowardly. The late King was equally averse to men of many difficulties, but it was from a conviction of his own superiority. Great talents, however, are little necessary to reign over your men of Topinamboo.

The memorial against the capitation tax, which has been signed by Messieurs Hertzberg, Heinitz, Arnim, and Schulemburg, concludes with these words: " This operation, which alarms all classes of Your Majesty's subjects, effaces in their hearts the epithet of WELL-BELOVED, and freezes the fortitude of those whom you have appointed to your Council." Struensee, on his part, has sent in two pages of figures, which demonstrate the miscalculations that will infallibly be discovered when the tax has been collected. Messieurs Werder, Gaudi, and probably Welner, persist; and the King, who neither has the power to resist a plurality of voices, nor that of receding, dares not yet decide.

On the 15th of February, he is to depart for Potsdam, where he proposes to continue the remainder of the year; that period excepted when he journeys into Silesia and Prussia.

POSTSCRIPT—*Evening.*—The King has to-day advanced the Duke of Brunswick to the rank of field marshal. This is indubitably the first honorable choice he has made; and everybody approves his having singly promoted this Prince.

January 2d.

The Dutch envoy has thrown me into a state of great embarrassment, and into astonishment not less great. He has asked me, in explicit terms, whether I consented that endeavors should be made to procure me credentials to treat with the Princess of Orange, at Nimeguen. If deception might be productive of anything, I should have imagined he only wished to induce me to speak; but the question was accompanied with so many circumstances, all true and sincere, so many confidential communications of every kind, and a series of anecdotes so rational and so decisive, that, though I might find it difficult to account for the whim he had taken, I could not possibly doubt of the candor of the envoy. After this first consideration, I hesitated whether I should mention the affair to you, from a fear that the presumption should be imputed to me of endeavoring to rival M. de Renneval; but, besides that my cipher will pass under the inspection of my prudent friend, before it will fall into the hands of the King or his Ministers, and that I shall thus be certain he will erase whatever might injure me to no purpose, I have imagined it was not a part of my duty to pass over a proposition of so singular a kind in silence. I ought to add further, referring to the ample details which I shall give, after the long conference which I am to have with him to-morrow morning, that, if France has no latent intention, and means only to weaken the Stadtholder, in such a manner as that his influence cannot hereafter be of service to the English, the patriots are by no means so simple in their intentions. I have proofs that, from the year 1784 to the end of 1785, they were in secret correspondence with Baron Reede; and that they ceased precisely at the moment when the Baron wrote to them: " Make your proposals; I have a *carte blanche* from the Princess, and, on this condition, the King of Prussia will answer for the Prince." I have also proofs that M. de Renneval cannot succeed, and that the affair will

never be brought to a conclusion, " so long as negotiation shall be continued instead of arbitration."
These are his words, and they appear to me remarkable. It is equally evident that the implacable vengeance of the Duc de la Vauguyon arises from his having dared to make love to the Princess, and his love
having been rejected. I shall leave those who are able
to judge of the veracity of these allegations; but it is
my duty to repeat verbally the following phrase of
Baron Reede: " M. de Calonne is inimical to us, and
his enemy opens his arms to receive us. What is it
that M. de Calonne wishes? Is it to be Minister of
Foreign Affairs? A successful pacification of the
troubles of Holland would render him more service,
in such case, than the continuation of those troubles,
which may kindle a general conflagration. I demand
a categorical answer to the following question: Should
it be proved to M. de Calonne that the Stadtholder is
in reality come over to the side of France, or, which
is the same thing, if he shall be obliged to come over,
will he then be against us? Has he any private interest which we counteract? Is it impossible he should
explain himself? The chances certainly are all in his
favor against M. de Breteuil, whom we have continually hated and despised. Wherefore will he spoil his
own game."

I necessarily answered these questions in terms rather vague. I informed him that M. de Calonne, in
what related to foreign affairs, continually pursued
the line marked out by M. de Vergennes; that the former, far from coveting the place of the latter, would
support him with all his power, if, which could not
happen, he had need of his support; that a comptroller-
general never could be desirous of anything but peace
and political tranquillity; that whether M. de Calonne
had or had not particular agents in Holland, was a

fact of which I was ignorant (this Baron Reede positively assured me was the case, and probably was the
reason of his afterward conceiving the idea of making
me their substitute); but that he would suppose me
a madman, should I speak to him of such a thing; and
therefore if, as seemed very improbable, it were true
that the Princess of Orange, on the recommendation
of Baron Reede, should be capable of placing any confidence in me, it was necessary she should give this
to be understood, through some medium with which
I should be unacquainted, as, for example, by the way
of Prussia; but it scarcely could be supposed that
there would be any wish of substituting a person unknown in that walk to those who were already in the
highest repute.

Baron Reede persisted, and further added, not to
mention that M. de Renneval could not long remain in
his station, the parties would undoubtedly come to a
better understanding when the Princess could speak
with confidence; that confidence was a sensation which
she never could feel for this negotiator. In fine, he
demanded, under the seal of profound secrecy, a conference with me, which I did not think it would be
right to refuse; and his whole conversation perfectly
demonstrated two things: the first, that his party supposes M. de Calonne is totally their enemy, and that
he is the Minister of influence in this political conflict;
and the second, that they believed him to be deceived.
I am the more persuaded these suppositions are true,
because he very strongly insisted even should I not
receive any orders to repair to Holland, I should pass
through Nimeguen, on my return to Paris; that, by
the aid of the pledges of confidence which I should
receive from him, I might sufficiently penetrate the
thoughts of the Princess, so as to be able to render
M. de Calonne a true report of the situation of affairs,

and what might be the basis of a sincere and stable conciliation. It is not, therefore, so much another person, instead of M. de Renneval, that they desire, as another Couette Toury, or some particular confidant of M. de Calonne. I shall conclude with two remarks that are perhaps important.

1. My sentiments and principles concerning liberty are so known that I cannot be regarded as one of the Orange party. There is, therefore a real desire of accommodation at Nimeguen. And would not the success of this accommodation be of greater consequence to M. de Calonne than the machinations of M. de Breteuil? Wherefore will he not have the merit of the pacification, if it be necessary? And is it not in a certain degree necessary, in the present political state of Europe?

2. The province of Friseland has ever been of the Anti-Stadtholder party, and it now begins to be on better terms with the Prince. Is it not because there has been the ill address of attacking the Stadtholder in some part hostile to the provinces, and in which neither the nobility nor the regencies do, or can, wish to see the constitution absolutely overthrown? Has not the province of Holland drawn others too far into its particular measures?

These two considerations, which I can support by a number of corroborating circumstances, perhaps are worthy the trouble of being weighed. I shall send you, by the next courier, the result of our conference; but, if there are any orders, information or directions, to be given me on the subject, it is necessary not to leave me in suspense; for my situation relative to Reede is embarrassing, since I dare neither to repel nor invite advances, which most assuredly I never shall provoke, and which, by the well-avowed state of the Cabinet of Potsdam, it was even impossible I should provoke, had I been possessed of so much temerity.

Noldé has already written several letters to me from Courland, and mentions an important dispatch in cipher, which is to be sent by the next courier. But the evident result is that it is too late to save Courland; that everything which ought to have been prevented is done, or as good as done, and that the best physicians would but lose their time in prescribing for the incurable. The bearer of the letter, which occasioned the departure of Noldé is a merchant of Liebau, named Immermann. He has been charged with the negotiation of a loan in Holland and elsewhere, but, as it is said, has met with no success. It is supposed in the country that the Duke has thrown impediments in its way. The Diet of Courland is to sit in January. It is worthy of remark that, for two years past, no delegate has been sent from Courland to Warsaw.

Good information is said to be received that four corps of Russian troops have begun their march, purposely to approach the Crimea at the time that the Empress shall be there; and this not so much to inspire the Turks with fear, as to remove the greatest and most formidable part of the military from the vicinage of Petersburg and the northern provinces of Russia; and especially from the Grand Duke, that there may not be any possibility of dangerous or vexatious events; for the unbounded love of the Russians for their Grand Duke is apprehended. Yet, if such terrors are felt, wherefore undertake so useless a journey, which will cost from seven to eight millions of rubles? So useless, I say, according to your opinions, for, according to mine, the Empress believes she is going to Constantinople, or she does not intend to depart.

The troops are to be divided into four corps, of forty thousand men each. The General of these armies will be Field-Marshal Potemkin, who will have the immediaate command of a corps of forty thousand men, and the superintendence of the others who are under him, to be led by General Elvut, Michaelssohn, and Soltikow. Prince Potemkin has under his particular and independent orders sixty thousand irregular troops in the Crimea. It is whispered he entertains the project of making himself King of the country, and of a good part of the Ukraine.

LETTER LXII

January 4th, 1787.

MY CONFERENCE with Baron Reede is over. It continued three hours and a half, and I have not the smallest remaining doubt concerning his intentions, after the confidence with which he spoke and the writings he showed me. He appears to be a good citizen, a constitutionalist by principle, a friend of liberty by instinct, loyal and true from character and habit, and rather the servant of the Princess of Orange from personal affection than from the place he holds under her husband; a person desirous of ending tumultuous and disquieting debates, because in pacification he contemplates the good of his country, and that of the Princess, whose confidence he possesses. He is, further, a Minister of passable talents, who has abstained from making advances so long as he presumed our political management of the Court of Prussia would greatly influence its intervention, and that he might prevail on that Court to speak firmly. At present, feeling that the respect in which the Cabinet of

Berlin was held is on the decline, and especially perceiving the King is disinterested in the affairs of
the Stadtholder, because he has no interest in anything, he knocks immediately at the door of reconciliation.

You may hold the following as probabilities:

1. That the Princess, who will finally decide what
the catastrophe is to be, at least in a very great measure, is, to a certain point, desirous of accommodation,
and to throw herself into the arms of France, because,
in fine, she dreads risking a stake too great, to the
injury of her family.

2. That she imagines M. de Calonne to be the Minister who influences the mind of the King, and the
personal enemy of her house.

3. That successful attempts have been made to
inspire her with very strong prejudices against his
sincerity.

4. That still she seeks his friendship, and is desirous of a correspondence with him, either direct or
indirect; and of an impartial trusty friend in Holland,
who should possess her confidence.

5. That not only nothing is more possible than to
retouch the regulations, without some modifications
in which the influence of the Stadtholder cannot be
repressed, but that this is what they expect, secretly
convinced of its justice, and politically of its necessity;
and that Baron Reede, as a citizen, and one of the
first of the first rank, would be much vexed were they
not retouched.

The reason of the sincere return of the Princess of
Orange, who indeed was never entirely alienated, is
that she seriously despairs of being efficaciously served
at Berlin.

That of her opinion of the enmity of M. de Calonne
is solely founded on his intimate connection with the

Rhingrave of Salm, which the latter exaggerates;
and the inconsiderable discourse of M. de C——,
which really surpasses all imagination, and who is
supposed to be the particular intimate of the Minister.

Her prejudices against M. de Calonne arise, in a
great part, from the calumny spread by one Vander-
mey, who had formed I know not what enterprise on
Bergue-Saint-Vinox (while this Minister was inten-
dant of the province), in which he failed in such a
manner as to cost the Stadtholder more than a hundred and sixty thousand florins; and, that he might
excuse himself, he threw the whole blame on the
opposition made by M. de Calonne. Add further, that
all these causes of discontent, suspicion, and animosity are still kept in fermentation by a M. de Portail,
the creature of M. de Breteuil, the which M. de Portail equally blames M. de Veyrac, M. de C——, the
Rhingrave of Salm, M. de Renneval, the Comte de
Vergennes, and all that has been done, all that is done,
and all that shall be done; but especially M. de
Calonne, whom he depicts as the incendiary of the
Seven Provinces, which, with all Europe besides, cannot be saved but by the meekness of M. de Breteuil,
the gentle, the polished, the pacificator.

With respect to the desire of the Princess to be on
better terms with M. de Calonne, it is, I think, evident.
Baron Reede is too circumspect and too artful to have
taken such a step with me had he not been authorized.
What follows will, perhaps, give you the genealogy of
his ideas, which may sufficiently explain the whole episode. He could easily know that I wrote in cipher.
He is the intimate friend of Hertzberg. And for
whom do I cipher? Whoever is acquainted with the
coast and the progress of our affairs must know it can
only be for M. de Calonne. On what principle do I

act? The Duke of Brunswick, who has had many conferences with him, cannot have left him in ignorance that my views on this subject were all for peace. Having been totally disappointed through the ignorance of Comte d'Esterno, which he affirms is complete in this respect, and which must, therefore, on this subject, redouble the native surliness of the Count; and by the stupidity of F——, who painfully comes to study his lesson with him, and returning does not always repeat it faithfully; well convinced that the influence of Count Hertzberg is null, the affection of the King cooled, and the credit of his Cabinet trifling, the Baron has proposed to the Princess to make this experiment.

With respect to her consent, whether express or tacit, and her serious determination to retouch the regulations, of this I have seen proofs in the letters of the Princess, and read them in the cipher of the Princess (for it will be well to know that she is very laborious, ciphers and deciphers herself, and with her own hand indites answers to all the writings of the contrary party), as I have done in those of Larrey and of Linden.

I did not think myself justified in disregarding such overtures. After having said everything possible in favor of M. de Calonne, his views, projects, and connections (nor, I confess, do I believe that the manner in which I am devoted to him left me at this moment without address), after having treated as I ought the perfidious duplicity of M. de Breteuil and his agents, and after having uttered what I thought on the prudence of M. de Vergennes, the delicate probity of the King, and the undoubted politics of our Cabinet, which certainly are to render the Stadtholder subservient to the public good, and the independence of the United Provinces, but which cannot be to procure his expulsion, it was agreed that I should write the day after to-morrow to demand a categorical answer from M. de Calonne, to know whether he wishes to begin a correspondence, direct or indirect, with the Princess; and whether he consents that any propositions for accommodation should be made him, for rendering which effectual his personal word should be accepted, when they shall be agreed on, and to an honorable pacification in behalf of the Stadtholder, suitable to the Sovereign.

Baron Reede, on his part, who is cautious, and wished to appear to act totally from himself, wrote to the Princess to inform her that this step was taken at his instigation, and to demand her prompt and formal authority to act. We are to meet to-morrow on horseback in the park that we may reciprocally show each other our minutes; it being certainly well understood that neither of us is to show the other more than the ostensible minutes we shall have prepared; and the whole is to depart on Saturday; because, said he, as not more than twelve or thirteen days were necessary for him to have an answer, this would be time enough, before yours should arrive, for us to form the proposed plan—at least, so far as to establish confidence.

This is the faithful abstract of our conversation. With respect to the propositions, I had only to listen; and as to the reflections, I have only to apologize. Should you be tempted to suppose I have been too forward in accepting the proposal to write, I beg the incident may be weighed, and that I may be informed how it may be possible, at the distance of six hundred leagues, ever to be successful, if I am never to exceed my literal instructions. And after all, what new information have I given the Baron? Who here, who is concerned in diplomatic affairs, has any doubt that

I cipher? And on what subjects do men cipher? Is it philosophy, literature, or politics? Neither have I told of what kind my business is; and my constant formulæ have been—I SHALL ENDEAVOR—I SHALL FIND SOME MODE—I SHALL TAKE AN OPPORTUNITY OF LETTING M. DE CALONNE KNOW, ETC.

At present, send me orders either to recede or to advance; and in the latter case give me instructions; for I have only hitherto been able to divine, and that the more vaguely because, as you must easily feel, it was necessary I should appear to the Baron to be better informed than I really am, and consequently to ask fewer questions than I should otherwise have done. Ask yourself what advantages might I not obtain, were I not obliged to have recourse entirely to my own poor stock.

In brief, what pledges do you desire of the sincerity of the Princess? What proofs of friendship will you afford her? What precautions do you require for the good conduct of the Stadtholder? What kind of restraints do you mean to lay him under? Will you in nothing depart from what was stipulated in the commission of the 27th of February, 1766? What are the modifications you propose? Must mediation be necessarily and formally accepted? Is it not previously requisite that the provinces of Guelderland and Utrecht should send their troops into their respective quarters? Will the province of Holland then narrow her military line? In this supposition, is there nothing to be feared from the Free Corps? and how may she answer for them? What will be the determinate constitutional functions of the Stadtholder? What the relations of subordination and influence toward the deputy counselors? What is the reformation intended to be made in the regulations?

These, and a thousand other particulars, are of

consequence to me, if I am to be of any service in the business; otherwise I need none of them. But it is to me indispensable that you should immediately and precisely inform me how I ought to act and speak, how far I am to go, and where to stop.

Be kind enough to observe that it is requisite this step should be kept entirely secret from Comte d'Esterno, and that the intentions and proceedings of Baron Reede certainly do not merit that the Baron should be betrayed.

A curious and very remarkable fact is that the Duke of Brunswick was the first who spoke to Baron Reede of the Prussian troops being put in motion, and asked him what effect he imagined it would have on the affairs of Holland if some regiments of cavalry were marched into, and should it be needful, if a camp were formed in, the principality of Cleves, which might be called a camp of pleasure. Baron Reede replied this was a very delicate step, and it was scarcely possible the Cabinet of Versailles could remain an unconcerned spectator. Does the Duke desire to be Prime Minister, be the event what it may? And has he unworthily deceived me? Or was it only his intention to acquire from Baron Reede such information as might aid him to combat the proposition of Count Hertzberg? The Dutch Ambassador wished to persuade me of the first. I imagine he is sincere; yet, to own the truth, the public would echo his opinion, for the Duke is in high renown for deceit. But here I ought to oppose the testimony of Count Hertzberg himself, who owned that the idea was his own, and who bitterly repeated, more than once, " Ah! had not the Duke deserted me! " It is necessary to have heard the expression and the accent to form any positive opinion on the subject, which to a certain point may be warranted.

January 5th.

I found Baron Reede at the rendezvous, in the same temper of mind; and, if possible, more fervent, more zealous. The only delicacy in acting he required was that I should not say he had written; in order, as he observed, that, should these advances still fail in their effect, a greater animosity might not be the result. He related to me an example of this kind, concerning the success of a confidential proceeding which happened, some years ago, between himself and M. de Gaussin, at that time *chargé d'affaires* from France to Berlin, and who, having described the business in terms too ardent to be accurate, receives a ministerial answer from M. de Vergennes, of the most kind and amicable complexion, which, passing directly to the Stadtholder, through the medium of the Cabinet of Berlin, was by no means found acceptable, as it might reasonably have been supposed it would have been; and that this produced an additional degree of coldness. True it is that the Prince of Orange had not, at that time, experienced the strength of his opponents; but this Prince is so passionate, and his mind is so perverse, that the Princess herself is obliged to take the utmost precautions when she has anything to communicate.

I promised Baron Reede to act entirely as he wished; yet have not thought it the less my duty to relate the whole affair, well convinced that people only of very narrow minds pique themselves on their policy; that M. de Calonne will think proper to know nothing of all this, except just as much as he ought to know; that in any case he will seem only to regard this overture as the simple attempt of two zealous men, who communicated a project which they supposed was most probable of success. In reality, though it may be the most pressing interest of the Stadtholder to obtain

peace, how can our alliance with Holland be more effectually strengthened than by the concurrence of the
Stadtholder? And with respect to the individual interests of M. de Calonne, should we happen to lose
M. de Vergennes, through age or ill health, who is
there capable of disputing the place with him, who
shall have promoted the commercial treaty between
France and England, and have accomplished the
pacification of Holland? Enough at present concerning the business in which I am engaged. Let us return to Prussia.

January 6th.

Lieutenant-Colonel Goltz has long been on cold
terms, and even has quarreled, with Bishopswerder.
They had once been reconciled by the King, who felt
that the first, being more firm of character, and more
enterprising, had great advantages in the execution
of affairs over the other, who was more the courtier,
and more the humble servant of circumstances. To
avoid domestic scandal, he has appointed M. von Han-
stein, who possesses dignity, or rather haughtiness,
and M. von Pritwitz, a man of mediocrity, and a victim to the caprices of the late King, to be general
aides-de-camp. Thus Bishopswerder, after he has
done everything in his power to remove all who had
more understanding than himself from about the person of the King, having accomplished his purpose and
secured the Monarch solely to himself, knows not what
he shall do with him.

Count Brühl has found neither arrangements ready
prepared, apartments furnished, nor persons placed in
the service of the Prince Royal. The consequences
were—ill-humor, a visit to Welner, not admitted, visit
returned late, and by a card, rising discontent, which

is encouraged by Bishopswerder, who suspects Welner to have been softened concerning the nomination of the two general aides-de-camp.

A fact which appears very probable is that Welner, who is christened by the people The Little King, knows not how to perform three offices at once; and, as he foolishly believed he might yield to the eagerness of speculators, and has had the meanness to enjoy the despicable flatteries of those who six months ago treated him like a lackey, his days have glided away in these perilous pastimes of vanity. Business has been neglected, everything is in arrear, and it is presumed that, when he shall have been sufficiently bandied by the intrigues of the malcontents, the ingratitude of those whom he shall have served, the arts of courtiers, and the snares of his own subalterns, his brain will be entirely turned.

It is at length determined the capitation tax shall not be enforced. Thus it is withdrawn after having been announced! Without conviction! Without a substitute! What confusion! What forebodings! From the short prospect of the morning of the reign, how portentous are the steps of futurity!

The sending an envoy to London; which Court has not yet returned the compliment.

Another envoy sent to Holland, who, in every step he has taken, has risked the reputation of his Sovereign. It certainly was necessary either to act consistently, or totally to abstain from acting.

The commission of inquiry on the administration of the finances, which has been productive of nothing but injustice and rigor toward individuals, without the least advantage to the public.

Another commission to examine the conduct of General Wartemberg, appointed with ostentation, and suspended in silence.

The suppression of the administration of tobacco and snuff, which must be continued.

The project of the capitation tax, which is obliged to be withdrawn at the very moment it was to commence.

The convocation of the principal merchants of Prussia and Silesia, which has generated nothing but discussion, such as are proper to unveil the absurdity of the rulers, and the wretchedness of the people.

Do not so many false steps, so many recedings, suppose administrators who have reflected but little, who are groping in the dark, and who are ignorant of the elements of the science of governing?

Amid this series of follies, we must nevertheless remark a good operation, which is truly beneficial. I speak of that at present unlimited corn trade, and an annual exemption in behalf of that miserable Western Prussia, the amount of which I do not yet know. The domestic fermentation of the palace begins to be so great that it must soon become public. The agent of the wishes, or, more properly speaking, of the secret whims, is in opposition to Bishopswerder and Welner, who are on cold terms with Mademoiselle Voss, who is desirous that Madame Rietz should be discarded, who will agree that Mademoiselle Voss should be a rich mistress but not a wife. Among this multitude of opposing wills, where each, except the King, acts for himself, we may enumerate his Majesty's chamberlain, and the counselor of Mademoiselle Voss, Reuss; and the pacificator, the mediator, the counselor, the temporizer, the preacher, Count Arnim.

The Sovereign, amid these rising revolts, weathers the storm to the best of his abilities. The jeweler Botson has laid a complaint against Rietz, which occasioned a quarrel that might have had consequences, had not the King recollected that ten years might be necessary to replace a confidant whom he might have discharged in a moment of anger. The birthday of the Count of Brandenburg was likewise a circumstance which the Rietz party made subservient to their interest. His Majesty sent for the mother to dinner, and peace was the restorer of serenity.

The master of the horse, who was said to have lost his credit, appears to have risen from the dead. Exclusive of his yellow ribbon, which he hung over his shoulders on the last Court day, and which excited bursts of laughter from everybody, even from the Ministers, he requested his nephew might be created a count, and was answered with a "So be it." The creating of a count is but a trifling evil, especially when so many have been created; but never to possess a will of one's own is a serious reflection.

Would you wish for a picture of the sinews of Government, and active facilities of the Governors? Take the following feature:

Various remonstrances had been made to the King finally to regulate the state of expenditure, and the salaries of his officers. He replied that he intended to keep a Court; and that, in order to regulate his expenses, he first desired to know the permanent state of his revenues, according as they should be collected and ascertained by his new financiers. After reflecting on various phases, in all of which was repeated the word ASCERTAINED, the Ministers, under whose charge the excise and the daily expenditure were, began to have their apprehensions. Hence followed a multitude of trifling taxes, ridiculous, hateful, and unproductive, which sprang up in a single night. Oysters, cards, and an increase on the postage of letters, on stamps, on wines, eight groschen per ell on taffetas, thirty-three per cent on furs. They even went so far as to suppress the franchises of the Princes of the household. Not one of these new imposts but was most gratuitously odious; for they retard what they are meant to effect, and are productive of nothing but a demonstration of the heavy stupidity of those who neither can procure money nor satisfy the public.

POSTSCRIPT.—I have received a voluminous dispatch in cipher from Courland, the contents of which it is impossible I should at present send. I can only confirm former intelligence, that the chamberlain Howen, who is at present Burgrave, disposes of the province, and is wholly Russian; the circumstances by the next courier.

LETTER LXIII

January 8th, 1787.

THE following is the substance of the news from Courland, as authentic as can possibly be procured.

The chamberlain Howen, an able man, the first and the only person of understanding in the country (for the chancellor Taubé, who might otherwise counterpoise his influence, is destitute of mind and character) ; Howen, I say, is become Ober Burgrave, by the sudden death of the Prime Minister, Klopman. After this event followed a torrent of re-placings and de-placings, in none of which you are interested, and concerning which it will be sufficient for you to know that every recommendation of the Duke has been absolutely rejected and contemned. The Baron of Mest-Machor, the Russian envoy by a formal and direct recommendation, occasioned the election to alight on Howen, who once was the violent enemy of the Russians, by whom he had been carried off from Warsaw, where he resided as envoy from Courland, and banished into Siberia. Here he remained several years. By a concurrence of circumstances he is become Russian. It appears that the Cabinet of Petersburg has preferred the gaining of its purpose by gentle measures, and intends amicably to accomplish all its designs on Courland. Howen is in reality Duke of Courland, for he executes all the functions of the dukedom, and converts or overawes all opponents. Woronzow, Soltikow, Belsborotko, and Potemkin are absolute masters of Courland, as they are of Russia; with this only difference, that Potemkin, who possesses a library of mortgages and bank bills, who pays nobody, corrupts everybody, who subjects all by the energy of his will and the extent of his views, soars above Belsborotko, who is politically his friend; above Woronzow, who is capable but timid; and above Soltikow, who is wholly devoted to the Grand Duke.

The Duke of Courland will probably return no more to his country, because he has ruined his affairs in Russia, is unable to alter anything which has been done in his absence, is entangled in lawsuits, and by complaints laid against him without number, and because the regency, which preserves a good understanding with the chiefs of the equestrian order, under the guidance of Howen, reigns with moderation, conformable to the laws of the land, and brings down benedictions on its administration; insomuch that the people, who were ready to revolt because they were threatened by, and already were suffering, famine, wish affairs to continue in their present train. It is to them of little import whether the government be or be not Russian, if misery be not entailed on them. There is no possibility of reversing a system thus stable. Some sixty considerable estates have been granted as fiefs or farms. All the vacant places have been bestowed on persons of the greatest influence, abroad and at home;

so that we may say the party of the administration of Howen or of the Russians in Courland, includes everybody. Several millions must be expended to counterpoise such a preponderance; and, if to counterpoise were to vanquish, victory itself would not be worth expenses so great.

One of the principal complaints against the Duke is the deterioration of Courland, which has been effected by the total impoverishment of the peasants and the lands, the ruin of the forests, and the exportation of the ducal revenues into foreign countries. But the grand crime, the crime not to be forgiven, is having displeased Russia. The Empress has been so enraged against him, by his anti-Russian proceedings in Courland, that she herself said: "The King of France would not have injured me as the Duke of Courland has dared to do." She probably meant, bestowing Courland on Prussia.

I cannot perceive how we can act better, in our present situation, than to wait with patience. Our young man will certainly have a place in his own country. Should it be thought proper to bestow on him the title of consul, with leave to wear our uniform, and a captain's commission, from which he might derive respect, he asks nothing more; and we should possess an intelligent, zealous, and incorruptible sentinel, who, from so well-situated a post, might inform us of whatever was passing in the North, and aid us in what relates to commerce.

I need not observe that great changes are not effected in a day. We may, however, depend upon a confirmation of the Maritime Company as a symptomatic anecdote of importance. Struensee has acted in a pleasant manner. "Gentlemen," said he, to the merchants of Königsberg and Prussia, "nothing can be more excellent than a free trade; but it is very just that you should buy all the salt in our warehouses." "True." "Very good. You must, therefore, give us security for one million, two hundred thousand crowns, as well as pay a hundred and twenty thousand crowns annually to the proprietors, in return for the ten per cent for which we are accountable; for public good will not admit an injury to be committed on private right." "True." "Very good. And, for the same reason, you must pay five per cent, which has been legally granted on the new shares." "True." "Very excellent, gentlemen. But who are to be your securities? Or, at least, where are your funds?" "Oh, we will form a company!" "A company, gentlemen! One company is as good as another. Why should not the King give the preference to the company that actually exists?"

All projects for the freedom of trade will, like this, go off in *fumo;* and, what is still more fatal, if possible, conclusions will be drawn, from the ignorance of the present administration, in favor of the impossibilty of changing former regulations. Such are Kings without a will; such is the present, and such will he live and die! The other was all soul; this is all body. The symptoms of his incapacity increase with aggravation. I shall have continual occasion to repeat nearly the same words, the same opinions, the same remarks. But here, however, may be added, what I think a fact of weight, which is that one of the causes of the torpor of interior administration is the misunderstanding which reigns in the Ministry. Four Ministers are in opposition to two, and the seventh remains neuter. Messieurs Gaudi and Werder, who keep shifting the helm of finance, are counteracted by Messieurs Heinitz, Arnim, Schulemburg, and Blumenthal. The former of the last four is accused of attempting to add the department of the mines to that of the finances. In the meantime the expediting of business continues with

Welner, and the impulse of influence with Bishops-werder.

The latter, either sincerely or insidiously, has become the associate of the plan to bring Prince Henry again into power, at least in military affairs. The Prince, for several years, has not been present at the manœuvres. It is affirmed that he not only will be this year, but that he will be made a kind of inspector general. The negotiation is carried on, with great secrecy, by General Moellendorf and the favorite.

The marriage of Mademoiselle Voss is again in report. Certain it is that every species of trinkets has been purchased, every kind of preparation has been made, and that a journey is rumored. Most of these circumstances are kept very secret; but I am well assured of their truth, because I have them from the Rietz family, who are very much interested in preventing the union being accomplished, under certain formalities, and who consequently are very actively on the watch. But I know not what form they will bestow on this half-conjugal, half-concubine state. Yesterday, however, when I supped with the King, I had ocular demonstration there was no longer any restraint laid on speaking together in public.

The King, at supper, asked me, "Who is one M. de Laseau?" "Du Saux, perhaps, Sire." "Yes, Du Saux." "A member of our academy of inscriptions." "He has sent me a large work on gaming." "Alas! Sire, you masters of the world only have the power of effecting the destruction of gaming. Our books will accomplish but little." "But he has embarrassed me by paying me a compliment which I by no means merit." "There are many, Sire, which you are too prudent to be in haste to merit." "He has congratulated me on having abolished the Lotto; I wish it were true, but it is not." "A wish from Your Majesty will effect much." "I am some thanks in your debt, on this subject, for this is one of the good counsels you gave me in a certain writing." (I made a low bow.) "But you must excuse me for a time. There are funds assigned on that vile Lotto; the military school, for example." "Fortunately, Sire, a momentary deficiency of fifty thousand crowns is not a thing to inspire the richest King on earth, in ready money, with any great apprehensions." "True; but agreements—" "Will not be violated when the parties are reimbursed, or have any proportionate remuneration. Surely, since despotism has so often been employed to do ill, it might for once effect good." "Oh, oh! then you are somewhat reconciled to despotism." "Who can avoid being reconciled to it, Sire, where one head has four hundred thousand arms?" He laughed with a simple kind of grin, was informed the comedy was going to begin, and here ended our conversation. You perceive, there is still some desire of being praised in this lethargic soul.

POSTSCRIPT.—Launay this night departed incognito. I imagine you will give very serious offense to the Cabinet of Berlin if you do not prevent him going to press, as is his intention.

LETTER LXIV

January 13*th,* 1787.

I BELIEVE I have at length discovered what the Emperor was hatching here. He has, *sans* circumlocution, proposed to suffer Prussia to appropriate the remainder of Poland to itself, provided he might act in like manner by Bavaria. Fortunately, the bait was too gross. It was perceived he offered the gift of a country which he had not the power to bestow, and the invasion of which would be opposed by Russia, that he might, without impediment, seize on another which had been refused him, and of which, if once acquired, he never after could have been robbed. Your Ambassador, probably, has discovered this long before me, from whom you will have learned the circumstances. To him the discovery has been an affair of no difficulty; for confidence is easily placed, in politics, when it is determined that the proposal shall be rejected; besides that it is a prodigious step in advance to have the right of conferring with Ministers, from whom that may be divined which is not asked. For my own part, I can only inform you intrigues and machinations are carried on, and the very moment I discover more, I shall consider it as my duty to send you intelligence. But I do not suppose I can give you any new information of this kind. I have only promised to supply you with the current news of the Court and the country. The rest is out of my sphere. I want the necessary means effectually to arrive at the truth. God grant it never should enter the head of the Emperor to allure the King of Prussia more adroitly, and to say to him, "Suffer me to take Bavaria, and I will suffer you to seize on Saxony; by which you acquire the finest country in Germany, a formidable frontier, and near two millions of subjects; and by which, in a word, you will extend, round, and consolidate your dominions. Neither shall we have any great difficulties to combat. All of them may be obviated by making the Elector King of Poland. The Saxon family possess the mania of royalty; and even should the kingdom become hereditary, wherein would be the inconvenience? It is good, or at least it very soon will be good, to possess a strong barrier against Russia."

Should they ever conceive such a project, it would

be executed, with or without the consent of all Europe. But this they have not conceived. One is too inconsistent, the other too incapable; and after some disputes, more or less serious, the Emperor will filch a village, perhaps, from Bavaria, and the King of Prussia continue to crouch under his nullity.

The misfortune is that to treat him thus is to treat him with indulgence. The following is a fact entirely secret, but certain; and which, better than all those my preceding dispatches contain, will teach you to judge the man. Within this fortnight he has paid a debt of a million of crowns to the Emperor. And what was this debt? The Empress-Queen had lent the Prince Royal, now King of Prussia, a million of florins; which by accumulating interest, had become a million of crowns. And when? In the year 1778, during the Bavarian campaign, under the fatigues of which they imagined themselves certain that Frederick II. would sink. Thus was Frederick William base enough to accept the money of Austria, which he has had the imbecility to repay. He had not the sense to say, "MY SUCCESSOR WILL REPAY YOU." No; he sanctions the act of the Imperial Court when lending money to the Princes Royal of Prussia. He imagines he has fulfilled his duties as a sovereign when he has had the honesty to pay his debts as an individual.

The sum total of these debts amounted to nine millions of crowns; and, though I do not indeed suppose that the agents are any losers, it is nevertheless true that the first months of his reign will cost Prussia thirty-six millions, exclusive of common expenses, gifts, gratifications, pensions, etc. The extraordinaries of the first campaign, in which it was necessary to remount all the cavalry, did not cost Frederick II. more than five millions, or five millions and a half, of crowns.

I have not yet depicted the Monarch as a warrior; the trade gives him the spleen, its *minutiæ* fatigue him, and he is weary of the company of generals. He goes to Potsdam, comes on the parade, gives the word, dines and departs. He went on Wednesday to the house of exercise at Berlin, uttered a phrase or two, bade the troops march, and vanished. And this is the house in which Frederick II., loaded with fame and years, regularly passed two hours daily, in the depth of winter, in disciplining, grumbling, cursing, praising, in a word, in keeping the tormented troops in perpetual action, who still were transported to see the Old One, for that was the epithet they gave him, at their head.

But a more important point is the new military regulations, which have been conceived, planned, approved, and, as it is said, are going to be printed, without either having been communicated to Prince Henry or the Duke of Brunswick. The tendency of this new plan is nothing less than the destruction of the army. The seven best regiments are converted into light troops, and among others that of Wunsch. I am yet unacquainted with the particulars of the changes made, but, according to the opinion of General Moellendorf, had Lascy himself been their promoter they would have been just as they are. The worthy Moellendorf is humbled, discouraged, afflicted. All is under the direction of Goltz, who is haughty, incapable of discussion, and who holds it as a principle that the army is too expensive, and too numerous, in times of peace. He is perpetually embroiled with Bishopswerder, often obliged to attend to business of this kind, and in some manner under the necessity of interfering in affairs in the conduct of which he is not supposed to be equally well versed.

The Duke of Brunswick does not come. He replied to some person who had complimented him on his promotion, and who, in a letter, had supposed he was soon expected to arrive at Berlin, that he had been exceedingly flattered by receiving a title, which, however, he did not think he had merited; that he never had, and never should, come to Berlin, unless sent for; and of this he saw no immediate prospect. I have very good information that he is exceedingly disgusted, and will doubtless be so more than ever, should the constitution of the army be reversed without his opinion being asked, who is the only field marshal of Prussia.

I do not scruple to affirm that, by the aid of a thousand guineas, in case of need, the whole secrets of the Cabinet of Berlin might be perfectly known. The papers which continually are spread upon the tables of the King might be read and copied by two clerks, four *valets de chambre,* six or eight footmen, and two pages, the women not included. For this reason the Emperor has an exact and daily journal of the proceedings of the King, and would be acquainted with all his projects, were he really to project anything.

Never did kingdom announce a more speedy decline. It is sapped on every side at once. The means of receipt are diminished, the expenses are multiplied, principles are despised, the public opinion sported with, the army enfeebled, the very few people who are capable of being employed are discouraged. Those even are disgusted, to please whom all others have been offended. Every foreigner of merit is kept at a distance, and the King is surrounded by the vulgar and the vile, that he may be thought to reign alone. This fatal frenzy is the most fruitful cause of all the evil which at present exists, and of that which is preparing for the future.

Were I to remain here ten years longer, I might furnish you with new particulars, but could not draw any new consequence. The man is judged; his creatures are judged; the system is judged. No change, no possible improvement, can take place, so long as there shall be no first Minister. When I say no change, I do not, by any means, wish you to understand no person shall be dismissed. Sand shall succeed to sand, but sand it still shall be, and nothing better, till piles shall be sunken on which a foundation may be laid. What, therefore, should I do here henceforth? I can be of no use; yet nothing but utility—great, direct, immediate utility—could reconcile me to the extreme indecency of the present amphibious existence which has been conferred upon me, should this existence be prolonged.

I am obliged to repeat that my abilities, what I merit and what I am worth, ought at present to be known to the King, and to the Ministry. If I am capable of nothing, and merit nothing, I am, while here, a bad bargain. If I am of some worth, and may effect some good purpose, if nine months (for nine months will have passed away before I shall return), if, I say, a subaltern test of nine months, most painful in itself, and during which I have encountered a thousand and a thousand impediments without once being aided, have enabled me to acquire some knowledge of men, some information, some sagacity, without enumerating the precious contents of my portfolio, I am, then, in duty bound to myself to ask, and either to obtain a place or to return to a private station, which will neither be so fatiguing to body nor mind, nor so barren of fame.

For these reasons I undisguisedly declare, or rather repeat, I cannot remain here, and I request my return may be formally authorized; whether it be intended to employ me hereafter or to restore me to myself. I certainly shall not revolt at any kind of useful occupation. My feelings are not superannuated, and though my enthusiasm may be benumbed, it is not extinct. I have in my sensations at this moment a strong proof to the contrary. The day which you inform me you have fixed for the convocation of the notables I shall regard as one of the most glorious days of my life. This convocation, no doubt, will soon be followed by a national assembly, and here I contemplate renovating order, which shall give new life to the monarchy. I should think myself loaded with honors were I but the meanest secretary of that assembly, the project of which I had the happiness to communicate, and to which there is so much need that you should appertain, or rather that you should become its soul. But to remain here, condemned to the rack, in company with fools, obliged to sound and to wade through the fœtid meanderings of an administration, each day of which is signalized by some new trait of cowardice and stupidity, this is beyond my strength; for I perceive no good purpose it can effect. Send me, therefore, my recall, and let me know whether I am to pass through Holland.

There, for example, I would accept a secret commission; because pacification there demands, as an indispensable preliminary, a secret agent, who can see and speak the truth, and who is capable of captivating confidence. I do not believe foreign politics afford any opportunity of rendering greater service to France. I fear, since it is necessary I should confess my fears, we rely too much on the ascendency which the aristocracy has gained, of late years, over the Stadtholdership. I think I perceive the system of the patriots has not acquired any decided superiority, except in the province of Holland, which does not disturb its co-estates, or at least inasmuch as it excites their animosities. Nay, at Amsterdam itself, the very hotbed of anti-Stadtholder sentiments, was not the Grand Council though the first to rise against the concession of the Scotch brigade to England, the first to plead in favor of military convoys, and to demand the dismission of the Duke Louis of Brunswick? Was it not also the first to vote for a separate peace with England, and for the acceptance of the mediation of Russia? Was not its admiralty, several of the members of which depend on the regency, highly involved in the plot which occasioned the failure of the Brest expedition? How can it be otherwise? The Sovereign Council is only in possession of an imaginary authority. It is the burgomasters, who are annually changed; or even the president of the burgomasters, who is changed once in three months; or rather, in fine, such among the burgomasters as gain some influence of understanding or character over the others, who issue those orders that direct the important vote of the city of Amsterdam, in the Assembly of the States. When we recollect that the college of sheriffs, old and new, from which the burgomasters are elected, contains a great number of English partisans, and depends in some manner on the Stadtholder, who chooses those sheriffs, I know not how we can depend upon the future system of that city.

It is for such reasons that I cannot understand why it should not be for our interest to bring these disputes to a conclusion, if we do not wish to annul the Stadtholdership, which cannot be annulled without giving birth to foreign and domestic convulsions. And is it possible we should wish for war? We ought not, doubtless, to suffer the family of the Stadtholder to remain possessed of legislative power, in the three provinces of Guelderland, Utrecht, and Over-Yssel, by what is called the rules of the regency; for this, added to the same prerogative in the provinces of Zealand and Groningen, inclines the balance excessively in his favor. Neither can it be doubted but that the power of the Stadtholder ought to be subservient to the legislative power of the States. It is of equal importance to our system, or rather to the regular system of foreign politics, that the legislative power of the States should be directed and maintained by the uniform influence of the people. But the pretensions and passions of individuals, and the private interests of the members of an aristocracy, have, in all countries, too often been supposed the public interest; which is peculiarly true here, where the union of the Seven Provinces was formed in troublesome times, and by the effect of chance, since the people did not think of erecting a republican government till the sovereignty has first been refused by France and England. Hence it resulted that the regents and the people never were agreed concerning the limitation of their rights and reciprocal duties. The regents have necessarily labored to render themselves independent of the people; and the people, supposing themselves absolute, since they never consigned over the sovereignty to the regents, nor have had any interest to support them, have on all critical occasions counteracted their attempts. This was the origin of the Stadtholder party, and that of fluctuation which has happened between the despotic will of an individual, the perfidious tergiversations of the wavering, the feeble aristocratical colleges, and the impetuosity of an enraged populace. Should ever a link of union exist between the citizens and the regents, the despotism of the Stadtholder and the caprices of the oligarchy will have an end; but, while no such union does exist, while the mode in which the people influence the Government remains undetermined, so long must the system of France remain insecure.

Preserve the confederate constitution, between the provinces and the republican form, in its reciprocal state. Or, to reduce the proposition to the most simple

terms, INSTEAD OF THE ODIOUS AND ILLEGAL RECOM-
MENDATIONS OF THE STADTHOLDER, OR OF A BURGO-
MASTER, SUBSTITUTE THE REGULAR AND SALUTARY
RECOMMENDATIONS OF THE CITIZENS.   Such should
be the palladium of the republic; such the pursuit of
our politics.

This restriction rather demands a concurrence of circumstances than the shock of contention.   And shall
we be able to effect it by those acts of violence which
are attributed to us, even though they should not be
ours, or by increasing fermentation on one part, and on
the other suspicion?   Have we not made our influence
and our power sufficiently felt?   Is it not time to show
that we wish only for the abolition of the Stadtholder
regulations, and not that of the Stadtholdership?   And
how shall we conclude without making the conclusion
tragical, since it is not in human wisdom to calculate
all possible consequences, if we cannot effectually persuade the persons at Nimeguen that such is our real
and sole system.

Such is the rough draft of my profession of faith,
relative to the affairs of Holland.   From what I have
said, and according to these principles, which I shall
more circumstantially develop, if required, in a written
memorial, it may be estimated whether I can or cannot
be useful in the country; further supposing me possessed of local information, which I shall with facility
acquire.

LETTER LXV

January 16th, 1787.

IN THE opinion of those who know that revolutions
effected by arms are not often those that overturn
States, it is truly a revolution in the Prussian mon-

archy to behold an example for the first time of a
titled mistress, who is on the point of sequestrating the
King, of forming a distinct Court, of exciting cabals
which shall be communicated from the palace to the
LEGIONS, and of arranging affairs, favorites, administration, and grants, after a manner absolutely unknown
to these cold and phlegmatic countries. The moment
of the disgrace, and the consequent elevation of Mademoiselle Voss approaches. Hence intrigues, sarcasms, opinions, and conjectures, or rather predictions.
Amid this mass of suppositions, true or false, the following is what I can collect, which seems to have
most probability. My translation is according to the
text of one of the former friends of Mademoiselle
Voss, to whom she has opened her heart.

This new Joan of Arc, on whose head devotion
would invoke the nuptial benediction, has been persuaded that it is her duty to renounce marriage, and
sacrifice herself, first to her country; in the second
place, to her lover's glory; and, finally, to her family's
advantage. The country, say her advisers, will gain a
protectress, will remove covetous and perverse counselors; the glory of the Monarch will not be tarnished
by a double marriage; and her family will not be exposed to the danger of beholding her a momentary
princess, and presently afterward exiled to an old castle, with some trifling pension. They affirm favor will
be the more rapturous should rapture not be secured by
the rites of Hymen, and that the instant this favor
commences she will rain gold on her relations, with
dignities and gratuities of every kind. Religious
motives have been added to motives of convenience. It
has been demonstrated that there was less evil in con-
descension than in contracting a pretended marriage
while the former one remained in full force. At length
it was concluded that this VICTIM TO HER COUNTRY'S

GOOD should be taken to Potsdam and offered up at Sans Souci. A house has been prepared, sumptuously furnished, say some, and simply, according to others, and at which are all the paraphernalia of a favorite.

An anecdote, truly inconceivable, which requires confirmation, and which I am still averse to believe, is circulated: that the King prostitutes his daughter, the Princess Frederica, to be the companion of his mistress.

Mademoiselle Voss has a kind of natural wit, some information, is rather willful than firm, and is very obviously awkward, which she endeavors to disguise by assuming an air of simplicity. She is ugly, and that even to a degree; and her only excellence is the goodness of her complexion, which I think rather wan than white, and a fine neck, over which she threw a double handkerchief the other day, as she was leaving Prince Henry's comedy to cross the apartments, saying to the Princess Frederica, " I must take good care of them, for it is after these they run." Judge what must be the manners of princesses who can laugh at such an expression. It is this mixture of eccentric licentiousness (which she accompanies with airs of ignorant innocence) and vestal severity, which, the world says, has seduced the King. Mademoiselle Voss, who holds it ridiculous to be German, and who is tolerably well acquainted with the English language, affects the Anglomaniac to excess, and thinks it a proof of politeness not to love the French. Her vanity, which has found itself under restraint when in company with some amiable people of that nation, hates those it cannot imitate, more especially because her sarcasms sometimes are returned with interest. Thus, for instance, the other day, I could not keep silence when I heard an exclamation, " Oh, Heavens! when shall I see, when shall we have an English play? I really should expire with rapture!" "For my part, Mademoiselle," said I, dryly, "I rather wish you may not, sooner than you imagine, stand in need of French play." All those who began to be offended by her high airs smiled, and Prince Henry, who pretended not to hear her, laughed aloud. Her face was suffused with blushes, and she did not answer a word; but it is easy to punish, difficult to correct.

She has hitherto declared open war against the mystics, and detests the daughters of the chief favorite, who are maids of honor to the Queen.

But, as amid her weaknesses she is transported by devotion even to superstition, nothing may be depended on for futurity. Should ambition succeed primary sensations, it is to be presumed her family will govern the State. At the head of this family stands Count Finckenstein, whose tranquillity would not be disturbed by the fall of the empire, but who would with inexpressible joy contemplate his children enacting great parts. Next in rank is Count Schulemburg; who has newly been brought into the Ministry; an active man, formerly even too busy, but who seems to perceive that those who keep most in the background become the principal figures. This family preserves an inveterate hatred against Welner, who formerly carried off or seduced one of their relations, who is at present his wife. To these we may add the president Voss, the brother of the beauty; who at least possesses that spirit of calculation, and that German avidity, by which such persons profit whenever fortune falls in their way. Should Mademoiselle Voss render her situation in any degree subservient to such purposes, she must, while at Potsdam, prepare the dismission of Bishopswerder and Welner, or render them useless; for it is more the mode in Germany to dispense with service than to dismiss. She herself may possibly be ill-guided, and may confide in the first who shall happen to be present, for she is indiscreet. She depends on the constancy of her lover; for she is yet inexperienced in the GRATITUDE of mankind. Having never yet obliged anybody, she never yet has rendered anyone ungrateful.

Should this happen, affairs will remain in their present state, or grow worse. The King will shut himself up at Potsdam; whence, however, he will frequently make excursions to Berlin, because he has contracted a habit of restlessness, and because his favorite seraglio will always be at a brothel. He will then be totally idle, will tolerate rapaciousness, and, as much as he is able, hasten the kingdom's ruin, toward which it tends as rapidly as present circumstances and the *vis inertiæ* of the German character will allow; which does not permit madmen to commit anything more than follies, and preserves men from the destructive delirium of the passions.

Add to this, the Emperor dares attempt nothing, is consistent in nothing, concludes nothing, that he approaches his end, and that all his brothers are pacific. I should not be astonished were the hog of Epicurus, who, at least, is not addicted to pomp, and consequently will not of himself ruin the Treasury, to acquire, thanks to circumstances and interested men, a kind of glory during his reign.

Military regulations are again mentioned. The regiments of the line are not to be ruined, but it seems there is an intention to form a certain number of battalions of chasseurs, who, under good regulations, may become useful; and this, indeed, was the design of Frederick II. Nothing yet can be affirmed on the subject, except that it is exceedingly strange that Frederick William should imagine himself able to effect any reform, the economical part excepted, in the military system and in the army of Frederick II.

Prince Henry probably will have some influence in the army. His name stands the first on the list, although a field marshal has been appointed. The King sent him the list yesterday to assure him it was so, by M. von Goltz himself. They have given the child a bauble. What his military influence is to be must remain a secret till the appearance of the new regulations. He is often visited by the general aides-de-camp. Whether this is or is not known to the King is doubtful, and, if known, it is evident deceit only is meant, which, indeed, is a very fruitless trouble. He has no plan contrary to the politics of the kingdom. I do not say of the Cabinet, for Cabinet there is none. Indeed, he has no plan whatever.

Count Goertz is recalled, of which Count Hertzberg was this morning ignorant. There cannot be a better proof that there is no desire to interfere in the affairs of Holland, or not openly; nor simply to expose the nation to a war, to promote the interests of the Stadtholder. Of this, unfortunately, the House of Orange is not persuaded, but of the contrary, if I may judge from the letter of the Princess, which came by the courier of this morning, a part of which I read as soon as it was deciphered. It is in this point of view that my journey to Nimeguen, under a borrowed name, and with secret authority, known only to her and me, may become useful. In this same letter I have read that the patriots are endeavoring to effect a loan of sixteen millions of florins, at three per cent, although the province of Holland has never given more than two and a half per cent, and that they find difficulty in procuring the money.

There are three Bishops here: the Bishop of Warmia, the Bishop of Culm (who is of the House of

Hohenzollern), and the Bishop of Paphos. The first, whom I mentioned to you in my account of the King's journey into Prussia, is the same whom Frederick II., robbed of near eighty thousand crowns per annum, by reducing the revenues of his bishopric to twenty-four thousand from a hundred thousand crowns; for such was its value previous to the partition of Poland. The Monarch one day said to him: "I have not, in my own right, any great claims on Paradise; let me entreat you to take me in under your cloak." "That I would willingly," replied the prelate, "if your Majesty had not cut it so short." He is a man of pleasure and of the world, and who is only acquainted with the fine arts, without other views or projects, religious or political.

The second has been in the service of France. He has the rage of preaching upon him and of being elo-quent; and the desire of doing good; but as he has also the rage of running in debt, and getting children, his sermons make no proselytes, and his charities relieve no distress. The latter is a suffragan of Breslau, for-merly a great libertine, and a little of an atheist; at present impotent and superannuated.

These three prelates, who are to be reinforced by the Bishop of Lujavia, and the new coadjutor, the Prince of Hohenloe, Canon of Strasburg, will hold no council; nor will they justify the fears the orthodox Lutherans, and all Saxony, who suppose the corner stone of the Protestant religion to be laid here, have entertained concerning the inclination of the King to popery. The one came to obtain the order of the Black Eagle, and is gratified; the other for a benefice, vacant by the death of the Abbé Bathiani; the Prince Bishop of Warmia for a money loan, at two per cent, which may be sufficient to satisfy his creditors.

Prince Henry, after having given a comedy and a

grand supper, concluded the banquet with a ball, which began gloomily enough, and so continued. While some were dancing in one room, others were gambling at the Lotto in another. The King neither danced nor gambled; his evening was divided between Mademoiselle Voss, and the Princess of Brunswick. He spoke a word to M. von Grotthaus, but not a syllable to anybody else. Most of the actors and spectators departed before him. The Bishop of Warmia and the Marquis of Lucchesini were not so much as remarked. I would have defied the most penetrating observer to have suspected there was a King in company. Languor and restraint were present, but neither eagerness nor flattery. He retired at half past twelve, after Mademoiselle Voss had departed. It is too visible that she is the soul of his soul, and that the soul which is thus wrapt up in a covering so coarse is very diminutive. You must expect this continual repetition; the place of the scene may change, the scene itself never.

POSTSCRIPT.—The news of the recall of Goertz is false; and, from the manner in which it was conveyed to me, either Comte d'Esterno wished to lay a snare for me, or had had a snare laid for himself. I am acquainted with circumstances which make me believe it possible the negotiation should again be resumed. I have not time to say more.

The Duke of Brunswick is sent for, and will be here in a few days.

Count Wartensleben, who has for five months been forgotten, yesterday morning was presented with between five and six hundred crowns per annum, and the command of the regiment of Roemer at Brandenburg.

LETTER LXVI

January 19th, 1787. The day of my departure. This will not be sent off sooner than to-morrow, but it ought to arrive before me.

COUNT SCHMETTAU, the complaisant gentleman of the Princess Ferdinand, the indisputable father of two of her children, had eight years quitted the army, which he left in the midst of war, angered by a disdainful expression from Frederick II., and holding the rank of captain. He has lately been appointed a colonel, with the pay of fifteen hundred crowns per annum. The nomination has displeased the army, and particularly the General Aide-de-camp Goltz, who had been in harness five-and-twenty years, and still only enjoys the rank of lieutenant colonel. Count Schmettau has served with honor, has received many wounds, nor does he want intelligence, particularly in the art of fortification. He has drawn a great number of plans which are much esteemed. A military manual is also mentioned with praise, in which he teaches all that is necessary to be done from the raw recruit to the field marshal. In fine, this infringement on rank might have been supportable, but there has been another which has excited the height of discontent.

The commission of one Major Schenkendorff, the governor of the second son of the King, who gives up his pupil, has been antedated, by which he leaps over six-and-thirty heads. This dangerous expedient, which Frederick II., never employed but on solemn occasions, and in favor of distinguished persons, and which his successor had before practiced in behalf of Count Wartensleben, does but tend to spread incertitude over the reality of military rank, and to be destructive of all emulation. It is, besides, infinitely dangerous when employed by a feeble prince, absurd when resorted to at the commencement of his reign, and must finally deprive the Monarch himself of one of his greatest resources, the point of honor.

He has deposited five hundred thousand crowns in the provincial treasury, and has sent the transfer to Mademoiselle Voss. Thus happen what may, she will always have an income of a thousand a year, besides diamonds, plate, jewels, furniture, and a house that has been purchased for her at Berlin; which is a pleasure house for she does not intend to inhabit it. Her royal lover has himself imagined all these delicate attentions, and the consequence is that the most disinterested of mistresses has managed her affairs better than the most artful of coquettes could have done. Time will show us whether her mind will aspire to the rank of favorite Sultana.

New taxes are intended to be laid on cards, wines, foreign silks, oysters, coffee, sugar,—contemptible resources! As the Ministry are proceeding blindfold on all these matters, they are kept in a kind of secrecy. It seems they will rather make attempts than carry them into execution.

To-day, the birthday of Prince Henry, the King has made him a present of a rich box, estimated to be worth twelve thousand crowns, has set out the gold plate, and has done everything which Frederick II. used to do, if we omit the rehearsal of a grand concert, the day before, in his chamber; for he has time for everything except for business.

"Let there be bawdyhouses on the wings, and I will easily beat him in the center." Beware that this saying of the Emperor does not become a prophecy. The prophet himself, fortunately, is not formidable; though I should not be astonished were he to be animated by so much torpor and baseness; but if he do not wait two years longer, the energy which the King wants may be found in the army.

POSTSCRIPT.—The Duke of Weimar is at Mayence, as it is said, for the nomination of a coadjutor; but, as he visits all the Courts of the Upper and Lower Rhine, it would be good to keep a watchful eye over him, in my opinion.

END OF THE SECRET HISTORY

LETTER OR MEMORIAL

PRESENTED TO

FREDERICK WILLIAM II.

KING OF PRUSSIA

ON THE DAY OF HIS ACCESSION TO THE THRONE

BY

COMTE DE MIRABEAU

———

Arcus et statuas demolitur et obscurat oblivio, negligit carpitque posteritas. Contrà contemptor ambitionis et infinitæ potestatis domitor animus ipsâ vetustate florescit; nec ab ullis magis laudatur quàm quibus minimè necesse est.

PLIN., Panegy.

ADVERTISEMENT

SOME imputations are at once so odious and absurd, that a person of sense is not tempted to make them any reply. If he be a worthy man, silence is his only answer when his calumniators are anonymous.

But, amid the abuse lately vented against me, and which I have enumerated rather among the rewards of my labors than estimated as a part of my misfortunes, there is one species of scandal to which I have not been insensible.

I have been accused of presenting the reigning King of Prussia with a libel against the immortal Frederick II.

Frederick II., himself sent for me, when I hesitated (much as I regretted, having lived his contemporary, to die unknown to him) lest I should disturb his last moments during which it was so natural to desire to contemplate a great man. He deigned to welcome and distinguish me. No foreigner after me was admitted to his conversation. The last time he thus honored me he had refused the just and eager request which some of my countrymen, who had repaired to Berlin to see his military manœuvres, testified to be admitted to his presence. And could I, in return for so honorable a distinction, have written a libel?

Frederick is of himself too great for me ever to be tempted to write his panegyric. The very word is, in my apprehension, highly beneath a great King; it supposes exaggeration and insincerity, the wresting or dissimulation of truth; a view of the subject only on the favorable side. Panegyric, in fine, is to disguise, or to betray, the truth; for this is one of its inevitable inconveniences; never was panegyric true or honorable that was devoid of reproof. I therefore have not, nor shall I ever have, written the eulogy of Frederick II., but I have for these two years past been endeavoring to raise a monument to his memory, that ought not to be wholly unworthy of the labors by which his reign has been illustrated, or of those grand lessons which his successes and his errors have equally taught. I have engaged in this considerable work, which will see the light in the course of the present year, and of which I make no secret.

The Memorial which I presented to Frederick William II., on the day of his accession to the throne was entirely foreign to this plan. It was intended only to lay before him the hopes of worthy men, who knew how many events, rather great than splendid, might take birth in Prussia under a new reign and a Prince in the prime of manhood.

The following is the Memorial in question, which has been attributed to me as a crime. I lay my case before the world, that the world may judge. I have not altered a line, though my opinion has varied considerably in some circumstances, as will be seen in my work on Prussia. But I should have reproached myself had I made any change, however trifling, in a Memorial to which the venom of malignity has been imputed.

It has been often asked what right I had to present such a Memorial.

Besides the thanks which the present King of Prussia graciously was pleased to send me in a letter, he has not disdained personally to address me, in a numerous assembly, at the palace of his royal uncle, Prince Henry, a week before my departure from Berlin. This I have thought proper to make public, not in answer to idle tales, which never could deceive any person, but because the courage to love truth is even more honorable to a King than that of speaking truth is to a private person.

LETTER OR MEMORIAL

PRESENTED TO

FREDERICK WILLIAM II.

SIRE, you are now King. The day is come when it has pleased the Creator to confide to you the destiny of some millions of men, and the power of bringing much evil, or much good, upon the earth. The scepter descends to you at a period of life when man is capable of sustaining its weight. You ought at present to be weary of vulgar enjoyments, to be dead to pleasures, one only excepted. But this one is the only great, the sole inexhaustible pleasure,—a pleasure hitherto interdicted, but now in your power. You are called to watch over the welfare of mankind.

The *epocha* at which you ascend the throne is fortunate; knowledge daily expands; it has labored, it continues to labor for you, and to collect wisdom; it extends its influence over your nation, which so many circumstances have contributed in part to deprive of its light. Reason has erected its rigorous empire. Men at present behold one of themselves only, though enveloped in royal robes, and from whom more than ever they require virtue. Their suffrages are not to be despised, and in their eyes but one species of glory is now attainable; all others are exhausted. Military success, political talents, the miraculous labors of art, the progress of the sciences, have each alternately appeared resplendent from one extremity of Europe to the other. But enlightened benevolence, which organizes, which vivifies empires, never yet has displayed itself pure and unmixed upon the throne. It is for you to seat it there. Yes, renown so sublime is reserved to you. Your predecessor has gained a sufficient number of battles, perhaps too many; has too much wearied fame and her hundred tongues; has dried up the fountain of military fame for several reigns, for several ages. Should accident oblige you to become his imitator, it is necessary you should appear worthy so to be, in which Your Majesty will not fail. But this is no reason why you should painfully seek honor in the beaten path, wherein you can but rank as second; while with greater ease, you may create a superior glory, and which shall be only yours. Frederick has enforced the admiration of men, but Frederick never obtained their love: Yes, SIRE, their love may be wholly yours.

SIRE, your mien, your stature, recall to mind the heroes of antiquity. These to the soldier are much; much to the people, whose simple good sense associates the noblest qualities of mind to beauty of person; and such was the first intention of Nature. In your person the heroic form is embellished by most remarkable tints of mildness and calm benevolence, which promise not a little, even to philosophers. You have a feeling heart, and the long necessity of behaving with circumspection must have tempered that native bounty which otherwise might have made you too compliant. Your understanding is just; by this I have often been struck. Your elocution is nervous and precise. You have several times demonstrated that you possess an empire over yourself. You have not been educated, but you have not been spoiled; and men possessed of energy can educate themselves. They are daily educated by experience, and thus are taught what they never forget. Your means are great. You are the only Monarch in Europe who, far from being in debt, is possessed of treasures. Your army is excellent, your nation docile, loyal, and possessed of much more public spirit than might be expected in so slavish a constitution. Some parts of the administration of Prussia, such as its responsibility and consistency, which are purely military, merit great praises. One of your uncles, crowned with glory and success, possesses the confidence of Europe, the genius of a hero, and the soul of a sage. He is a counselor, a coadjutor, a friend, whom Nature and destiny have sent you, at the moment when you have most need of him, at the time when the more voluntary your deference for him shall be, the more infallibly will it acquire your applause. You have rivals in power, but not a neighbor who is in reality to be feared. He who seemed to proclaim himself the most formidable has too long threatened to strike. He has been taught to know you. He has hastily undertaken, and as hastily renounced. He will again renounce his new projects. He will require all, will obtain nothing, and will never be anything more than an irresolute adventurer, a burden to himself and others. To preserve yourself from his attempts, you need but to suffer his contradictory projects to counteract each other.

You, SIRE, are the only Prince who is under the indispensable necessity of performing great things, and from whom great things are expected; and this necessity, this expectation, ought to be enumerated among your best resources. How admirable is your situation! How inestimable are the advantages you bring to that throne whereon being seated your power is boundless! A power formidable even to the possessor! But be it remembered that grand institutions, important changes, and the regeneration of empires, appertain only to absolute Monarchs. Deign, oh, deign, to accept the good that Providence has strewn beneath your feet! Merit the benefactions of the poor, the love of the people, the respect of Europe, and the approbation of the wise! Be just, be good; and you will be happy and great.

GREAT.—This, SIRE, is the title you wish; but you wish it from history, from futurity; you would disdain it from the lips of courtiers, whom you HAVE heard, and whom you SHALL hereafter much oftener hear, prodigal of the grossest praise. Should you do that which the son of your slave could have hourly done better than yourself, they will affirm that YOU HAVE PERFORMED AN EXTRAORDINARY ACT. Should you obey your passions, they will affirm—YOU HAVE WELL DONE. Should you pour forth the blood of your subjects as a river does its waters, they will pronounce —YOU HAVE DONE WELL. Should you tax the free air, they will assert—YOU HAVE DONE WELL. Should you, puissant as you are, become revengeful, still would they proclaim you had DONE WELL. So they told the intoxicated Alexander when he plunged his dagger into the bosom of his friend. Thus they addressed Nero, having assassinated his mother.

But, SIRE, you need only to feel those sentiments of justice which are native to your bosom, and that enlightened consciousness of benevolence which you possess; your own heart will be your judge; and its decrees will be confirmed by your people, by the world, and by posterity. The esteem of these is indispensable; and how easily may their esteem be obtained! Should you indefatigably perform the duties of the day, and not remit its burdensome labors till the morrow; should you by grand and prolific principles know how to simplify these duties, so that they may be performed by a single man; should you accord your subjects all the liberty they are capable of enjoying; should you protect property, aid industry, and root out petty oppressors, who, abusing your name, will not permit men to do that for their own advantage which they might without injury to others; then will the unanimous voice of mankind bestow blessings on your authority, and thus render it more sacred and more potent. All things will then become easy to you, for every will and every power will unite with your will and your power, and your labors will daily acquire new enjoyments. Nature has rendered labor necessary to man; but she has also bestowed on him this precious advantage, that the change of labor is at once a recreation to him and a source of pleasure. And who more than a Monarch may live according to this order of Nature? A philosopher has said, " No man was so oppressed by languor as a King." He ought to have said a SLOTHFUL KING. How can languor overcome a Sovereign who shall perform his duties? How may he better maintain his body in health, or his mind in vigor than when by labor he preserves himself from that disgust which all men of understanding must feel, amid the babblers and the parasites who study but to corrupt, lull, benumb, and pilfer Princes? Their whole art is to inspire him with apathy and debility; or to render him impotent, rash, and indolent. Your people will enjoy your virtues; for by these only can they prosper or improve. Your courtiers will applaud your defects; for on these depend their influence and their hopes.

Habit, SIRE, no less than accident, influences men; and habit is determined by the beginning. Therefore is the commencement of a reign of such value. Everything is hoped, and the slightest effort seconds and confirms that hope, increasing it a hundredfold. By the pleasure of having done, we are strengthened in the love of doing, good; and that which is wished is rendered more easy by that which has been effected.

The beginning, SIRE, depends absolutely on yourself. Acquire none but good habits; give no encouragement to those that are frivolous. Display the man of order, the lover of the public welfare. You will soon be joined by all your Ministers and all your courtiers. Emulation will spring forth, and wisdom will inevitably be the result. Emulation will aid you to judge the understandings of those by whom you shall be approached. It may sometimes excite or produce a happy project, and you will even turn that propensity to flattery, which cannot totally be expelled from Courts, to the good of your people.

You may immediately ascertain to yourself that liberty of mind which grand affairs require, by interfering only with such as appertain to the sovereign authority, and by leaving to your Magistrates and Ministers all those which naturally should come under their consideration.

More than one estimable Monarch has rendered himself incapable of reigning with glory by overburdening his mind with private affairs. As, SIRE, it will become you always to govern well, it will also be worthy of you not to govern too much. Wherefore should a King concern himself with civil government which can be better exercised without his aid? Authority once established, external safety ascertained, civil and criminal justice administered alike to all classes of citizens, landed property accurately estimated so as to be judiciously assessed, and public works, roads, and canals wisely attended to; what more has government to transact? It has but to enjoy the industry of the people, who, while active for their own interest, are also acting for the interest of the State and the Sovereign.

The King who shall examine whether it be not the most wise not to lay any restraint on the general affairs and business of men is yet to be born; yet this is the King who would govern like a God; and, by the ministry of reason, leaving the interest of each individual to himself, would ascertain to all the fruits of their industry and their knowledge. Where men are most free, there will they be most numerous; and there, also will they pay the most submission, and have the greatest attachment, to authority; for authority is essentially the friend of that freedom which it protects. No man would require more than to be left AT LIBERTY AND IN PEACE.

You surely, SIRE, are not to be told that the mania of enacting and restraining laws is the characteristic of inferior minds; of men incapable of generalizing, who feed on timidity, and shake with ridiculous apprehensions. This important truth will indicate to you the reformation you ought to make; and how much better you will govern than your predecessors and rivals, by governing less.

There are, doubtless, a multitude of good, useful, necessary, and even urgent things, which it will be impossible you should immediately execute. You must first learn them, must combine, and leave them to ripen. And wherefore should you confide in the opinion of another? This is one of the grand errors of which you ought to be aware, as you ought also of being obliged to retract what you have done. The inconsistency of that Sovereign, among your rivals, who has attempted the most, has been more injurious to the political respect in which he might have been held than his worst errors. Not only, therefore, must you learn what is to do, but, which is more difficult, you must, perhaps, instruct your Ministers, and certainly your people. Let persuasion precede legislation, SIRE; and you will meet no contradiction, and scarcely any impediments in those operations which require moments of greater calm, and less business, than are those of the beginning of a reign. But there are things which you may instantly execute, and which, by propagating a high opinion of your worth, will acquire the fruits of confidence to your own profit, and facilitate the grand changes with which your reign ought to abound.

Suffer a man who loves you—pardon the freedom for the truth of the expression—suffer a man who loves you, for the good you may do, and for the grand example you shall afford of the evil that may be avoided, to point out a few of those things which a single voluntary act of yours may perform, and which can only be productive of good, without inconvenience, while they shall display the morning of the most paternal reign which has ever blessed mankind.

Among these, SIRE, and in the first rank, I shall enumerate the abolition of military slavery; that is to say, the obligation imposed in your States on all men from the age of eighteen to sixty and upward, if able, to serve for threepence a day.

This fearful law, originating in the necessities of an iron age and a half-barbarous country; this law which depopulates and exhausts your kingdom, which dishonors the most numerous and the most useful class of your subjects, without whom you and your ancestors would only have been slaves more or less feathered and painted; this law, which is abused by your officers, who enroll more men than the military conscription permits, this law does not procure you a soldier more than you would acquire by an increase of pay, which might easily be made from the additional revenue which you would gain by the just suppression of those ruinous enlisters whom Frederick II. maintained in foreign countries; and by a sage mode of recruiting the Prussian army, in a manner that should elevate the mind, increase public spirit, and preserve the forms of freedom instead of those of brutalizing slavery.

Throughout Europe, SIRE, and in Prussia particularly, men have had the stupidity to deprive themselves of one of the most useful instinctive feelings on which the love of our country can be founded. Men are required to go to war like sheep to the slaughterhouse; though nothing could be more easy than to unite the service of the public with emulation and fame.

Your subjects are obliged to serve from eighteen to sixty; and this they, with good reason, suppose to be the rigorous subjection of servility. The militia of France is the same, and though less cruel, is hateful to the people. Yet the Swiss have a similar obligation, which commences at the age of sixteen, and they believe themselves to be free men.

In fact, that natural confederacy which induces citizens of the same condition to repel the enemy, and to defend their own and their neighbor's inheritance, is so manifest, and the exercise of it is so pleasingly attractive to youth, that it is inconceivable how tyranny could be so weak as to render it a burden.

Impart, SIRE, to this obligation the forms of freedom and of fame, by making it voluntary, and necessary in order to merit esteem, by rendering it a point of honor; and your army will be better conditioned, while your subjects shall imagine they are, and shall really be, relieved from a yoke most odious.

Begin by remitting ten years of service; your army then will not be debilitated by age.

Let your peasants afterward form national companies, in all parishes, that shall exercise every Sunday.

Let such national companies choose their own grenadiers; and from these let the recruits for your regiments be selected,—not by your officers, not by the Magistrates, but by the plurality of votes among their comrades. Arbitrary proceedings would vanish, choice would become distinction, and the parishes responsible for the soldiers they have supplied. Being obliged to fill up their own vacancies when drafts are made, the regiments would be always complete, without effort, without tyranny, and without murmur.

Kings who have created power, impatient of enjoyment, have not confided in general principles. They have feared that the people they have invited into their countries should too soon be disgusted by the difficulties they must have to encounter at the beginning. Hence those tyrannical regulations, by the aid of which they have intended to fix the wretch to the soil on which he had been planted. In the present state of your kingdom there is no pretext for the continuance of this error. It is time to eradicate slavery at which the heart revolts, which drives away good subjects, or inspires them with the desire of escaping. Banish, therefore, all unnecessary constraint; and this, which of all others is the most unnecessary.

Yet, before deciding on any plan for the recruiting of the army, it is requisite to consider, with all the attention which it merits, that of the most worthy of your Ministers, Baron Hertzberg, who, to a comprehensive knowledge of the wounds of Prussia, and the means of prosperity and cure, joins the highest degree of public spirit and patriotic love. He supposes it possible to recruit the army by itself, so as to provide for everything that the most restless state of politics can require. Perhaps, and probably, his plan and mine may coalesce. It is incontestably one of those which ought to be executed at the very beginning of your reign; but let it be preceded by a law of enfranchisement, which shall procure your efforts the universal suffrages of mankind, and their combined aid.

It is not to a man so worthy as you, SIRE (and what greater praise can be bestowed upon a King?), it is not necessary to recommend, with respect to enrollments, the religious observation of all the stipulations so unworthily violated by your predecessors, or the pious rewarding of soldiers who have distinguished themselves by long and loyal service. Alas! SIRE, I have seen alms bestowed, under the windows of your palace, upon men who, while you were yet in your cradle, have shed their blood in defense of your family. Your generous equity doubtless will soften the rigor of their destiny. Remember also the duty, the necessity, of educating the children of soldiers, who at present are perishing in the most deplorable manner, in the orphan house of Potsdam, where more than four thousand are huddled together. Humanity implores your protection of these wretched victims, and provident policy, which but too loudly affirms how requisite a great army will long be to the Prussian States, will point out the real value of these children.

Men ought to be happy in your kingdom, SIRE; grant them liberty to leave their country, when not legally detained by individual obligations. Grant this freedom by a formal edict. This, SIRE, is another of the eternal laws of equity, which the situation of the times demands should be put in execution; which will do you infinite good, and which will not rob you of one enjoyment; for your people can nowhere seek a better condition than that which it depends on you to afford them; and could they be happy elsewhere they would not be detained by your prohibitions. Leave such laws to those Powers that have been desirous to render provinces prisons, forgetting that this was but to make them hateful. The most tyrannical laws respecting emigration have only impelled the people to emigrate, against the very wish of Nature, and perhaps the most powerful of all wishes, which attaches man to his native soil. How does the Laplander cherish the desolate climate under which he is born! And would the inhabitant of a kingdom enlightened by milder suns pronounce his own banishment, did not a tyrannical administration render the benefits of Nature useless or abhorred? Far from dispersing men, a law of enfranchisement would but detain them in what they would then call their GOOD COUNTRY; and which they would prefer to lands the most fertile; for man will submit to everything that Providence imposes; he only murmurs at injustice from man, to which, if he does submit, it is with a rebellious heart. Man is not a tree rooted to the earth in which he grows; therefore pertains not to the soil. He is neither field, meadow, nor brute; therefore cannot be bought and sold. He has an interior conviction of these simple truths; nor can he be persuaded that his chiefs have any right to attach him to the glebe. All powers in vain unite to inculcate a doctrine so infamous. The time when the sovereign of the earth might conjure him in the name of God, if such a time ever existed, is past; the language of justice and reason is the only one to which he will at present listen. Princes cannot too often recollect that English America enjoins all governments to be just and sage, if governors do not wish to rule over deserts.

Abolish, SIRE, the *traites foraines,* and the *droits d'aubaine.* Of what benefit to you can such remains of feudal barbarism be? Do not wait for a system of reciprocity, which never has any other effect than that of longer detaining nations in a state of folly and warfare. That which is good for the prosperity of any country needs no reciprocity. Objections of this kind are but the foolish objections of vanity. Should the tyranny which is exercised over man and property in one State be to the loss of another, this is an additional reason why the latter should put an end to such absurd customs. Similar absurdities, perhaps, have obliged its own subjects to seek their fortune elsewhere, and have even made them forbear to return and bring the fruits of their labors back to the country that gave them birth. As nothing is wanting but that some one should begin, how noble, how worthy is it of a great King to be first! Your commercial subjects who are somewhat wealthy could not acquire their wealth at home, they were obliged to seek it in foreign countries; who, therefore, SIRE, is more interested than you are to set the example of abolition, where to exact is so atrocious? Have England and Holland waited to renounce such rights till you should have renounced them in their behalf?

One of the most urgent changes which demands your attention, and which a word may accomplish, is a law to restore to the plebeians the liberty to purchase patrician lands, with all their annexed rights. The execution of the strange decree by which they were deprived of this liberty has been so iniquitously inflicted that, if a patrician estate was sold for debt, and a plebeian was desirous of paying all the creditors, with an additional sum to the debtor, he was not allowed so to do, without an express order from the King. This order was generally refused by your predecessor; and the patrician by whom the creditors were defrauded, and the debtor kept without resource, had the preference. What was the consequence of this absurd law? The debasement of the price of land, that is to say, of the first riches of the State, and highly to the disadvantage of the noble landholders; the decay of agriculture, which was before discouraged by so many other causes, and of credit among the gentry; the aggravation of that fearful prejudice which wrongs the plebeian and renders the patrician stupid, by making him suppose his honorable rights are a sufficient source of respect, and that he need not acquire any other; in fine, the absolute necessity that those plebeians should quit the country who had acquired any capital; for they could not employ their money in trade, that being ruined by monopoly; nor in agriculture, because they were not allowed to hope they ever might be landholders. Is not Mecklenburg full of the traders of Stettin and Königsberg, etc., who have employed the wealth they gained, during the last maritime war, in the purchase of the estates of the ruined nobility of that country? This, SIRE, would be a heavy loss to you, were Mecklenburg always to be separated from your kingdom; a loss beyond the powers of calculation, were the same regulations hereafter to subsist. It is a remark which could not escape sagacious travelers, that wealthy merchants have delighted, in retirement, to betake themselves to agriculture. The most barren land becomes fruitful in their possession. They labor for its improvement, and bear with them that spirit of order, that circumstantial precision, by which they grew rich in trade. Wherever merchants can purchase, and wherever trade is honorable, there the country flourishes, and wears the face of abundance and prosperity. Commercial industry awakens every other kind of industry, and the earth requires that ingenious tillage which animates vegetation in the most ungrateful soil. Ah! SIRE, deign to recollect this tillage never was invented on patrician lands; for this we are indebted to those countries where illustrious birth vanishes when merit and talents appear.

Abolish, SIRE, those senseless prerogatives which bestow great offices on men who, to speak mildly, are not above mediocrity; and which are the cause that the greatest number of your subjects take no interest in a country where they have nothing to hope but fetters and humiliations. Beware, oh! beware, of that universal aristocracy which is the scourge of monarchical States, even more than of republics; an aristocracy by which, from one end of the earth to the other, the human species is oppressed. It is the interest of the most absolute Monarch to promulgate the most popular maxims. The people do not dread and revile Kings; but their Ministers, their courtiers, their nobles; in a word, the aristocracy. "OH, DID THE KING BUT KNOW!" Thus they exclaim. They daily invoke the royal authority, and are always ready to arm it against aristocracy. And whence is the power of the Prince derived, but from the people; his personal safety, but from the people; his wealth and splendor, but from the people; those benedictions which alone can make him more than mortal, but from the people? And who are the enemies of the Sovereign, but the grandees: the members of the aristocracy, who require the King should be only THE FIRST AMONG EQUALS, and who, wherever they could, have left him no other pre-eminence than that of rank, reserving power to themselves? By what strange error does it happen that Kings debase their friends, whom they deliver up to their enemies? It is the interest and the will of the people that the Prince should never be deceived. The interest and the will of the nobility are the very reverse. The people are easily satisfied: they give and ask not. Only prevent indolent pride from bearing too heavily upon them; leave but the career open which the Supreme Being has pointed out to them at their birth, and they will not murmur. Where is the Monarch who could ever satisfy the noble, the rich, the great? Do they ever cease to ask? Will they ever cease?

SIRE, equality of rights among those who support the throne will form its firmest basis. Changes of this kind cannot be suddenly made; yet there is one of these which cannot be too suddenly: let no person who wishes to approach the throne, whatever may be his rank in life, be impeded by the prerogatives of the great. Let men feel the necessity of equal merit to obtain preference. It is for you to level distinctions, and seat merit in its proper place.

Declare open war on the prejudice which places so great a distance between military and civil functions. It is a prejudice which, under a feeble Prince, such as your august family, like every other, may some time produce, will expose the country, and the Crown itself, to all the convulsions of pretorian anarchy. The officer and the soldier, SIRE, should only be proud in the presence of the foe. To their countrymen they should be brothers; and, if they defend their fellow-citizens, be it remembered they are paid by their fellow-citizens. In a kingdom like yours, perhaps, the warrior ought to have the first degree of respect; but he ought not to have it exclusively. If you have an army only you will never have a kingdom. Render your civil officers more respectable than they were under your predecessor. Nothing is more just, or more easy to accomplish. The Prince who reigns over the affections engages them by the simplest attentions. Frederick II. had the frenzy of continually wearing a uniform, as if he were the King only of soldiers. This legionary habiliment did not a little contribute to discredit the civil officer. How happened it he never felt it was impossible a Sovereign should render men estimable, for whom he never would testify esteem? He who attempts to make those incorruptible to whom he will not assure pecuniary independence will be equally unsuccessful. Let the civil officer be better paid, and never forget, Sire, that ill pay is ill economy. Among a thousand examples, I will but cite the enormous frauds that the Prussian Administrators have, for some years, committed on the public revenue. By an inconsistency, which is important in its effects, the financiers have been held in too much contempt, and those who have been convicted of acts the most dishonest have been too slightly punished. Such partiality could only raise the indignation of the poor, and encourage the fraudulent, who soon learned that to bribe an accomplice was to diminish the danger.

Prompt and gratuitous justice is evidently the first of Sovereign duties. If the Judge have no interest to elude the law, and can receive only his salary, gratuitous justice is soon rendered, and will be equitable, should your inspection be active and severe, and should you never forget that severity is the first duty of Kings. This grand regulation of rendering justice entirely gratuitous will, fortunately, not become burdensome in your States, for your people are well inclined, and not addicted to litigious disputes. But, burdensome or not, that which is strict equity is always necessary. Justice, Sire, precedes utility itself; or, rather, where justice is not, there is there no utility. The Judge ought to be paid by the public, and not to receive fees. To deny this were absurd; for must not Judges subsist, though there should not, for a whole year, be a single lawsuit?

Be you, Sire, the first to render the administration of justice gratuitous.

Be you also the first in whose States all men who wish to labor shall find work. All who breathe ought to feed by labor. It is the first law of Nature, and prior to all human conventions. It is the bond of society. The Government that should neglect to multiply the products of the earth, and that should not leave to each individual the use and profits of his industry, would be the accomplice or the author of all the crimes of men, and never could punish a culprit without committing a murder; for each man who offers labor in exchange for food, and meets refusal, is the natural and legitimate enemy of other men, and has a right to make war upon society.

Everywhere, in country as well as in town, let houses of industry be kept open at the expense of Government; that any man, of any country, may there gain his livelihood by his labor; and that your subjects there may be taught the value of time and industry.

Such institutions, SIRE, would be no burden; they would pay themselves. They would open a road to trade, facilitate the sale of natural products, enrich your lands, and improve your finances.

Such, SIRE, are the institutions which become a great King; and not manufactures protected by exclusive privileges, which only can be supported by injustice and mountains of gold, and which do but contribute to enrich a very small number of men; or to endow hospitals, which, if there were no poor, would create paupers.

There are, alas! too many poor in Prussia, especially at Berlin, and the poverty of whom demands your attention. In your capital it cannot be said without a painful emotion, a tenth of the inhabitants receive public alms; and this number annually augments. It is, no doubt, necessary to limit the extent of cities, where excessive population is productive of the worst consequences. In them not only poverty takes birth, but the worst of poverty, because it is not known how it may be remedied. The poor of cities are beings that have lost all good properties, moral and physical. But, speaking in general, the best opponent to this increasing poverty would be the houses of industry before mentioned, where all men who have arms may labor; and not those useless trades which are wretched in their pomp, and serve but to encourage the luxury of splendor, which already eats up your kingdom; nor those hospitals, fruitful sources of depredation, of benefit only to their directors, which engulf sums so considerable; while your schools, especially those of the open country, are so neglected and so miserable that the salaries of some of the headmasters scarcely amount to fifteen crowns a year. Let Your Majesty fit your subjects for labor by a proper mode of instruction, and they will have no need of hospitals.

You are not ignorant, Sire, that to instruct is one of the most important duties of the Sovereign, as it is one of his greatest sources of wealth. The most able man could do nothing without forming those who surround him, and whom he is obliged to employ; nor without teaching them his language, and familiarizing them with his ideas and his principles. The entire freedom of the Press, therefore, ought to be enumerated among your first regulations, not only because the deprivation of this freedom is a deprivation of natural right, but because that all impediment to the progress of the human understanding is an evil, an excessive evil, and especially to yourself, who only can enjoy truth, and hear truth, from the Press, which should be the Prime Minister of good Kings.

They will tell you, Sire, that with respect to the freedom of the Press you can add nothing at Berlin. But to abolish the censorship, of itself so useless, and always so arbitrary, would be much. If the printer's name be inserted in the title-page it is enough, perhaps more than enough. The only specious objection against an unlimited freedom of the Press is the licentiousness of libels; but it is not perceived that the freedom of the Press would take away the danger, because that, under such a regulation, truth only would remain. The most scandalous libels have no power except in countries that are deprived of the freedom of the Press. Its restrictions form an illicit trade, which cannot be extirpated; yet they lay restraints on none but honest people. Let not, therefore, that absurd contrast be seen in Prussia, which absolutely forbids foreign books to be inspected, and subjects national publications to so severe an inquisition. Give freedom to all. Read, SIRE, and suffer others to read. Knowledge will everywhere expand, and will center on the throne. Do you wish for darkness? Oh, no! Your mind is too great. Or, if you did, you would wish in vain; would act to your own injury, without obtaining the fatal success of extinguishing light. You will read, SIRE; you will begin a noble association with books; books that have destroyed shameful and cruel prejudices; that have smoothed your paths; that were beneficial to you previous even to your birth. You will not be ungrateful toward the accumulated labor of beneficent genius. You will read; you will protect those who write; for without them what were, what should be, the human species? They will instruct, they will aid you, will speak to you unseen, without approaching your throne; will introduce august Truth to your presence, who shall enter your palace unescorted, unattended; and, having entered, she will ask no dignities, no titles, but will remain invisible and disinterested. You will read; but you would wish your people should read also. You will not think you have done enough by filling your academies with foreigners. You will found schools, especially in the country, and will multiply and endow them. You will not wish to reign in darkness. Say but, " Let there be light," and light shall appear at your bidding; while her divine beams shall shine more resplendent round your head than all the laurels of heroes and conquerors.

There is a devouring plague in your States, SIRE, which you cannot too suddenly extirpate; and no doubt this good deed will nobly signalize the first day of your accession to the throne. I speak of the lottery, which would but be the more odious and more formidable did it procure you the wealth of worlds; but which, for the wretched gain of fifty thousand crowns, hurries the industrious part of your subjects into all the calamities of poverty and vice.

You will be told, SIRE, what some pretended statesmen have not blushed to write, and publish, that the lottery ought to be regarded as a voluntary tax. A tax? And what a tax! One whose whole products are founded either on delirium or despair. What a tax! To which the rich landholder is not obliged to contribute. A tax which neither wise nor good men ever pay. A voluntary tax? Strange indeed is this kind of freedom! Each day, each minute, the people are told it depends only on themselves to become rich for a trifle: thousands may be gained by a shilling. So the wretch believes who cannot calculate, and who is in want of bread; and the sacrifice he makes of that poor remaining shilling which was to purchase bread, and appease the cries of his family, is a free gift!—a tax, which he pays to his Sovereign!

You will be further told—yes, men will dare to tell you—that this horrible invention, which empoisons even hope itself, the last of the comforts of man, is indeed an evil; but that it were better you should yourself collect the harvest of lottery than abandon your subjects to foreign lotteries. Oh! SIRE, cast arithmetic so corrupt, and sophisms so detestable, with horror from you. There continually are means of opposing foreign lotteries. Secret collectors are not to be feared. They will not penetrate far into your States when the pains and penalties are made severe; and in such instances only are informers encouraged without inconvenience, for they only inform against an ambulatory pestilence. The natural penalties against such as favor adventurers in foreign lotteries are: infamy, an exclusion from municipal offices, from trading companies, and the right of coming on 'Change. These penalties are very severe, and no doubt sufficient; yet if violent remedies are necessary to impede the progress of such a crime, the punishment of death, that punishment at which my mind revolts and my blood is frozen, that punishment so prodigally bestowed on so many crimes, and which perhaps no crime can merit, would be rendered more excusable from the fearful list of wretchedness and disorder, which originate in lotteries, than even from the most exaggerated consequences of domestic theft.

But, SIRE, the great, first, and immediate operation which I supplicate from YOUR MAJESTY, in the name of your dearest interest and glory, is a quick and formal declaration, accompanied with all the awful characteristics of sovereignty, that unlimited toleration shall prevail through your States, and that they shall ever remain open to all religions. You have a very natural, and not less estimable, opportunity of making such a declaration. Publish an edict which shall grant civil liberty to the Jews. This act of beneficence, at the very commencement of your reign, will make you surpass your illustrious predecessor in religious toleration, who was the most tolerant Prince that ever existed. Nor shall this excess of beneficence be without its reward. Exclusive of the numerous increase to population, and the large capitals which Prussia will infallibly acquire, at the expense of other countries, the Jews of the second generation will become good and useful citizens. To effect this they need but be encouraged in the mechanic arts and agriculture, which to them are interdicted. Free them from those additional taxes by which they are oppressed. Give them access to the courts of justice equal to your other subjects, by depriving their Rabbis of all civil authority. Oh! SIRE, I conjure you, beware of delaying the declaration of the most universal tolerance. There are fears in your provinces of rather losing than gaining in this respect. Apprehensions are entertained concerning what are called your prejudices, your preconceived opinions, your doctrine. This, perhaps, is the only part in which you have been seriously attacked by calumny. Solemnly prove the falsehood of those who have affirmed you are intolerant. Show them that your respect for religious opinions equals your respect for the great Creator, and that you are far from desiring to prescribe laws concerning the manner in which He ought to be adored. Prove that, be your philosophic or religious opinions what they may, you make no pretensions to the absurd and tyrannical right of imposing opinions upon others.

After these preliminary acts, which, I cannot too often repeat, may as well be performed in an hour as in a year, and which consequently ought to be performed immediately, a glance on the economical and political system by which your kingdom is regulated will lead you to other considerations.

It is a most remarkable thing that a man like your predecessor, distinguished for the extreme justness of his understanding, should have embraced an economical and political system so radically vicious. Indirect taxes, extravagant prohibitions, regulations of every kind, exclusive privileges, monopolies without number! Such was the spirit of his domestic government, and to a degree that, besides being odious, was most ridiculous.

Is it not astonishing, for example, that a man like Frederick II., could waste his time in regulating, in such a city as Berlin, the rates that should be paid at inns; the pay of *laquais de louage*, and the value of all the necessaries of life; or that ever he should conceive the project of prohibiting the entrance of French apples into the march of Brandenburg, which is only productive of wood and sands? As if the apples of his provinces were in dread of rivals! Thus, too, he asked, when he prohibited the eggs that were brought from Saxony, " Cannot my hens lay eggs? "—Could he forget that the eggs of the hens of Berlin must first be eaten before the inhabitants would send as far as Dresden for others? His prohibition, too, of the mouse traps of Brunswick! As if the man had ever before been born who founded his hopes of fortune on a speculation in mouse traps! It would be endless to collect all his singularities of this kind. Who can reflect, without pain and pity, that four hundred and twelve monopolies exist in your kingdom? So interwoven was this equally absurd and iniquitous system with the spirit of the government of Frederick II. Or that a great number of these monopolies are still active; at least that the prohibitive ordinances are effective, which bestowed such exclusive privileges on persons many of whom have since been ruined, and have become bankrupts or outlaws? Or that, in fine, the number of prohibited commodities greatly exceeds that of commodities that are permitted? These things would

appear incredible to men even most accustomed to indulge the regulatory and fiscal delirium. Yet thus low
could even a great man sink, who was desirous of
governing too much.

Is it not equally astonishing that a Monarch so active,
so industrious in his royal functions, should leave the
system of direct taxation exactly in the state in which
it was under Frederick I., when the clergy were taxed
at a fiftieth of their income, the nobility at the thirty-
third, and the people at the seventeenth; a burden at
that time excessive, but which, by the different variations in value and the signs of property, is almost reduced to nothing? So that industry and trade have
been most unmercifully oppressed by your predecessor,
at the very time that he was establishing manufactures
at an excessive expense.

How might this same King, so consistent and pertinacious in what he had once ordained, at the time that
he settled new colonies by granting them franchises and
the right of property, the necessity of which to agriculture he consequently knew, suffer the absurd regulation to subsist which excludes all right of property in
the greatest part of his kingdom? How was it that he
did not feel that, instead of expending sums so vast
in forming colonies, he would much more rapidly have
augmented his revenues and the population of his
provinces, by enfranchising those unfortunate beasts
of burden who, under the human form, cultivate the
earth, by distributing among them the extensive tracts
called domains (which absorb almost the half of your
estates) in proprietaries, and on condition of paying
certain hereditary quitrents in kind?

All these particulars, and a thousand others of a like
kind, are strange, no doubt; yet it is not totally impossible to explain such eccentricities of mind in a great
man. Without entering here into a particular inquiry

concerning that quality of mind whence it resulted that
Frederick II. was much rather a singular example of
the development of great character, in its proper place,
than of an elevated genius, bestowed by Nature, and
superior to other men, it is easy to perceive that, having
applied the whole power of his abilities to form a grand
military force, with provinces that were disunited, par-
celed out and generally unfruitful; and, for that purpose, wishing to outstrip the slow march of Nature,
he principally thought of money, because money was
the only engine of speed.   Hence originated with him
his idolatry of money; his love of amassing, realizing,
and heaping.   Those fiscal systems which most effectually stripped the people of their metal were those in
which he most delighted.   Every artifice, every fiscal
extortion, that has taken birth in kingdoms the most
luxurious, which, unfortunately, in this as in other
things, gave the fashion to Europe, were by turns
naturalized in his States.   Frederick II. was the more
easily led to pursue this purpose, because such was the
situation of some of his provinces that they were almost necessarily a market for the products of Saxony,
Poland, etc., and thus the multiplicity and severity of
his duties were less rapidly destructive of the revenue
arising from the tolls.   Besides that, his nation, but
little active, and still, perhaps, tainted by the Germanic improvidence which neglects or disdains to
save, did not afford him any other immediate resource
than what might be found in the Royal Treasury.   He
imagined the Prussians were in need of being goaded
by additions, which, however, could only tend to
slacken their pace.   He supposed they might be taught
wisdom by monopolies; as if monopolies were not injurious to the progress of knowledge.   Having taken
his first steps, his unconquerable spirit of consistency,
which was his distinguishing characteristic; the multi-

tude of his affairs, which obliged him to leave whatever
did not appertain to the military system on the same
basis, and with similar institutions, in which he found
it; his habit of not suffering contradiction nor discussion; his extreme contempt for mankind, which, perhaps, will explain all his success, all his errors, all his
conduct; his confidence in his own superiority, which
confirmed him in the fatal resolution of seeing all, of
all regulating, all ordaining, and personally interfering
in all—these various causes combined have rendered
fiscal robbery, and systematic monopoly, irrefragable
and sacred in his kingdom; while they were daily aggravated by his despotic temper and the moroseness of
age.

Evils so various and so great had indeed some com-
pensations. To his numerous taxes Frederick II.
joined a rigorous economy. He raised heavy contributions on his enemies. His first wars were paid by
their money. He conquered a rich province, where
great and wealthy industry, reduced no doubt by a
government more sage than his, had previously been
established. He drew subsidies from his allies; the
folly of granting which is no longer in fashion. During four-and-twenty years of peace, he enjoyed a degree of respect which rather resembled worship than
dread. He continually reserved, in his States, some
part of the money he extorted. His new military discipline, a species of industry of which he was the
creator, not a little contributed to his puissance; and his
wealth, in the midst of indebted Europe, would have
been almost sufficient for all his wishes; for, had the
ardor of his ambition longer continued, what he could
not have conquered he would have bought. Who,
indeed, can say whether Frederick II., was not indebted, for a great part of his domestic success, to the
deplorable state of the human species in Germany;

through most of the States of which, if we except
Saxony, the inhabitants were still more wretched than
in Prussia?

Yet, SIRE, with efforts so multiplied, what is the inheritance that has been left you by this great King?
Are your provinces rich, powerful and happy? Deprive them of their military renown and the resources
of the Royal Treasury, which soon may vanish, and
feeble will be the remainder. Had the provinces of
which your kingdom is composed been under a paternal government, and peopled by freemen, the acquisition of Silesia might have been more distant; but how
different would have been the present state and wealth
of the whole remaining nation!

Your situation, SIRE, is entirely different from that
of your predecessor. The destructive resources of
fiscal regulation are exhausted. A change of system is,
for this reason, indispensable. An army cannot always,
cannot long, constitute the basis of the Prussian puissance. Your army must, therefore, be supported by all
the internal aids which good administration can employ, built on permanent foundations. It is necessary
that you should truly animate the national industry, in
ably profiting by those extraordinary and perishable
means which have been transmitted to you by your
predecessor. These, it is to be presumed, you may
long enjoy. It is not, therefore, absurd to advise you
to sow in order that you may reap. Should momentary
sacrifices, however great, be necessary to render the
Prussian States (which hitherto have only constituted
a vast and formidable camp) a stable and prosperous
monarchy, founded on freedom and property, the im-
mensity of your treasure will render such sacrifices infinitely less burdensome to you than they would be
to any other Sovereign, and the barter will be pro-

digiously to your advantage, even should the rendering of men happy be estimated at nothing.

The basis of the system which it is your duty, SIRE, to form, must rest on the just ideals which you shall obtain of the true value of money, which is but a trifling part of national wealth, and of much less importance than the riches which annually spring from the bosom of the earth. The incorruptibility and the scarcity of gold have rendered it a pledge, and a mode of exchange between man and man; and this general use is the chief source of the deceitful opinions that are entertained of its value. The facility with which it may be removed, when men are obliged to fly, especially from places where tyranny is to be dreaded, has given every individual a desire of amassing gold; and the false opinions concerning that metal have been strengthened by this universal desire. No less true is it that, gold being an engine or agent in trade, and that the multiplicity of agents is the increase of trade, and still further that the increase of trade is the prosperity of nations, to imprison gold, or to act so as to oblige others to imprison it, is madness. What would you say of a Prince who, desiring to become a conqueror, should keep his army shut up in barracks? Yet Kings who amass gold act precisely thus. They render that lifeless which is of no value except when in motion.

But just ideas concerning the value of gold are necessarily connected with those of the government that shall respect property, and shall pursue principles of rigorous justice; such as shall inspire unshaken confidence, and render to each individual the most perfect security; for, without this, the true use of gold is traversed by innumerable accidents, that deprive it of the utility which would otherwise render national industry so fruitful.

Whatever you may do, SIRE, to inspire confidence, it still remains for you to observe that nations have commercial connections; and that gold forms one of those, because of its necessity to trade. It must flow here or there, according to the indefinite combinations of merchants. Hence no nation can unite sound opinions concerning trade with restraint on the exportation of gold. Each man must finally pay his debts, and no person gives or receives gold, from which little is to be gained, except when every means of paying in merchandise is exhausted; for from these, profits are derived to buyer and seller. What would you think, SIRE, of a Prince who should encourage the merchants of his kingdom to establish numerous manufactures, consequently to employ numerous agents, yet should forbid those agents to leave the kingdom that they might purchase the materials of which the manufacturers stand in need? This, however, is the picture of the Prince who should prevent, or lay restraint on, the exportation of gold; such would his frenzy be. But in what does this originate? In his fear that the gold will never come back. And wherefore? Because he secretly feels that his subjects are not perfectly secure of their property. Thus, SIRE, you perceive justice, security, respect for men, and a declaration of war against all tyranny, are indispensable conditions to every play of prosperity.

When your subjects shall be at ease in this respect, entertain no apprehensions should gold seem to vanish; it is but gone in search of gold, and to return with increase. Forget not, SIRE, that the value of gold is lost, irretrievably, when it is not absolutely subjected to the will of trade, which alone is its monarch. By trade I here understand the general action of all productive industry, from the husbandman to the artist.

What has been done in kingdoms where the security

of the citizen is perfect, and where men have been convinced that gold never can be fixed, nor acquired in sufficient abundance for the supply of exchange? Why, in such kingdoms, banks have been imagined, and bills have been brought into circulation, which, from the conviction that they may at any time be turned into specie, have become a kind of coin, which not being universal has been an internal substitute for gold, and induced men not to disturb themselves concerning its external circulation.

Of such establishments you, SIRE, should be ambitious. Happy the State in which the Sovereign, having habituated his subjects to the opinion of perfect internal security, can cause sufficient sums to issue from his treasury for the establishment of such banks, to his own advantage. How many fiscal inventions, produced by the spirit of pilfering, under the protection of ignorance and the laws, how many absurd and tyrannical taxes might be annihilated, by gaining the interest of that money of which this confidential currency should be the representative? And what tax ever could be more mild, more natural, more productive, or more agreeable to the Monarch, than the interest of money which he may gain by a currency which cost him nothing? Such a tax is cheerfully paid, for industry is the borrower; and, wherever industry finds its reward, each individual wishes to be industrious.

The outline I have here traced, and which you, SIRE, may strengthen by so many circumstances of which I am ignorant, and by so many others that would be too tedious to recapitulate at present, will naturally lead you—

1. To the distribution of your immense domains among husbandmen, whom you will supply with the sums they want, and who will become real landholders, that shall pay a perpetual quitrent in kind, in order that

your revenues may augment in proportion to the augmentation of wealth.

2. To the due lowering (till such time as they may be wholly abolished) of indirect taxes, excise duties, customs, etc., the product of which will continually increase in an inverse ratio to the quantity of the duty and the vigor with which it is collected; for illicit trade, excited by too tempting lures, gains protectors among those by whom it ought to be repressed, and agents who had been appointed its opponents. Such disastrous taxes might likewise find substitutes in the natural and just increase of direct taxes; as on land, from which no estate ought to be free; for land finally bears the whole burden of taxation, which burden is the heavier the more the means of laying it on are indirect. How many disputes, shackles, inquisitions, and disorders would then vanish! Plagues which are more odious, more oppressive, than the burden of the tax itself; and even more intolerable from the mode of assessment than from the value! That artificial vice which, before the last reign, was unknown in your kingdom, the vice of illicit trade, which makes deceit the basis of commerce, depraves the manners, and inspires a general contempt for the laws, then would disappear. To the regions of hell itself would then be banished the infernal power which your predecessor conferred on the administrators of excise duties and tolls, of arbitrarily increasing the penalties and punishments inflicted on smugglers.

3. You will firmly and invariably determine on the system of favoring, by every possible means, the TRANSIT TRADE, which must find new roads should foreigners longer be vexed; or rather, has already found new roads. The impositions and minute examinations, which are occasioned by the manner of levying duties on this trade, and the fatal vigilance that has been

employed not to suffer contraband goods to find entrance at the fair of Frankfort on the Oder, has produced this fatal effect, that the Poles, who formerly carried on a very considerable trade at Frankfort and at Breslau, at present totally avoid both places, and condemn themselves to a circuit of near a hundred German miles through a great part of Poland, Moravia, and Bohemia, that they may arrive at Leipsic; for which reason this last city, which is much less favorably situated than Frankfort on the Oder, where there is a great river, has within these fifteen years become flourishing; while the former, from the same cause, has fallen to decay; which decay continues increasing, and that at the very moment when the revolution in America threatens the North with so powerful a rivalship. Profit, Sire, by the last stage in which perhaps, the transit trade can be an object of any importance. Favor it by taking off the chief of the duties which shackle it at present, and impart a confidence befitting of your candor and generous benevolence. How might you find a more fortunate moment in which to manifest such intentions than that wherein your neighbors are signalizing themselves by so many prohibitive frenzies?

4. To you, Sire, is reserved the real and singular honor of abolishing monopolies, which are no less injurious to good sense than to equity; and which, in your kingdom, are so perpetual a source of hatred and malediction. The Prussian merchants, incited by the example of monopolizing companies (Nature, desirous of preserving the human race, ever causes evil itself to produce good), and, thanks to the excellent situation of your States, have made some progress, in despite of every effort to stifle their industry, on the first ray of hope that monopolies should disappear; and these merchants will, by voluntary contributions, af-

ford a substitute for a part of the deficiency which the new system may at first occasion in your revenues.

5. You will, finally, arrive at the greatest of benefits, and at the most useful of speculations in politics and finance. You will set industry, arts, manufactures, and commerce free; commerce, which only can exist under the protection of freedom; commerce, which prefers no request to Kings except not to do it an injury. When you shall seriously have examined whether those manufactures which never can support a foreign rivalship deserve to be encouraged at an expense so heavy, prohibitions will then presently vanish from your States. The linens of Silesia never were otherwise favored than by exempting the weavers from military enrollment; and, of all the objects of Prussian trade, these linens are the most important. In none of your provinces are any manufactures to be found more flourishing than in that of Westphalia; namely, in the county of Marck; yet never has Government done anything to encourage the industry of this province, except in not inflicting internal vexations. I repeat, internal, for all the products of the industry of Prussian subjects, beyond the Weser, are accounted foreign and contraband, in all the other provinces; which odious and absurd iniquity you will not suffer to subsist. You will enfranchise all, SIRE, and will grant no more exclusive privileges. Those who demand them are generally either knaves or fools; and to acquiesce in their requests is the surest method of strangling industry. If such are found in England, it is because the form in which they are granted renders them almost null. In Ireland they are no longer admitted. The Government and the Dublin Society afford support and give bounties, but on condition that no exclusive privilege is asked. The most magnificent, as well as the most certain, means of possess-

ing everything Nature bestows is freedom, SIRE. It is the prodigality with which she bestows that attracts men, by moral feeling and physical good. All exclusive grants wound the first, and banish the second.

I entreat, SIRE, you would remark that I do not propose you should suddenly, and incautiously, lop away all the parasite suckers which disfigure and enfeeble the royal stock which you were born to embellish and strengthen; but I likewise conjure you not to be impeded by the fear of meeting your collectors with empty hands; for this fear, being solely occupied concerning self, they will not fail to increase. The only man among them who really possesses an extensive knowledge of the general connections, of commerce, and from whom you may expect able services, whenever your system shall invariably be directed to obtain other purposes than those to which his talents have hitherto been prostituted, STRUENSEE, will confirm all my principles. He will indicate various means to Your Majesty, which may serve as substitutes to fiscal extortions. Thus, for instance, the commutation of duties, which is a new art, may, under the direction of a man so enlightened, greatly increase your revenues by lightening the public burden.

England, formed to afford lessons to the whole earth, and to astonish the human mind by demonstrating the infinite resources of credit, in support of which everything is made to concur—England has lately made a fine and fortunate experiment of this kind. She has commuted the duties on tea by a tax on windows, and the success is wonderful. Acquire a clear knowledge of this operation, SIRE. It is preserved, with all the effects it has produced, in a work which will open vast prospects to your view. Your generalizing mind will take confidence in the industry of the honest man, and in the resources of his sensibility, aided by experience and talents; though the misfortune of heavy taxes and the vicious mode of assessment should necessarily be prolonged.

But, SIRE, were you obliged to accept that heavy interest which Powers in debt are obliged to pay, as a substitute for duties that, though destructive, are not commutable, where would be the misfortune? What advantage might not result from treasures employed to obtain the payment of interest by which monarchies the most formidable are enfeebled? Wherefore not seize the means which they themselves furnish at their own expense, no longer to stand in awe of them? Do not you perceive, SIRE, that you would thus without danger make them pay you tribute? For the governments which might be mad enough to wish to rob their creditors would be unable, thanks to the general intercourse of trade.

It remains to inquire to whom you would confide labors so difficult, yet so interesting. It is not for a stranger to estimate the worth of your subjects. Yet, SIRE, is there one whose talents are esteemed in France and England, and him, therefore, I may venture to name. Baron Knyphausen is well acquainted with men and things, in those countries in which he has served, and particularly with the system of the public funds.

But more especially, SIRE, summon the merchants. Among them are most commonly found probity and abilities. From them is derived the theory of order; and without order what can be accomplished? They are in general men of moderation, divested of pomp, and for that reason merit preference. Be persuaded, SIRE, that the most enlightened, the most wise, and the most humane of mankind, would depart from you were their reward to consist in the vain decorations which titles bestow. These cannot be accepted without trampling on principles to which men are indebted for the glory of having merited reward; nor without paying with contempt the class they honor. The merchant who is worthy of your confidence will dread making himself guilty of such ingratitude toward his equals; and this is one of the characteristics by which he will be distinguished. In the title of Lord Chatham the great Pitt expired; nor did the lord ever console himself for having acted thus traitorously toward his own glory. The services of the merchants you may employ, far from multiplying, must destroy the monstrous inequalities which disorganize and deform your States. Thus will men like these find their reward, and not in silly titles, or the vain decorations of nobility.

But, SIRE, I have too long intruded upon the precious moments in which the scepter has so lately been confided to your hands. What can I add which your own reflections, increased by facts that daily must fall under your notice, will not convey a thousand times more forcibly than any words of mine can? I have imagined it might not be wholly fruitless to awaken these ideas at the moment of a change so new, under a variety of affairs so great, and a multitude of interests and intrigues which must traverse and combat each other round your throne, and which may deprive you of that calm of mind that is necessary to abstract and to select. Should you in any degree be affected by my frankness, I dare hope it will not be unpleasantly. Mediate, O FREDERICK! on this free, sincere, but respectful remonstrance, and deign to say:

" Here I find what no man has informed me of, and perhaps the reverse of what I shall be daily told. The most courageous present truth to Kings under a veil; I here behold her naked. This is more worthy of me than the venal incense of rhymers, with which

I am suffocated; or academical panegyrics, which assaulted me in the cradle, and scarcely will quit me in the coffin. I was a man before I was a King. Wherefore then take offense at being treated like a man; or because a stranger, who asks nothing from me, and who soon will quit my Court, never to behold it more, speaks to me without disguise? He lays before me what inspection, experience, study, and understanding have collected. He gratis gives me that true and liberal advice of which no man stands so much in need as he who is devoted to the public good. Interest to deceive me he has none; his intentions cannot be evil. Let me attentively examine what he has proposed; for the simple good sense, the native candor of the man, whose only employment is the cultivation of reason and reflection, may well be of equal value with the old routine of habit, artifice, forms, diplomatic chimeras, add the ridiculous dogmas of those who are statesmen by trade."

May the eternal Disposer of human events watch over your welfare; may your days be beneficent and active; employed in those consolatory duties which elevate and fortify the soul; and may you, till the extremest old age, enjoy the pure felicity of having employed your whole faculties for the prosperity of the people for whose happiness you are responsible, for to you their happiness is intrusted!

THE END